War In Peace

Volume 5

War In Peace

The Marshall Cavendish Illustrated Encyclopedia of Postwar Conflict.

Editor-in-Chief
Ashley Brown

Editorial Board
Brig-Gen. James Collins Jr (USA Retd.)
Vice-Admiral Sir Louis Le Bailly KBE CB
Ian V Hogg; David Floyd
Professor Laurence Martin
Air-Vice Marshal SWB Menaul CB CBE DFC AFC

MARSHALL CAVENDISH
NEW YORK, LONDON, TORONTO

Reference Edition Published 1985

Published by Marshall Cavendish Corporation
147 West Merrick Road
Freeport, Long Island
N.Y. 11520

Printed and Bound in Italy by L.E.G.O. S.p.a. Vicenza.

British Library Cataloguing in Publication Data

Brown, Ashley
   War in peace : the Marshall Cavendish
   illustrated encyclopaedia of post-war conflict.
   1. History, Modern—1945-   2. War—History
   —20th century
   I. Title   II. Dartford, Mark
   909.82   D842

   ISBN 0-86307-293-3
      0 86307 298 4   vol. 5

Library of Congress Cataloging in Publication Data

Main entry under title:

War in peace.

   Includes bibliographies and index.
   1. Military history, Modern—20th century.   2. Military
art and science—History—20th century.   3. World politics—1945-
I. Marshall Cavendish Corporation.
U42.W373 1984   355'.009'04   84-19386
ISBN 0-86307-293-3
      0 86307 298 4   vol. 5

Editorial Staff

Editor	Ashley Brown
Editorial Director	Brian Innes
Editorial Manager	Clare Byatt
Editorial Editors	Sam Elder
	Adrian Gilbert
Sub Editors	Sue Leonard
	Simon Innes
Artwork Editor	Jonathan Reed
Artwork Buyer	Jean Morley
Picture Editor	Carina Dvorak
Picture Consultant	Robert Hunt
Design	EDC

Reference Edition Staff

Editor	Mark Dartford
Designer	Graham Beehag
Consultant	Robert Paulley
Indexers	F & K Gill
Creation	DPM Services

Editorial Board

Contributors

David Blue served with the CIA in various countries of Southeast Asia, including Laos, and is a writer on and a student of small wars.

Gordon Brook-Shepherd spent 15 years in Vienna, first as lieutenant-colonel on the staff of the British High Commission and then as a foreign correspondent for the *Daily Telegraph*. A graduate in history from Cambridge, he is currently Chief Assistant Editor of the *Sunday Telegraph*.

Jeffrey J. Clarke is an expert on recent military history, particularly the Vietnam War, and has written for the American Center of Military History.

Major-General Richard Clutterbuck OBE has been Senior Lecturer in politics at Exeter University since his retirement from the army in 1972. His works include *Protest and the Urban Guerrilla, Guerrillas and Terrorists* and *Kidnap and Ransom*.

Alexander S. Cochran Jr is a historian whose area of research is modern Indochinese affairs with particular reference to the war in Vietnam since 1945. He is at present working in the Southeast Asia Branch of the Center of Military History, Department of the Army.

Colonel Peter M. Dunn is a serving officer in the USAF. His doctoral thesis is on the history of Indochina during the mid-1940s.

John B. Dwyer served both with the infantry and with armoured units in Vietnam. He was editor and publisher of the Vietnam veteran's newsletter *Perimeter* and has been a writer and correspondent for *National Vietnam Veteran's Review* for the past few years. His particular interest are Special Forces and Special Operations.

Brenda Ralph Lewis has specialised in political and military history since 1964. She s a regular contributor to military and historical magazines in both Britain and the United States.

Hugh Lunghi served in Moscow in the British Military Mission and the British Embassy for six years during and after World War II. He was interpreter for the British Chiefs of Staff at the Teheran, Yalta and Potsdam conferences, and also interpreted for Churchill and Anthony Eden. He subsequently worked in the BBC External Services and is a former editor of *Index on Censorship*.

Charles Messenger retired from the army in 1980 to become a fulltime military writer after 21 years service in the Royal Tank Regiment. Over the past 10 years he has written several books on 20th century warfare, as well as contributing articles to a number of defence and historical journals. He is currently a Research Associate at the Royal United Services Institute for Defence Studies in London.

Billy C. Mossman is a well-known American writer and historian. He is currently working on a volume on the Korean War for the US Army Center of Military History.

Bryan Perrett served in the Royal Armoured Corps from 1952 to 1971. He contributes regularly to a number of established military journals and acted as Defence Correspondent to the *Liverpool Echo* during the Falklands War. His recent books include *Weapons of the Falklands Conflict* and *A History of Blitzkrieg*.

Chapman Pincher is one of England's leading authorities on international espionage and counter-intelligence. He is the author of political novels and books on spying, the most recent of which is *Their Trade is Treachery*, which deals with the penetration of Britain's secret services by the Russian secret police.

Yehoshua Porath is a noted scholar at the Hebrew University in Jerusalem. He has made a special study of the Palestinian problem and is the author of two books on the subject, the most recent of which is *The Palestinian Arab National Movement 1929—39*, which was published in Britain in 1977.

Contributors

Antony Preston is Naval Editor of the military magazine *Defence* and author of numerous publications including *Battleships, Aircraft Carriers* and *Submarines*.

Brigadier-General Edwin H. Simmons, US Marine Corps, Retired, is the Director of Marine Corps History and Museums. At the time of the Inchon operation and the Chosin Reservoir campaign, he, as a major, commanded Weapons Company, 3rd Battalion, 1st Marines. Widely published, he is the author of *The United States Marines*.

Ronald Spector is an expert on Vietnam and has recently completed a book on that subject for the Center of Military History in the United States.

Andres Suarez served in the Cuban ministry of education from 1948–1951, took part in the Cuban revolution, and served in the ministry of housing from 1959. From 1965, he has been Professor of Latin American Studies at the University of Florida. Other publications include *Cuba and the Sino−Soviet Rift*.

Sir Robert Thompson KBE, CMG, DSO, MC is a world authority on guerrilla warfare, on which he has written extensively. He was directly involved in the Emergency in Malaya in the 1950s and rose to become permanent Secretary for Defence. From 1961 to 1965 he headed the British Advisory Mission to Vietnam and since then he has advised several governments, including the United States, on counter-insurgency operations Sir Robert Thompson is a Council member of the Institute for the Study of Conflict, London. His books include *Defeating Communist Insurgency and Revolutionary War in World Strategy, 1945−69.*

Patrick Turnbull commanded 'D' Force, Burma during World War II. His 29 published works include a history of the Foreign Legion.

Contents of Volume

Brunei in revolt

When the Queen's Own Highlanders saved a sultan

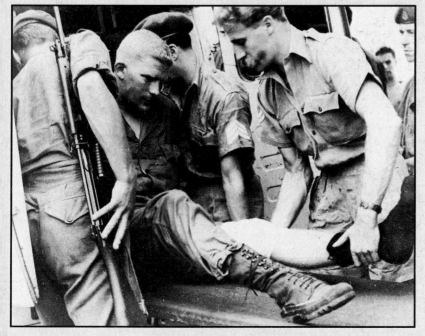

In December 1962 Brunei, a small oil-rich state on the northwest coast of Borneo (Kalimantan), was faced with a vital choice about its future. The Sultan, Sir Omar Ali Saifuddin, was under heavy pressure to bring his tiny kingdom into the Federation of Malaysia which was to be set up in 1963. The British, who were responsible for Brunei's defence and had a high commissioner in the country, were in favour of the Malaysia concept. They had already agreed that their colonies of Sarawak – in which Brunei formed two small enclaves – and nearby North Borneo (now Sabah) should join the new Federation.

But feeling in Brunei was not necessarily in favour of the move. At recent elections, all 16 elected seats in Brunei's 33-seat legislative assembly had gone to the Partai Ra'ayat (People's Party) which was in favour of Brunei joining Malaysia, but only as a single state with Sarawak and Sabah, and with the Sultan reigning over the whole as a constitutional monarch. Despite the elections, the People's Party had no power, since 17 members of the assembly were appointed by the Sultan.

The more radical adherents of the People's Party were not prepared to accept their exclusion from power or the prospect that the Sultan might accede to Malaysia. As a result they formed a secret military wing: the Tentera Nasional Kalimantan Utara (TNKU) – the North Kalimantan National Army.

The leader of this radical group was A.M. Azahari. He was 34 years old in 1962 and born in Brunei of Arab/Malay parents. As a child during World War II he had been sent by the Japanese to study in the occupied Dutch East Indies and, following the Japanese defeat in 1945, he fought with the Indonesian Nationalists against the Dutch. He finally returned to Brunei in 1952. Thereafter he became increasingly active in politics and his major opportunity to advance came with the formation of the TNKU in 1962. While Azahari was much influenced by the Indonesian President Sukarno, it remains a matter of debate whether he was actually working for him. With hindsight it seems that, seeing a chance to overthrow the Sultan's government and to replace it with one of his own, he grabbed at the opportunity.

By December 1962 the TNKU could boast an ill-assorted, ill-equipped, ill-trained and, as events were to show, ill-led army of some 4000 men. Only about 1000 of them were armed with guns; the rest carried only parangs or knives. The somewhat extravagantly titled 'commander-in-chief' of this army was Yassin Effendi. Rather strangely, when the rebellion broke out both Azahari and Effendi were in the Philippines, far from the action, although the latter returned after the revolt was under way.

The immediate aims of the rebellion were to capture more effective weapons from the police while seizing control of all police stations, to take over the oilfields and to capture the Sultan himself. The revolt began at 0200 hours on 8 December 1962, when large groups of the TNKU stormed the main power-station in the capital, Brunei Town, and attacked the Astana (the Sultan's palace) and the prime minister's house. The attack on the power-station was a success and the whole town was plunged into darkness but, thanks to prompt action by the commissioner of police acting on a tip-off, neither the Astana nor the prime minister's house fell to the rebels. The police quickly drove the rebels from the power-station and left the commissioner generally in control of the situation in Brunei Town. But elsewhere the rebels were more successful. Outside the capital they seized the townships of Limbang (actually in Sarawak), Bangar and Tutong, and the oilfield complex at Seria on the coast.

The initial British military response was not very urgent because of the seeming ability of the police to contain the situation. First reports only mentioned the events in Brunei Town itself and the widespread nature of the uprising was not at first appreciated.

Situation critical

Still, within two hours of the initial attacks in the early hours of 8 December, 99 Gurkha Infantry Brigade in Singapore was placed on 48 hours notice to move. At 0930 hours as increasingly alarming reports came in, elements of 1/2nd Gurkhas (one of 99 Brigade's battalions) were ordered to move immediately. The second-in-command of the battalion arrived with C and D Companies at Seletar airfield in Singapore by midday. Transport aircraft were not immediately available and it was not until 1500 hours

that the group was airborne and heading across the South China Sea bound for Brunei. They travelled in three Beverleys and a Britannia, all of which had only recently flown into Singapore.

The force intended to land at Labuan, a small island off the coast of Borneo, as it was not known whether Brunei airport was in government hands. During the flight, however, news came through that Brunei was safe for landing and the Beverleys were diverted there. The Britannia continued on to Labuan, being in need of the longer runway on the island.

The landings were made without incident and by 2300 hours the Gurkhas had set up headquarters at the police station in Brunei Town. The size of the problem quickly became evident to Major Lloyd-Williams, the Gurkha detachment commander. He soon realised that two companies of troops were scarcely sufficient to bolster the police effort in

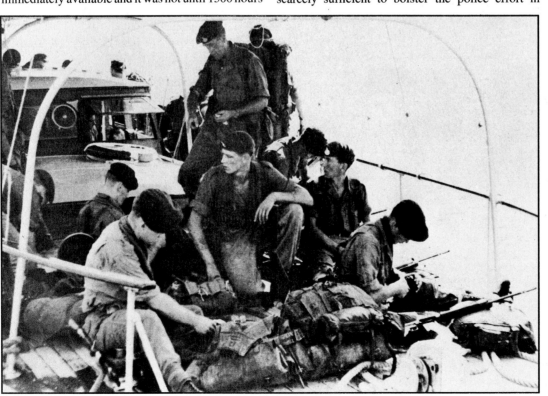

Previous page, top: British troops guard the Sultan's palace in a Saladdin armoured car mounting a 76mm gun. Previous page below: A Royal Marine Commando officer, wounded during the fighting in Brunei.

Above: Sultan Saifuddin. Left: Royal Marines of 42 Commando check their equipment while on river patrol in Brunei.

Brunei Town itself, let alone recapture the oilfields at Seria some 80km (50 miles) away, where the rebels were established in strength with a large number of hostages. Straightaway a platoon was dispatched to guard the Sultan's palace and curfew patrols were sent into the town in support of the police.

Night ambush

The commander decided to wait until first light before attempting the relief of Seria. To have travelled in darkness along unknown roads, all of which were perfectly suited to ambush, would have been to invite disaster. But in the early hours of the morning a telephone call was received warning that the rebels were about to attack the police station in Panaga near Seria, using hostages as a screen to shield their advance.

Brunei government Land Rovers were commandiered and C Company, 1/2nd Gurkhas, set off down the treacherous road. They drove fast and furiously towards Seria, shooting their way through two rebel road-blocks and several villages in rebel hands. At last the convoy was forced to halt at Tutong, a small town half way between Brunei Town and Seria. The company commander's Land Rover was fired on and his driver was wounded, causing the vehicle to leave the road. A firefight ensued. It was soon realised that little would be achieved by such a small group attempting to go further and running the risk of yet more casualties.

Back in Brunei Town the night had produced its own problems. A number of patrols had been fired on by rebels occupying buildings and fierce battles had broken out with both sides suffering casualties. The situation remained tense and uncertain as dawn broke on 9 December. Major Lloyd-Williams ordered the

Left: British soldiers armed with 7.62mm SLRs crawl towards enemy positions in Brunei Town. Below: A detachment of the Queen's Own Highlanders in Seria, soon after the landings near the town.

Seria breakthrough party back to Brunei to reinforce his heavily pressed men until the arrival of further troops from Singapore.

The seriousness of the situation was by this time well understood in Singapore and reinforcements began to arrive in increasing numbers. First to come was the battalion commander of the 1/2nd Gurkhas with another of his companies; close on his heels followed the commanding officer of the Queen's Own Highlanders, Lieutenant-Colonel McHardy, with his first company. Brigadier J.B.A. Glennie, a staff officer from Headquarters Far East Land Forces (FARELF), also arrived with a small HQ to take over command of all troops in Brunei. His first order to the commander of the Queen's Own Highlanders was to take Seria while causing minimum casualties to the hostages. Lieutenant-Colonel McHardy quickly flew out to reconnoitre the ground and on return devised an ambitious and daring plan to relieve the oilfields.

Landing at Panaga

Part of his battalion flew in small twin-engined Twin Pioneers to land on a grass clearing near Panaga with the aim of recapturing the police station. Conditions at the landing site were atrocious: a sudden tropical downpour turned the ground into a quagmire as the aircraft landed in torrential driving rain. The remainder of his available soldiers carried out an even more daring attack. Boarding one of the giant Beverleys they flew to Seria and landed on Anduki airfield close by. The RAF pilot touched down, off-loaded his human cargo and was in the air again before the rebels in possession of the airfield managed to open fire on his aircraft. Only superficial damage was done to the Beverley and the Queen's Own Highlanders, taking advantage of their enemy's surprise, soon seized control of the area.

Early on the morning of 11 December further sub-units of the Queen's Own Highlanders landed at Anduki to be followed by men of the 1/2nd Gurkhas. By the evening of the next day Seria was in their hands and the hostages had been released.

On 12 December a company of 42 Commando, which had just arrived in Brunei, was given the task of ejecting the rebels from the town of Limbang which lies on a river in Sarawak between the two separate wedges of Brunei. The Marines made their way up river from the coast in two small craft requisitioned in Brunei Town. They moved under cover of darkness, relying for navigation on a Brunei government officer who knew the river. They arrived at Limbang just at first light and were met with a hail of fire from the police station and other buildings where a large group of rebels was hidden. Despite suffering casualties, including two Marines killed, a party from the first boat got ashore. The second craft continued up river beyond the town where the Marines on board landed and made their way back to the other party already on land. Once both groups were together they proceeded to clear Limbang of rebels and, despite the loss of three more men, the town was returned to government control by the end of the day.

Further reinforcements of British and Gurkha infantry and Marines were sent in over the course of the following week and on 19 December Major-General Walter C. Walker arrived to take control of operations as Commander British Forces Borneo Territories.

The enemy had been put to flight in a series of more or less severe skirmishes; it now remained to be seen if

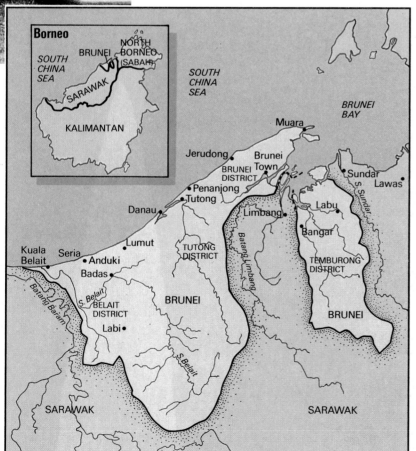

Borneo

SOUTH CHINA SEA

BRUNEI
NORTH BORNEO (SABAH)

SARAWAK

KALIMANTAN

SOUTH CHINA SEA

BRUNEI BAY

Muara

Jerudong
Brunei Town

BRUNEI DISTRICT

Sundar
Lawas

Penanjong
Tutong

S. Sundar

Danau

Labu

Limbang

Bangar

Batang Limbang

Lumut

Kuala Belait
Seria
Anduki

TUTONG DISTRICT

Badas

TEMBURONG DISTRICT

S. Belait

BRUNEI

Batang Baram

S. BELAIT DISTRICT

BRUNEI

Labi

S. Belait

SARAWAK

SARAWAK

the rebel forces could be hunted down and their organisation broken up. General Walker redeployed his forces to seek out the rebels and prevent the troubles spreading deeper into neighbouring Sarawak where there was already a considerable body of opposition to the formation of Malaysia.

The police Special Branch and army patrols soon established that, while many of the rebel army rank and file had returned home hungry and disillusioned, the hardcore elements of the movement had taken refuge in the jungle not far from Brunei Town itself and in the mangrove swamps that bordered the Brunei River. In February 1963 the Special Branch got hold of information which resulted in two of Azahari's brothers being caught.

The painstaking army patrolling went on and slowly the noose tightened as more and more information came in. By April the names of virtually all the remaining members of the secret army were known to the security forces. Then in May an informant agreed to lead a patrol of the 2/7th Gurkhas into the Brunei River swamps where he knew there was a rebel camp. Two platoons of Gurkhas were deployed in an extended cordon where the swamp edge met dry land and an assault party in canoes silently made their way into the swamp from the river. After four hours searching they came to the camp, saw the enemy and opened fire. One rebel surrendered and the remainder were put to flight. Four of the fugitives reached the line of the cordon where only a single Gurkha soldier was posted. The soldier waited until they were within 20 metres of him and then opened fire. His first shot passed through both the two leading men, killing them instantly. The other two dropped to cover and opened fire on the soldier. He managed nonetheless to shoot and wound both of his remaining adversaries and take them prisoner.

The end of a rebellion

All the four men thus eliminated were top members of the TNKU and one of those wounded turned out to be Yassin Effendi himself. The operation dealt a mortal blow to the TNKU and the rebellion collapsed almost overnight. In any case, the Sultan of Brunei decided not to join the Malaysian Federation – it would now appear that he never seriously intended to sink his personal power in a larger entity.

Not that this meant an end to disturbances in the region generally. Sukarno's support for the TNKU had not benefitted him in any way, but now, in pursuit of his aim of preventing the formation of Malaysia, he ordered extensive operations against both Sabah and Sarawak. This confrontation, coupled with internal problems caused by Chinese groups in Sarawak, led to a further British military build-up in Borneo and a dramatic widening of the area of operations.

Major F.A. Godfrey

Above: Iban tribesmen bring in rebels captured up river from Limbang. Right: An aerial view of the jungle terrain illustrates the difficulties of foot patrolling. The photograph shows a settlement on the Belait River.

The undeclared war

Indonesian confrontation with Malaysia

Above: Malaysian police use strong measures against demonstrators in Sarawak protesting against the Federation. Absorption into Malaysia was not always welcomed by the peoples of the states concerned. Below: The Indonesian troops who infiltrated into Sarawak were not all regulars and while some were quite well armed (with support weapons including mortars and 12.7mm machine guns) others only carried spears or machetes. Here guerrillas are shown after being captured by Malaysian troops in August 1964.

In 1962 Sukarno achieved a final triumph over the Dutch, against whom Indonesia's nationalist liberation struggle had been fought. By a mixture of military and diplomatic pressure, he forced the Dutch to hand over West Irian, their last colony in the archipelago. This victory added greatly to Sukarno's prestige as a world statesman and his popularity in his own country.

Sukarno's power in Indonesia rested on two pillars, the army and the Indonesian Communist Party. This close connection with communists naturally worried the British (who had just defeated a communist revolt in Malaya) and their American allies (who were extremely concerned about communist insurgency in South Vietnam, Laos and Thailand), although the confused internal politics of Indonesia made it difficult to predict Sukarno's actions.

The road to confrontation

In May 1961 Malaya and Britain began moves to create a Malaysian federation which would join the British colonies of Singapore, Sarawak and North Borneo (Sabah), and the British protectorate of Brunei, to Malaya. In British eyes, this would enable them to decolonise the area without leaving small states exposed to outside pressure. A British Commonwealth military presence would guarantee newly-created Malaysia's independence.

After initial hesitation, Sukarno came out strongly against the planned federation. But a British commission established that a majority of the inhabitants of the northern half of Borneo were in favour of, or at least not opposed to, joining Malaysia. The main internal opposition came from the Sarawak United People's Party, with a large following amongst the local Chinese population and a significant communist element, and from the Brunei People's Party.

In December 1962 the armed wing of the Brunei People's Party launched an armed rising against the government of Brunei. President Sukarno espoused their cause, promising help in the shape of volunteers and unleashing an all-out propaganda offensive against the British and Malayan governments. Britain quickly put down the Brunei revolt (although the Sultan of Brunei decided not to join Malaysia) but the war of words between Sukarno on the one hand and Britain and Malaya on the other was soon to be translated into action. Sukarno promised to crush the fledgling confederation by all possible means, 'before the sun rose on 1 January 1965'.

In support of his political offensive, the Indonesian ruler called for volunteers to enter training camps in Indonesian Kalimantan before setting out on missions against Sarawak and British North Borneo (soon to be called Sabah). Most of these volunteers were from the Indonesian communist PKI and the left-wing of the Sarawak United People's Party. In April 1963 the first raid occurred when a party of volunteers attacked a police post near the village of Tebedu in Sarawak. Earlier warnings by the Director of Operations,

The conflict between Indonesia and British and Commonwealth forces in Borneo (Kalimantan) from 1963 to 1966 was one of the strangest wars the British have ever fought. Naval ships and fighter planes patrolled the seas and skies, while artillery and regular infantry units were deployed along the border by both sides. After 1964 the clashes were invariably between regular units using modern weapons. And yet diplomatic relations continued between the adversaries for much of the time, while both sides shunned publicity for their military operations. The extent of the conflict was deliberately obscured.

In the early 1960s the future shape of Southeast Asia emerging from colonialism was still unclear. President Sukarno of Indonesia had cast himself in the role of an anti-colonialist national leader dedicated to freeing the region from European and American dominance. He aspired to extend his influence over the neighbouring states of Malaya and the Philippines.

Above: Sukarno, the Indonesian leader whose fall from power in 1965 led to the end of confrontation.

Below: Maintaining radio contact with their spotting team, British gunners pound enemy positions with 105mm Model 56 pack howitzers.

Major-General Walter C. Walker, were not taken seriously by the politicians in London and Kuala Lumpur until the raid on Tebedu; then it was realised that Sukarno meant business.

When Malaysia was officially formed in September 1963, there were severe anti-British riots in Djakarta. A crowd attacked the British embassy, stoned the staff and set fire to the building. British businesses and property fell victim to angry demonstrators. More raids across the border were bound to follow.

The urgent defence of Sarawak, Sabah and Brunei posed a considerable problem for the small British Security Force under General Walker's command. Almost everything seemed in the guerrillas' favour; the long border of 1560km (970 miles), which in many places had not been accurately mapped, ran through hostile country with few tracks and no roads; fast-flowing rivers were navigable in many parts, enabling intruders to ferry men and supplies into Sarawak or Sabah; thick jungle provided a canopy under which men could move without being seen from the air. With a string of bases along the border, often no more than a kilometre inside 'safe territory', the guerrillas had the initiative and could strike where and when they wanted.

Watching the border

The problem of surveillance along the border had been exercising the mind of General Walker. He did not have troops to spare for this important task; indeed, even if he had had more soldiers, it would have been the height of folly to have strung them in penny packets along the border. With the small force under his command he could not prevent hostile incursions but by stationing units and sub-units at strategic points, and using the hard-worked helicopters to their maximum ability, he administered some telling rebuffs which sent the infiltrators reeling back across the border in disarray. But the Indonesian still retained the initiative, and to complicate matters some alarms proved to be rumours or reports exaggerated by the local people, so

that many valuable hours were wasted on abortive operations.

By the end of 1963, General Walker was calling it an 'Undeclared War'. The United Nations made persistent efforts to institute a ceasefire so that the two sides could talk rather than shoot at one another, but when a ceasefire was finally arranged in early 1964 it did not stop the Indonesian terrorists from making incursions across the border. The situation became farcical, especially when the Indonesian government made it clear that the 'volunteer terrorists', sponsored by them, were not bound by any rules whatever. As far as the British Security Forces were concerned there was considerable relief when the ceasefire ended. Their relief was short-lived because Sukarno decided to step up his confrontation and regular units of the Indonesian Army were deployed at various points along the border with Sarawak. The threat to Kuching, the capital of Sarawak, and other strategic points became very real; no longer could General Walker claim that he was able to carry out the mission given him by the British and Malaysian governments. By the end of 1964, the Indonesians had advanced their camps and bases up to within yards of the actual border. The British, Gurkha and Malay soldiers under General Walker's command could not react until the enemy crossed the border; for them it was a frustrating business.

If political clearance had not been given for cross-border operations, then Sukarno's tactics might have won the day and the concept of Malaysia might have failed. Not surprisingly, it took a considerable time for this political clearance to be given, but Sukarno's ill-conceived decision to raise the level of his military confrontation by sending armed raiders against the mainland of Malaya helped the politicians make up their minds. Those raids, including parachute drops, were abortive and the groups of Indonesians were rounded up in a remarkably quick time. The raiders themselves were disillusioned when they were not greeted as liberators, something they had been led to expect by Sukarno. Meanwhile, thoroughly shaken by these open acts of hostility, the Malaysian government pressed their British partners into sanctioning restricted cross-border operations, with a distance of 4500m (5000 yards) into Indonesian territory as an initial limit.

There was no public announcement and these operations were always carried out under maximum secrecy. Each raid had to be authorised by the Director of Operations himself; only trained troops could be used; the depth of penetration was strictly limited, although the limit was eventually raised to 9000m (10,000 yards) – and on one or two special occasions to 18,000m (20,000 yards). All such operations were authorised to prevent the Indonesians from launching any major offensive, not in retaliation or solely to inflict casualties; and in order to win over the local tribes, when targets were selected, care was taken not to risk civilian lives. Each operation had to be self-contained because no close air support was authorised except in dire emergency. There was to be no flying over the border. General Walker's aim was to drive the guerrilla forces back deep into their own territory, but not to escalate the confrontation into an all-out war with Indonesia.

Everything had to be meticulously planned, and every man taking part down to the most junior soldier had to be thoroughly rehearsed before crossing the border. The exacting instructions governing these operations were called 'The Golden Rules', and the mental and physical strain on the commanders and troops taking part was considerable. At first little of

Above: Protected by troops, British staff leave the embassy in Djakarta, after it had been sacked by Indonesian demonstrators.

note was achieved, but eventually the Indonesian bases along the border were pushed back further and further into their own territory. Gradually the Security Forces began to dominate lengthy tracts of the border and, of equal importance, large areas of the jungle.

With the Indonesians forced to abandon their forward positions, defeat in the long term became inevitable. Their logistic and supply arrangements were primitive, although their soldiers fought with gallantry on numerous occasions. But deprived of efficient medical or administrative support, their morale was sapped as time passed and conditions worsened in their jungle bases.

Sukarno's fall

Within Indonesia itself, Sukarno's *konfrontasi* added considerably to the parlous economic problems which crippled the country and gave rise to ever-growing discontent. In late September 1965 'The Night of the Generals' coup failed, ushering in a bloodbath in which the Indonesian Army massacred at least 200,000 Indonesian communists. Sukarno was stripped of effective power and although he continued to shout that Malaysia should be quashed, the new government under General Suharto realised that the *konfrontasi* could not be won. Peace came in 1966, with effective Indonesian acceptance of the status quo.

The stamina and health of the British, Gurkha, Australasian and Malay soldiers had withstood the stress and rigours of operating for long periods in some of the toughest terrain in the world. The Gurkhas were singled out for special praise, as each of the eight Gurkha battalions had carried out at least four six-month tours during the confrontation. One young lance-corporal, Rambahadur Limbu, was to win the Victoria Cross. Because of the secrecy at the time, his citation showed him winning the award on the Malaysian side of the border when in fact the company with which he was serving was on a raid deep into Indonesian territory. This in itself illustrates the strange Undeclared War that was fought far away from the media – quite the opposite of what was to occur in Vietnam. **E. D. Smith**

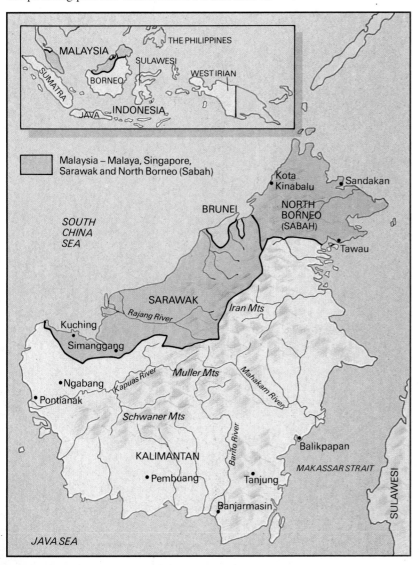

Malaysia – Malaya, Singapore, Sarawak and North Borneo (Sabah)

MALAYSIA
THE PHILIPPINES
SULAWESI
BORNEO
WEST IRIAN
SUMATRA
JAVA
INDONESIA

Kota Kinabalu
Sandakan
NORTH BORNEO (SABAH)
BRUNEI
Tawau
SOUTH CHINA SEA
SARAWAK
Iran Mts
Rajang River
Kuching
Simanggang
Ngabang
Kapuas River
Muller Mts
Mahakam River
Pontianak
Schwaner Mts
Barito River
Balikpapan
KALIMANTAN
MAKASSAR STRAIT
Pembuang
Tanjung
SULAWESI
Banjarmasin
JAVA SEA

Raid on Labang

A cross-border operation by the Gurkhas

The cross-border operations carried out under the stringent 'Golden Rules' of British Army conduct were code-named 'Claret' and each and every one was carefully planned. The raid on Labang in January 1965 was a typical example of the many raids carried out across the border, raids which remained unpublicised outside of classified reports, but which were to turn near defeat into victory.

C Company of the 2nd/7th Gurkhas was stationed in Sarawak. The company's duties were similar to those carried out by the other companies stationed along the border areas – foot and helicopter-mounted patrols, joint operations with the SAS, ambushes, and so on. They were not, however, permitted to cross the border. This was a great disappointment because C Company knew a great deal about the enemy and the whole company wanted to go on to the offensive.

Eventually, the major commanding C Company was invited to build up information on Indonesian targets in his sector with a view to launching a possible attack against them. The authority for such an attack was to be given at the highest level. C Company's main target would be Labang, a small longhouse on the east bank of the River Temburong; the river was the only supply line for the Indonesian forces in that sector. A successful attack against Labang would not only neutralise their base but would also disrupt supplies to other Indonesian forces up river, and thus be a severe blow to their morale.

It was known that the Indonesians had between 50 to 60 men at Labang armed with light machine guns, mortars and one 12.7mm heavy machine gun. Their post was a renovated longhouse in a cleared bowl about 300 metres away from the river on the west bank. Using newly acquired air photographs, a detailed model was made of the area. Then 8 Platoon commander led a recce party into the area guided by a local border scout. The following day the company commander joined the party and fire positions as well as routes were selected in anticipation of permission being given for an attack to be made against the Indonesian outpost. As the river could not be crossed, the attack would be by fire, without coming to close quarters with the enemy.

Over a month elapsed before authority for the attack was given by the director of operations. C Company was helicoptered into a landing zone (LZ) which had been secured beforehand by a party of SAS. All the men were heavily laden and carrying mortar bombs as well as their own ammunition and arms. After a march of approximately 8km (5 miles), a secure base was established with the mortars and 9 Platoon nearby but about a thousand metres from the River Temburong. Only then was it realised that the jungle canopy above the mortar position was thicker than had been anticipated and that some trees would have to be cut down. In the meantime, 7 Platoon moved down to an ambush position by the river while C Company Headquarters and 8 Platoon carried on for

a further 300 metres further north, again following the river. At the same time 8 Platoon went to the main fire position which had been selected earlier.

At about 1400 hours and while these moves were being completed, torrential rain cascaded down. The company commander gave the order for the Mortar Platoon to fell one tree at their location, and when it was realised that the noise was not carrying the order was repeated until half a dozen large trees had been felled, thus making an opening in the canopy through which the mortars could fire. After all fire positions, weapons and communications had been checked, the attacking force settled down for the long night's vigil.

Attacking the longhouse

The plan for the morning was that 8 Platoon and the mortars would make a fire attack against the Indonesians in the longhouse, across the river; meanwhile, 7 Platoon would provide left flank protection and ambush any Indonesian movement along the river. The signal to 'open fire' would be given only when Indonesians had been spotted by Company Headquarters and 8 Platoon at their various locations.

There was a heavy mist in the valley when dawn broke next morning. The mist was not to clear fully until 0800 hours, when the company commander gave orders for the mortars to open fire. As the first bomb exploded, 8 Platoon's two general-purpose machine guns began to fire at about 12 Indonesians who were eating their breakfast, sitting outside the longhouse. The Indonesians reacted quickly; their mortars and machine guns returned 8 Platoon's fire within seconds. Nevertheless, they were unable to pinpoint the platoon's position and there were no casualties among the Gurkhas. The company's mortars were soon on target and bombs landed one after another on and around the longhouse. Then, unaccountably, their accurate shooting deteriorated; only later was it found that the mortars' base plates had sunk over a metre (three feet) into the soft hillside. Eight Platoon continued to fire for another 12 minutes until the Indonesians had ceased to retaliate. The company commander waited a further 15 minutes but as complete silence prevailed, he gave the order for a general withdrawal.

Labang was never used as a base by the Indonesians thereafter. An unspectacular raid, yes: but meticulously planned and carefully rehearsed, because each and every soldier taking part in the raid had been briefed using an accurate model of the area. The importance of the Labang raid, and the many others that were taking place at various points along the border with Kalimantan, lay in the fact that the Indonesians were being driven further and further back into their own territory, so that it was soon to prove impossible for them to mount any offensive raids against Sarawak and Sabah. In such a way was the military confrontation won in Borneo.

E.D. Smith

A British major briefs Malaysian troops on the areas to be covered in search of terrorist units (below right). The dense nature of the jungle terrain provided no readily discernible physical features, thus making it necessary for patrolling units to constantly check their position (inset right). Similarly the jungle easily obscured the presence of enemy units, making even a river crossing a dangerous task requiring constant cover from the man at the rear (inset far right).

With silence and stealth

British tactics during confrontation

In the stealthy jungle war between Britain and Indonesia the tactical advantage lay with the man who kept still rather than the man on the move. The inevitable noise, however slight, of soldiers moving through jungle made it almost impossible for them to surprise a lurking enemy. As a result the war was resolved by a series of ambushes and preparation of a successful ambush was the tactical gambit of prime importance in the densely forested area where the clashes occurred.

The British and their allies realised that this would be the position from the inception of the struggle and their formula for winning the war makes an intriguing contrast to that of the Americans in their parallel war in Vietnam. The people who could observe this most closely were the Australian SAS men who served in both wars and attempted to fulfill the same role in each. In Borneo the SAS specialised in immensely demanding covert operations, observing their enemy and signalling details of his movements to support forces. When news of enemy movements reached this support, highly trained infantry would be moved to ambush and cut off positions as secretively as possible. In Vietnam, by contrast, the helicopter-borne support would come pouring noisily out of the sky backed by gunships and air strikes. The Australians observed that far fewer enemy formations escaped the stealthy ambush techniques of Borneo than the cavalier tactics of Vietnam. However, it was also true that only the most experienced of fully professional infantry units were good enough to command success in Borneo so that the Americans, with a largely conscript army, did not have a realistic option of using that approach.

In addition the British did have a few months to prepare for their campaign. The Brunei Revolt of December 1962 together with the rhetoric of the Indonesian President Sukarno gave a clear indication of trouble to come. Obviously the 1560km (970 mile)

jungle frontier could not be effectively guarded by the five battalions at the disposition of the commander, so the border area was seeded with tiny SAS patrols of two to five men. The British had learned lots of painful lessons about jungle warfare during their recently concluded war against communist guerrillas in Malaya and some of their most valuable tutors had come from the head-hunting population of Borneo. These Iban tribesmen had an almost supernatural tracking ability coupled with the superbly alert senses of people untouched by modern civilisation: their sense of smell, for instance, was as acute as that of many wild animals. Tribesmen similar to these admired allies inhabited the longhouse of the hinterland of Borneo and the SAS lost no time in making contact with them and enlisting their help in locating cross-border raiding parties.

Search and destroy

When the raids began the tribesmen of the rain forest were auxiliary eyes and ears to the SAS, but the task of destroying the enemy fell to the infantry battalions. Here the British were particularly well served by their Gurkha soldiers who were ferociously dedicated and superbly trained in jungle warfare, but British and later Australian and New Zealand infantry also played their part. These forces were held as a mobile reserve and rushed to deal with intruders by road, if there was any, by river or, most frequently, by helicopter. The idea was usually to ambush the enemy

Above: A typical encampment deep in the heart of the jungle. By remaining in such locations for long periods of time British troops found it easier to monitor the movements of Indonesian units. Left: Troops dismount from a helicopter at speed in pursuit of the enemy. Below: Natives look on as British troops prepare to evacuate an area after a successful operation. The use of helicopters for both rapid deployment and collection of troops did much to overcome the problems posed by dense vegetation.

force and this was made easier when the SAS had already reconnoitred suitable ambush positions. However, if the enemy had to be pursued, Iban or Iban-taught trackers preceded the infantry's cautious progress.

As the Indonesians were brave and tough soldiers who also used native trackers, the game of stalking them through the jungle was grim and extremely taxing. The highly developed senses of the trackers meant that any soldier who smoked, washed, used toothpaste or hair oil would give away an ambush position by his alien smell. In addition the slightest noise could alarm the quarry so that men who were liable to snore or talk in their sleep were constantly checked by sentries, a man with a cough would not be sent out on patrol and even whispering was forbidden for long stretches of time. Naturally, holding an ambush for days at a time or moving through jungle under these conditions was a great strain on the men involved, but high motivation and training brought spectacular results.

Clashes between Indonesian and British troops swiftly became a very one-sided affair with a disproportionately large number of casualties on the Indonesian side. At the same time it became evident that neither the British nor the Indonesian governments were prepared to let much news of these clashes out. The British did not want their success to be construed as aggression while the Indonesians were not proud of their failure. Under cover of this news blackout, the British commander was able to undertake a more offensive role.

Patrolling the jungle

Movement through the jungle was immensely difficult and the Indonesian raiding parties were often supplied along rivers and jungle trails. The British infantry were moved to ambush positions to cut these supply routes. These stealthy fighting patrols were very much on their own in the jungle but, wherever possible, artillery support for them was laid on. Gun batteries were established at defended bases and an artillery officer went with the patrol to call down fire where necessary. The sudden arrival of a barrage helped British forces to make a clean break with Indonesian counter-attackers after a clash. However, this onslaught on the Indonesian lines of communication, together with attacks on their raiding parties, could not wipe out their ability to make further raids – that could only be done by extinguishing the base camps on the Indonesian side of the border.

Because of the lack of media coverage the British felt able to take their campaign across the frontier. To do this they followed the same tactical mixture as before: SAS scouts went ahead to pinpoint the targets and to explore routes by which the infantry could safely and secretly approach them. With this difficult task accomplished, strong fighting patrols were sent out to attack and destroy the enemy bases. The technique was still a variant of the ambush tactic – the achievement of surprise was all important.

By these means the British achieved superiority and as much control as was possible over the disputed jungle area. It was obvious which side was winning the war. By the time a peace agreement was signed in August 1966 an estimated 2000 Indonesians had been killed while British and Gurkha dead numbered 59. The intensive training and meticulous attention to detail had proved worthwhile. **P.J. Banyard**

Hitting the target

Weapons firing techniques in theory and practice

The rules for the use of weapons to be found in infantry manuals the world over are designed to achieve maximum effectiveness against the enemy.

Priority is always given to the prevention of accidents. The weapon is always switched to safety except when a firefight is actually in progress. And weapons are always carried muzzle down. Then, when the enemy is encountered, the infantryman can move into one of four classic firing positions.

The most widely used position both in support of an assault and in defence is the prone position. This position is usually accepted as the most comfortable and the steadiest. Consequently it is also the most accurate and inflicts heavy casualties on the enemy.

Lying face down on the ground, the soldier ensures that the rifle, his spine and his right leg are directly aligned. His left leg is spread out to the side and both feet are lain as flat as can be physically achieved. From the stomach forward the body begins to rise, and the weight is supported on the elbows. The right hand pulls the weapon into the shoulder and the left is placed well under the stock to give maximum support. This is an excellent firing position in that it presents the enemy with very little in the way of a target although it does have a restricted field of fire.

Firing from the ground

Often in a firefight, a series of low obstacles between the firer and the enemy prevent the use of the prone position. To cope with this situation, the infantryman adopts a sitting or kneeling position. For the sitting position the body is turned 45 degrees to the right, the knees are raised and the feet are placed some 60cm (24in) apart. The left elbow is placed on the left knee with the forearm extended to support the weapon while the right elbow is rocked slightly inward allow-

ing the right hand to pull the butt well into the shoulder, support the weapon and operate it. A variation is the cross-legged sitting position. In this case support for the weapon comes from the elbows which are placed in the crook between the upper and lower leg. These positions are difficult to use for extended periods, and again the field of fire is restricted.

Kneeling is a position which can be of use for firing over low obstacles; also, in an assault dropping to the kneeling position can be effective for firing off a few quick, fairly accurate rounds. The left knee is raised and the left elbow, placed slightly forward as in sitting, gives the support. The right elbow is pushed outwards and upwards to bring it parallel with the weapon. The soldier sits either on the point of the right heel or the right instep. This position is accurate for only a short period of time before muscle fatigue sets in.

The final firing position is the standing or offhand position. This provides the least support of the four and is difficult to maintain steadily for more than a few seconds. The left foot is placed forward of the right with the knee slightly bent and the weight upon it. The left hand grips the stock with the arm providing what support it can. The right elbow is pushed upwards and outwards, as in the kneeling position. Although unstable and difficult to maintain, the standing position has a wide field of fire, allowing the soldier to engage targets in almost any elevation or dispersal.

While these positions are basic to infantry training the world over, there are inevitably times when they are not appropriate. Consequently, certain methods for the use of the modern weapon have evolved which, while they may not be in an infantry manual, are extremely effective.

The first principle of these less orthodox firing

Above: A Polisario guerrilla demonstrates the sitting firing position. Although offering a degree of support to the weapon, this position has both a restricted field of fire and is difficult to maintain for any period of time.

Action in Vietnam

The modern infantryman has developed unorthodox techniques for weapons firing. As this anonymous testimony from the machine-gunner with a US infantry platoon in Vietnam shows, speed of response can be the key to survival.

'When it hit, I was firing rolling with the machine gun going off. I had learned to fire in bursts of only three. I had to learn to fire only three shots at a time so the enemy at a little distance couldn't tell who had the M-60.

'We were moving steady. My assistant gunner said, "left eleven o'clock." He made me practice to respond to his voice commands. All he had to do was find my targets. I would gear on them. We were running it and hitting it. He says, "run it" and we would run. "Okay, down!" I'm down and then I'm up again. He was just hollering commands. "Ammo up". The first squad had to do whatever they had to do to get a couple of hundred rounds to me, whatever amount I needed....

'So we ran and we ran and we ran. Then all of a sudden, we heard capping by us – Cap-cap. Cap-cap. We turned around. That whole squad almost got killed by me. As I spun around, I saw a little spark coming out of the trees. I opened that M-60 up and just ran it back and forth, spraying. Everybody behind me had to hit the ground lying flat. I was firing thinking, "damn these fools, these suckers ain't getting me."'

A US soldier with an M60 prepares to advance.

Firing positions

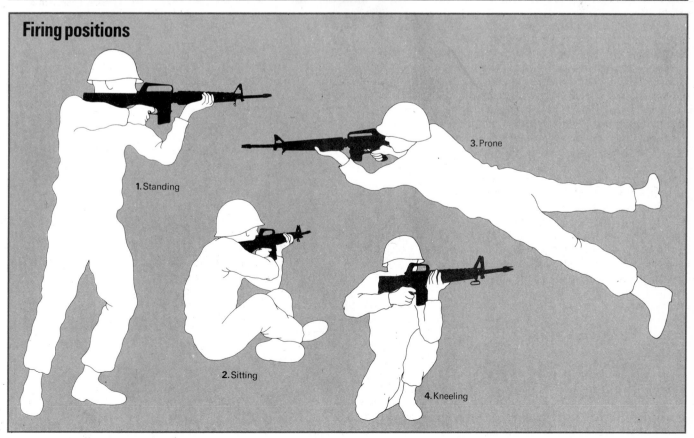

1. Standing

2. Sitting

3. Prone

4. Kneeling

techniques is the automatic response, the concept that the weapon is both a physical and mental extension of the body. Immediately the target is viewed, the weapon moves and the trigger is pulled. As the mind registers target hits, so it must subconsciously search for a new point of impact. It is also extremely important that at all times, without conscious thought, the body is balanced and the feet are never far apart – the recognised maximum in tactical patrolling is 60cm (24in). This allows the weight to be forward and the knees to be slightly bent.

Responding to the assault

The most basic of the weapons firing techniques in an assault situation is the instant response to right or left. If an enemy comes within the line of vision but is not aware of one's presence, range will affect the mode of response. At close quarters an immediate response with a burst of fire is most effective, but at a distance the soldier can adopt a fire position which will ensure him both cover and arc of fire. The response itself consists of a reflex action where the soldier pivots on the balls of his feet, twisting his torso and hips in the required direction. The weapon is pushed forward towards the target and a burst of fire released. When the left foot is forward and the response is made to the left, the left foot remains still and the right pivots on the ball; both knees are bent, slightly, in the direction of the target. Should the response be to the right, both feet pivot to bring the target into the line of fire. The arc of fire allowed by this movement is roughly 200 degrees, 100 degrees to either side of the assault line.

Above: Sitting on the point of his right heel, with his right elbow pushed outwards, a soldier adopts the classic kneeling position to cover a street in Belfast. This position allows some cover from the corner wall.

Below: South Vietnamese troops adopt the prone position during range practice with Browning automatic rifles. The prone position is easily maintained for extended periods and gives good support and improves accuracy; heavy casualties can be inflicted against the enemy while giving the firer a protective low profile.

Because weapons are usually carried to the right, there is considerable difference between responses to the left and right. In the response to the right, the fact that the right arm will automatically hug the stock of the weapon and that the left is stretched in its support both mean that the muzzle of the weapon is forced down, dropping the optimum point of aim. To compensate for this, the weapon is pushed forward from the body, forcing the muzzle up. The arc of fire can also be increased by letting go of the muzzle with the left hand and allowing the swing to continue to the right. In the response to the left, the stock of the weapon naturally moves away from the body and similarly increases the arc of fire but without the loss of the support of the left hand; consequently the response to the left may be more accurate.

Another effective firing technique is the drop to a squat, usually employed while on an assault march under ambush conditions. The infantryman brings his feet parallel and drops to his haunches, at the same time releasing a short (three to four rounds) burst of fire. As his thighs hit his calves a second burst is fired and as he bounces back upwards he fires a third burst. From this moment on, he continues to fire at the target while quickly advancing to a position of cover. Generally the first burst will be low, the second will be correct and the third allows the shooter to advance.

When moving against known enemy positions in a final assault, different techniques are applied. The most common of these is the assault position which can be used for rifles, sub-machine guns, light machine guns and, if the gunner is strong enough, heavy machine guns. The weapon is held with the butt against the side of the body just above the hip bone. With a sub-machine gun, the weight of the running body thrown over the barrel tends to prevent it twisting off target. With a light machine gun, usually supported from the shoulder by a sling, bursts of fire can be accurately delivered and provide substantial support for the advance.

Finally, another excellent assault technique is the use of what the Americans term 'point shooting'. This involves throwing the weapon to the shoulder and engaging the target without actually using the sights. As well as being effective for quick response, this technique is particularly good in battle conditions with adverse lighting, allowing the infantryman wider fields of vision than are possible through the aperture of a conventional sight.

Alexander McNair-Wilson

The S-TANK

When it first appeared in 1961, the Swedish Strids-vagn 103 MBT, or S-Tank, represented a revolutionary concept in tank design; not only because it was turretless, but because the entire vehicle was so engineered as to provide both the elevation and traverse for the fixed main armament.

In the late 1950s Sven Berge, head of tank design in the Swedish Army Ordnance Vehicle Division, set out to design a new armoured vehicle of radical design and low silhouette. Influenced by the French pre-World War II Char B and the more modern AMX-13 which mounted its main armament in an oscillating turret, and exploiting experience gained in the design of self-propelled guns, Berge proceeded to design an assault gun – the IKV-103. This vehicle, which mounted a 105mm gun, was built by AB Landsverk and Bofors, and was later used as a test bed for the S-Tank concept to examine the problems of accurate alignment of the main gun. The IKV-103's system of two hydraulically-powered external levers which acted on the hull and individual tracks provided a means of precise control over track movement. Test results were encouraging and further trials were made using an American M4 Sherman medium tank chassis in which the hydraulic rams were placed inside the vehicle and the levers situated between the tracks and the hull.

In mid-1958 Bofors received the contract to develop the new tank. Although relatively inexperienced in vehicle design, the firm had amassed considerable knowledge in weapon systems design and, assisted by Volvo and Landsverk, proceeded with the development. In 1957 Landsverk had produced two prototypes for the KRV medium tank (which was discontinued) and their chassis were used as test beds for the hydro-pneumatic suspension and hydrostatic steering system of the forthcoming S-Tank. The first two prototypes were ready in 1961 and an order was placed with Bofors for 10 production models even before these had appeared.

The suspension system incorporated four Centurion road wheels on each side (without track return rollers) with a front drive sprocket and rear idler.

Top: S-Tanks advance across the battlefield supported by infantry and Swedish-built Pbv 302 APCs. Above: S-Tanks on the assembly line at the Bofors works. Since the late 19th century, Sweden has had an important arms industry. Left: The driver/gunner's position in the S-Tank showing the steering and suspension control unit with loading and firing buttons for the 105mm main armament and 7.62mm machine guns. Right: An S-Tank on winter manoeuvres puts its secondary armament to the test.

Previous page: An S-Tank accelerates up an incline on a forest training ground.

Rubber inserts on the dry pin tracks were added later. The road wheels are mounted on a system of hydraulically operated arms and by the elevation and depression of these arms the entire hull with its fixed gun may be raised or lowered to plus 12 degrees or minus 10 degrees while track length is compensated as it does so. Aiming in traverse is achieved by slewing the tank in its tracks. The concept is unusual but has proved perfectly satisfactory in operation through sound engineering and rugged components. Steering the tank and aligning the gun is controlled by a single unit fitted with handlebars, allowing the driver/gunner to operate the vehicle and engage targets with great speed. The commander is provided with a second control unit and can override the driver/gunner if necessary. The S-Tank is highly manoeuvrable and, because of its extremely low and flat silhouette, presents a very small target.

The third crew member, the radio operator, faces to the rear of the vehicle and is provided with controls which enable him to drive the tank backwards, a highly desirable characteristic in armoured warfare. He also increases the tank's visual protection by maintaining a rearward watch which gives the commander constant all-round observation.

The S-Tank is powered by the Rolls-Royce K60 engine which, like the Israeli Merkava's powerplant, is mounted forward in the hull and increases crew protection. A second 'booster' engine, the Boeing 533 gas turbine, is provided for negotiating rough terrain or for use in battle when rapid acceleration might be required. The gas turbine also aids cold-weather starting and provides an additional power source in case of diesel failure. Fuel tanks are mounted externally above the tracks.

Main armament consists of a rifled 105mm L74 gun which passes between the driver/gunner and the commander in the fighting compartment. It is a longer Bofors-manufactured version of the British 105mm L7 and is provided with an automatic loading device

Above: A pre-production prototype of the S-Tank with the original, domed, commander's cupola. Right and below: The S-Tank was the first tank to be fitted with a flotation screen permanently fixed to the hull. Once in position the vehicle can swim at 5.5km/h (3mph) propelled by its tracks.

Left: By dispensing with a turret, and mounting the main armament within the hull itself, the S-Tank's designers achieved a far lower silhouette for the vehicle than that of the conventional turreted tank. Compared with the Centurion on the right, the S-Tank offers a very limited target area and is ideally suited to operating in the hull down position.

Left and bottom: Two views of the S-Tank showing the elevation and depression of the fixed main armament. Pitch of the hull is precision-regulated by the vehicle's hydro-pneumatic suspension system. This innovation, however, does not allow the vehicle to fire on the move.

which feeds the 50 rounds available by hydraulic power from a magazine into the breech. The magazine is in two halves and various types of rounds can be employed including APDS, HE, HESH and smoke. Spare ammunition is stored at the rear of the vehicle. The efficiency of the automatic loader provides a rate of fire of between 10 and 15 rounds per minute which is substantially higher than most manually-loaded conventional tank armament. At the moment of firing additional stability is provided by the locking of suspension and tracks. The empty shell cases are automatically ejected from the rear of the vehicle.

Secondary armament in the early versions consisted of four Ksp-58 7.62mm machine guns box-mounted in pairs on the glacis and firing along the axis of the main armament. For a time the box to the driver's right was fitted with a 0.5in ranging gun, but this was later deleted. A further 7.62mm machine gun, mounted on the commander's cupola, was also provided. Eight smoke dischargers are fitted and some S-Tanks are fitted with Bofors Lyran flare launchers which can provide night-time battlefield illumination.

The S-Tank offers a high level of protection to its crew. In addition to the very flat profile of the glacis plate, ribbing on it decreases the possibility of rounds penetrating. As the pre-production models were evaluated further improvements were incorporated including a clamp for the protruding barrel of the main

gun and a fume extractor fitted to the barrel, as on the Centurions in Swedish service. In addition two track return rollers were fitted on each side.

In the field of optics, the driver/gunner and commander are provided with a Jungner OPS-1 periscope/sight with wide angle vision and up to x18 magnification. With his cupola gyro-stabilised laterally and his OPS-1 in elevation, the commander enjoys a consistently high level of vision, assisted by four periscopes. The driver/gunner is provided with one periscope and the radio operator with two periscopes with armoured visors which can be lowered from inside the tank. A laser rangefinder has been developed, and this has led to an improvement in accuracy. Infra-red driving lights are standard though the vehicle has no infra-red searchlight.

Since deep-water obstacles abound in Sweden, the S-Tank is equipped with a flotation screen which is normally stowed flat around the tank's upper decking and can be erected in about 15 minutes to enable the tank to swim, powered by its tracks. This flotation gear was introduced as standard on the Stridsvagn 103B and retrofitted to the earlier A-series models. The vehicle is also fitted with a bulldozer blade which can be folded beneath the glacis plate when not required and manually brought into position for the excavation of a fire position. Stowage bins are provided at the rear of the tank.

The Stridsvagn 103A was formally adopted by the Swedish Army in July 1964 and the first of the 300

Bottom: A view of the S-Tank which clearly shows the bulldozer blade stowed beneath the hull front. The blade can be manually lowered and locked into position by the crew in five minutes and is used for digging out a firing position (inset) or clearing heavy obstacles. The depth of the cut made by the blade is controlled by altering the pitch of the hull.

vehicles now in service began to equip units in 1966. Production continued until 1971, and currently the tank equips six of the nine Swedish armoured brigades while the remaining three have the Centurion. Although the S-Tank has not been employed outside Sweden, the United States, Great Britain and West Germany have all evaluated it. The tank is extremely cost-effective and has proved reliable in service, a tribute to both advanced design and sound Swedish engineering. At present 275hp Detroit Diesel 6V 53T engines are being installed which will prolong the tank's life until its planned successor appears in the late 1980s. This new AFV is likely to owe much to the S-Tank and is being developed jointly by Bofors and Häggland and Söner.

Although to date it has not been proved in battle, there is no doubt that the S-Tank provides the Swedish Army with an effective and well-armed vehicle which offers its crew good protection and will remain the mainstay of the Swedish Armoured Corps until the new MBT appears.

Armament and crew positions

7.62mm machine gun · automatic loading system · smoke dischargers · commander · radio operator · driver/gunner · 105mm main gun · two 7.62mm machine guns

Stridsvagn 103B MBT

Crew 3
Dimensions Length (gun included) 8.9m (29ft 2½in); width 3.4m (11ft 2in); height (including machine gun) 2.5m (8ft 2½in)
Weight Combat loaded 39,000kg (85,979lb)
Engines One Rolls-Royce K60 water-cooled multi-fuel engine developing 240hp at 3650rpm; one Boeing 533 gas turbine developing 490shp at 38,000rpm

Performance Maximum road speed 50km/h (31mph); range 390km (245 miles); vertical obstacle 0.9m (2ft 11in); trench 2.3m (7ft 6in); gradient 60 per cent; water speed 6km/h (4mph)

Armour Details classified
Armament One 105mm L74 automatic gun; two 7.62mm machine guns mounted on the left hull front; one 7.62mm machine gun mounted on the commander's cupola; two four-barrelled smoke dischargers

Above: A rear view of the S-Tank. Ammunition is stored for safety at the rear of the vehicle; the S-Tank and the Israeli Merkava are among the few MBTs that include this feature. The S-Tank is also provided with additional stowage bins mounted on the hull rear. Left: The addition of ribbed armour in the form of a series of rectangular horizontal bars to the well-shaped glacis plate provides the S-Tank with considerably increased protection against high-velocity armour-piercing rounds.

Uncle Sam's backyard

War and revolution in Latin America

At the end of World War II the United States was unquestionably the dominant power throughout the Americas. Latin America fell automatically into the US sphere of influence, a situation formalised by the foundation of the Organization of American States (OAS) by the US and Latin American countries in 1948. Economically and militarily unrivalled, the US should have had an easy ride in the region; instead Latin America has been the bugbear of successive administrations in Washington up to the present day. If the US has had to devote so much time, thought and money to an area in which its ascendancy should have been assured, the reason lies in the instability and fragility of Latin American economies and governments. Like the Soviet Union in eastern Europe, the US has found that governments favourable to its interests have been unable to satisfy their own peoples' aspirations to prosperity and national pride.

A glance at the recent history of almost any of the Latin American countries will reveal the chronic political instability to which they are a prey (Mexico is the glaring exception, having forged some measure of effective government out of the traumas of revolution and civil war in the early 20th century). A welter of coups, uprisings, changes of constitution and regime, testifies not to any transformation of the countries concerned, but rather to frustration at the failure of genuine change to occur. Fuelled by accelerating population growth and rising expectations, desire for change is strong; but the forces of inertia are generally stronger. Any attempt at reform runs into the vested interests of large landowners, an urban elite of entrepreneurs, lawyers and financiers, and the US-based multinationals which control a remarkable share of Latin America's industry, mining and agriculture. Even if vested interests are defeated, the brutal inequalities of wealth and poverty, and economic dependence on the US, are not easily overcome.

Three figures have emerged in the struggle for change in the postwar political scene: the demagogue, the modernising military leader, and the revolutionary. The dominant national leader in the immediate aftermath of World War II was the Argentinian, Colonel Juan Perón. Despite his military rank, Perón achieved power as a politician of mass appeal. Impressed by European fascism in the 1930s, Perón advocated a corporate state. He rose to a government position in Argentina in 1943 and used the opportunity to build up support amongst the disorganised mass of new immigrant workers through spreading non-socialist unionism and promoting welfare measures. Afraid of his growing influence, military leaders had Perón arrested in October 1945, but mass demonstrations by his supporters secured his release. In February 1946 he was elected president.

Aided by his actress-wife Eva, Perón held the allegiance of the *descamisados* (shirtless ones) of the slums. He nationalised British-owned railways and

Above: A poster of Luís Somoza, defaced in the streets of Managua, the capital of Nicaragua. Somoza's family had dominated Nicaragua since a successful coup in 1934. The means by which they took power, the nature of their repressive, conservative regime, and their eventual defeat by an armed revolutionary group (the Sandinistas) typify the problems of political legitimacy in Latin America.

utilities, while at the same time making torture a standard part of police procedure and depending heavily on the army. It was the army which, in 1955, overthrew Perón and drove him into exile. Yet such was his charismatic appeal that for many years a guerrilla movement operated in his name, and when he was at last allowed to return to Argentina, an old man, in 1973, he easily reassumed the presidency. Even after his death the following year, his second wife Isabel was able to rule for almost two years on the strength of the Perón name alone.

Perón's flamboyant career illustrates vividly several important aspects of the Latin American situation. One is the personal influence exercised by a very small number of national politicians, sometimes through a whole lifetime of spectacular ups and downs. In Ecuador, for example, José María Velasco Ibarra – a man who claimed that if you gave him a balcony he would achieve political power – was five times president and four times deposed by military coups over a period of 30 years. An unpoliticised and often illiterate population, untouched by weak party organisations, could be mobilised by a strongly projected personality.

Another lesson of Perón's rule is the preponderant

role of the military in political life, including of course Perón himself. The Peruvian poet Manuel Gonzalez Prada described the presidency as the ultimate rank in a successful military career. Of course, the presence of a colonel or general as head of state does not necessarily imply a military – or undemocratic – regime. Many officers are elected and run civilian governments. But direct military interventions in government have certainly been common enough.

The military coup is a Latin American institution. Most coups are very formal affairs and completely bloodless – typically, in the Ecuadorian coup of 1972 the only casualty was a passer-by run over by a tank at a street corner. The causes of military action often have an element of personal interest – in 1962 units of the Guatemalan air force bombed the presidential palace when tighter income tax laws were introduced. But in general the high level of military involvement reflects the armed forces' view that they are responsible for the national interest.

The classic timing for a military coup is directly after presidential elections. Under most Latin American constitutions, the president must be elected by over 50 per cent of votes cast. If no one has a clear majority – which often happens with more than two candidates – the congress has to decide who shall be president. At this point, so often, the army intervenes

Above: Members of the Guatemalan Liberation Army march past a church, during the CIA-organised uprising of 1954. Right: General Juan Perón whose mixture of personal charisma and ruthlessness made him both respected and feared as a political leader.

Latin America

The 'Football War'

Open hostilities between the regular armies of Latin American states have been rare since 1945. The largest-scale conflict was the 'Football War' of 1969 between Honduras and El Salvador.

Relations between the two countries were tense because some 350,000 peasants from overpopulated El Salvador had settled in Honduras. When the two national football teams were drawn against one another in a World Cup qualifier, hostility boiled over. The two legs of the tie both ended in violent attacks on away supporters. As tempers mounted, Salvadoran settlers were forced to flee Honduras.

On 14 July, Salvadoran troops armed with light tanks, mortars and bazookas invaded Honduras. The Honduran army was no match for the Salvadorans, but Honduran peasants armed with machetes harassed the invaders' communications. By 18 July, when hostilities ceased, some 2000 people were dead. Lengthy peace negotiations ensued.

El Salvador qualified for the World Cup.

Below: Tempers rage among the civilian population in Peru as communist supporters assault an anti-communist protester. Bottom: A dramatic scene during the 1962 revolt at Puerto Cabello in Venezuela. The soldier on the far right has just been hit by a rebel bullet (he died later) while his comrade drops into a crouch just prior to locating and killing the sniper. In front of them lie three colleagues, early casualties of the attack.

to prevent, or insist on, a candidate taking office.

Such interventions are normally temporary and can be very frequent. But since the 1960s some more decisive military takeovers have been carried out. In 1964 the military seized power in Brazil, traditionally a country of civilian government. They did not install a personalised dictatorship, but a technocratic regime in which progressive but authoritarian officers strove to modernise the country's economy while repressing left-wing movements. Argentina, Uruguay and Chile all saw decisive moves to military control in the 1970s. General Augusto Pinochet's unusually bloody coup against the left-wing Chilean President Salvatore Allende in 1973 ended a tradition of democracy stretching back to the 19th century.

These new military regimes reflected a sharpening of cold-war ideological divides in Latin America.

Until the 1960s it was often difficult to describe the continent in terms of 'left' and 'right'. The personal rule of the Somoza family in Nicaragua, for example, hardly fitted modern political terminology, being more like a form of gangsterism than a 'right-wing' dictatorship. The links of General Alfredo Stroessner's Paraguay with ex-Nazis suggests a clearer political alignment, but his regime shows none of the main features of a fascist state except the brutality.

The US, however, was intent on seeing Latin America in terms of the defence of freedom against international communism. The first postwar *cause célèbre* was Guatemala. In 1950 elections brought the reforming government of Colonel Jacobo Arbenz Guzmán to power. He embarked on a programme of land reform which involved redistributing unused holdings of the United Fruit Company – the US giant which owned not only vast tracts of Guatemala's land but also the railway and main port – amongst the peasantry. But Jacobo Arbenz was supported by the Guatemalan communists. In 1954 at Caracas the US declared that since any communist government was a servant of international communism, the presence of communists in positions of power represented outside interference in Latin American affairs. Following the Monroe Doctrine that the US would resist interference by any outside power in the Americas, the US justified its own intervention. The CIA organised an invasion of Guatemala in June 1954 by Guatemalans opposed to Arbenz and he was overthrown.

Terrorism and torture

The ideological conflicts clarified after Castro's victory in Cuba in 1959. To the US, Castro's espousal of communism and acceptance of Soviet influence confirmed their worst fears; to many Latin Americans, however, Castro offered an inspiring example of how true independence could be won and a degree of social justice achieved. The rise of revolutionary guerrilla movements with a consciously left-wing ideology was met by the new-style military regimes, and by new techniques of counter-insurgency often surpassing the traditional cruelties of Latin American dictatorships. Right-wing terrorist movements specialising in the assassination of trade union leaders and other left-wingers grew up in countries as far apart as Argentina and El Salvador.

For the left, the overthrow of Allende's democratically-elected left-wing government in Chile marked the end of notions of orderly change. The failure of guerrilla movements in the 1960s and early 1970s produced a temporary lull, but the successful mass uprising in Nicaragua against the Somoza dictatorship in 1978-79 ushered in a new phase of instability in Central America. The Nicaraguan Sandinista regime soon showed its left-wing colours, and in conjunction with a very similar civil war in neighbouring El Salvador caused consternation in Washington.

The US problem is severe. Brutal regimes breed violent opposition. As long as poverty confronts conspicuous wealth in Latin America's mushrooming cities, and as long as peasants are denied the land they crave, governments cannot be stable. The tradition of endless coups and swashbuckling revolutionary bands is slowly dying, but only to be replaced by deeper-rooted conflicts. Latin America is heading from a past of comic opera into a future heavy with tragic possibilities. **R.G. Grant**

The violent continent

Military intervention and popular revolt have been the hallmark of Latin-American politics since 1945. This list includes only successful coups and uprisings.

ARGENTINA
1946 *May* Colonel Juan Perón Sosa elected president.
1955 *September* Perón overthrown in military coup led by General Eduardo Lonardi. *November* Lonardi deposed by General Pedro Aramburu in bloodless coup.
1962 *March* Military coup overthrows civilian government of President Arturo Frondizi.
1966 *June* Military coup installs General Juan Carlos Onganía, in place of civilian government of President Arturo Illia.
1970 *June* Military junta deposes Onganía, installs General Levington.
1971 *March* Levington replaced by General Lanusse.
1973 *September* Perón returns to presidency.
1974 *July* Perón dies, succeeded by his wife Isabel.
1976 *March* Isabel Perón overthrown by General Jorge Rafael Videla installing military regime

BOLIVIA
1946 *July* Colonel Villarroel deposed by popular uprising backed by elements of the army.
1951 *May* Army takeover after MNR election victory.
1952 *April* Popular rising overthrows military government; MNR leader Victor Paz Estenssoro becomes president.
1964 *November* The vice-president, General René Barrientos Ortuño, deposes Paz Estenssoro by military coup.
1969 *September* Coup led by General Alfredo Ovando Candía overthrows President Siles.
1970 *October* General Juan José Torres deposes General Ovando.
1971 *August* Military coup brings Colonel Hugo Banzer to power.
1978 *July* Coup led by General Juan Pereda Asbún. *November* Further coup led by General David Padilla Aranciba.
1979 *November* After indecisive elections Colonel Alberto Natusch Busch seizes power, but withdraws in 15 days.
1980 *July* Coup by General Luis García Meza after further indecisive elections.
1981 *August* Military uprising replaces General García with General Celso Torrelio Villa.
1982 *October* Hernán Siles Zuazo, victor in 1980 elections, installed as president.

Peru, 1962 – a bloodless coup

'In the early morning hours of July 18, a cordon of tanks and 200 army rangers, in camouflaged battle dress, encircled the Palace of Pizarro. After the guards refused to admit them to the grounds, a tank crashed through the heavy iron gate. From that point onward, the rite was formally correct. Colonel Gonzalo Briceno led two four-man columns into the president's office. Displaying eight armed hand grenades and two satchels of TNT, the commandos "invited" Prado to come with them. Seated at his desk with his family and friends standing behind him, the beleaguered chief of state declined their request. In a voice that at first trembled but then firmed, he made a brief address, protesting the military's violation of the constitution. There were cheers and some angry shouts.... The fallen leader and his family were taken to the Callao naval base where they were held until the expiration of Prado's term on July 28. The military then permitted the ex-president to fly to Paris, where he died four years later.'

Extract from David P. Werlich, Peru.

BRAZIL
1945 *October* Bloodless military coup deposes President Getúlio Vargas, dictator for 15 years.
1950 *October* Vargas elected president.
1954 *August* Vargas commits suicide after army calls for his resignation.
1964 *April* Coup led by General Humberto Castelo Branco overthrows left-wing President João Goulart; military government established.

CHILE
1973 *September* Military coup led by General Augusto Pinochet Ugarte overthrows left-wing government of Salvatore Allende Gossens, ending long period of Chilean democracy.

COLOMBIA
1953 *June* Civilian president deposed by General Gustavo Rojas Pinilla.
1957 *May* Military junta overthrows Rojas Pinilla, prepares the way for return of elected government.

COSTA RICA
1948 *April* Civil war ends with overthrow of President Picado; Colonel José Figueres takes power, establishes democracy.

CUBA
1952 *March* Coup reestablishes direct rule of General Fulgencio Batista, who had previously held power from 1933 to 1946.
1959 *January* Guerrilla war brings Fidel Castro Ruz to power.

DOMINICAN REPUBLIC
1961 *May* General Rafael Trujillo Molina, effective ruler since 1930, assassinated.
1963 *September* Military coup overthrows elected President Juan Bosch.
1965 *April* Supporters of Bosch topple civilian junta, but after US intervention they are ousted from power.

ECUADOR
1947 *August* Colonel Carlos Manchero replaces President José María Velasco Ibarra in bloodless coup. *September* Counter-coup defeats Manchero.
1961 *November* Fighting between military factions leads to replacement of President Velasco Ibarra by his vice-president, Carlos Julio Arosemena Monroy.
1963 *July* Military junta of Rear-Admiral Ramón Castro Jijon seizes power.
1966 *March* Armed forces overthrow junta, install civilian

Below: Well-armed Brazilian troops occupy positions outside the Ministry of War in Rio de Janeiro on 31 March 1964 just before the military coup led by General Castello Branco.

Above: A street vendor in Bogota, Colombia, makes little secret of her political preferences as she displays electoral posters for Rojas Pinilla.

government.
1972 *February* President Velasco Ibarra, elected in 1968, is deposed in military coup led by General Guillermo Rodríguez Lara.
1976 *January* Military junta deposes President Rodríguez Lara.
1979 *April* Return to elective government.

EL SALVADOR
1948 *December* Army coup overthrows President General Castañeda Castro.
1960 *October* Coup led by Colonel César Urias deposes Colonel José María Lemus.
1961 *January* Army installs new junta led by Colonel Arturo Armando Molina.
1979 *October* Junta of civilians and army officers overthrows the president, General Carlos Humberto Romero.

GUATEMALA
1954 *June* Reforming government of Colonel Jacobo Arbenz Guzmán toppled by CIA-backed coup; Colonel Carlos Castillo Armas takes power.
1957 *July* President Castillo assassinated. *October* After disputed elections military junta seizes power; in fresh elections General Miguel Ydígoras Fuentes becomes president.
1963 *March* Military coup led by Colonel Enrique Peralta overthrows elected President General Miguel Ydígoras Fuentes.
1982 *March* General Efraín Ríos Montt seizes power in coup after disputed elections.
1983 *August* Military coup deposes Ríos Montt.

Above: President Carlos Castillo Armas who headed the CIA-backed coup in Guatemala in June 1954.

HAITI
1946 *January* Military coup deposes President Elie Lescot.
1950 *May* Military coup deposes President Dumarsais Estime, General Paul Magloire subsequently becomes president.
1956 *December* President Magloire flees riots and general strike.
1957 *May* Army assumes power as disturbances continue. *September* Dr François Duvalier ('Papa Doc') elected president.

HONDURAS
1954 *October* Julio Lozano Diaz deposes elected president Villeda Morales.
1956 *October* Military junta overthrows Lozano Diaz.
1963 *October* Villeda Morales deposed again, this time by Colonel Oswaldo López Arellano.
1972 *December* López Arellano returns to power in second coup.
1975 *April* López Arellano overthrown in coup by Colonel Melgar Castro.
1978 *August* Melgar Castro deposed by military junta headed by General Policarpo Paz García.

MEXICO
Governments have succeeded one another constitutionally since 1945.

Below: Sandinista forces belie their guerrilla origins wearing their Number One ceremonial dress on parade in Nicaragua.

NICARAGUA
1947 *May* Newly-elected President Leonardo Arguello overthrown in coup led by General Anastasio Somoza Debayle, previously president for 10 years.
1956 *September* General Somoza assassinated, succeeded by his son.
1979 *July* Somoza regime toppled by Sandinista National Liberation Front after prolonged civil war.

PANAMA
1949 *November* Police Chief Colonel José Remón deposes President Chanis, installs Arnulfo Arias Madrid as president.
1951 *May* Nationwide revolt topples President Arias.
1955 *January* Remón, president since 1952, assassinated.
1968 *October* General Omar Torrijos Herrera, commander of National Guard, overthrows President Arias after 11 days in office.

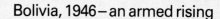

Bolivia, 1946 – an armed rising
Serious fighting began when armed students and workers attacked and captured the police barracks, taking big supplies of arms and ammunition. The troops at first did not intervene and were spectators. Later the majority of the La Paz garrison went over to the side of the revolutionaries, and soldiers and workers together attacked the police, who, accompanied by some loyal troops, defended the presidential palace and poured continuous fire from machine-guns and other automatic weapons into the revolutionary ranks....

Five thousand men stormed the palace and resistance collapsed when the attackers, led by two tanks, breached the defences. The mob entered the palace and seized Colonel Villarroel, already wounded by a bullet in the chest, and threw him from the balcony into the street, where he was shot dead....

Colonel Villarroel's body was stripped of its clothes, wrapped in a sheet, and hung on a lamp-post in the Plaza Murillo in front of Government House.... As a macabre and suggestive addition a military boot was tied on the corpse under the left arm.

Reports in The Times, *21-23 July 1946.*

PARAGUAY
1948 *June* President General Higinio Morinigo overthrown in bloodless military/civilian coup. *December* Bloodless coup deposes President Natalicio Gonzalez.
1949 *February* Bloodless coup overthrows President General Rolon.
1954 *May* Military/civilian revolt deposes President Federico Claves; General Alfredo Stroessner, commander-in-chief, becomes president.

PERU
1948 *October* General Manuel Odria carries out military coup against President Bustamente.
1962 *July* General Perez Godoy seizes power to block election of Haya de la Torre to presidency.
1963 *March* Junta removes Godoy, Belaúnde Terry becomes president.
1968 *October* Military coup led by General Juan Velasco Alvarado.
1975 *August* General Velasco Alvarado overthrown in bloodless military coup by General Fransisco Morales Bermúdez.

URUGUAY
1973 *February* President Juan María Bordaberry accepts armed forces' demand for predominant military role in government.
1976 *June* Military council deposes Bordaberry, appoints Aparicio Méndez president.

VENEZUELA
1945 *October* President General Isaias Medina overthrown in military/civilian coup led by Rómulo Betancourt, leader of Acción Democratica.
1948 *November* Democratically-elected President Gallegos deposed by Colonel Marcos Pérez Jiménez.
1950 *November* President Chalbaud assassinated, replaced by another Jiménez nominee.
1952 *December* Jiménez seizes power.
1958 *January* Jiménez regime toppled by popular revolt supported by some military leaders; Acción Democratica wins subsequent elections.

The great illusion

Latin American guerrillas of the early 1960s

Left: Fidel Castro (centre) whose successful guerrilla campaign in Cuba sparked off a whole series of attempted revolutions. Venezuela was one of the first countries to experience the new-style of revolutionary attack; President Betancourt (right) was able to meet the challenge, however, and his great triumph was the successful defence of the democratic elections of 1963. Above: Caracas during the run-up to the 1963 election.

When Fidel Castro entered Havana and took over the government of Cuba in January 1959 he provided the radicals of Latin America with the greatest and most appealing insurrectionary example of the postwar era. The charismatic Fidel had waged guerrilla war from the Sierra Maestra in the impenetrable heart of the island and with astonishingly few men had overcome the legions and the tanks and planes of the dictator Fulgencio Batista. But as important as victory itself was the way it had been achieved. Castro's forces had conducted a campaign notable for its lack of atrocities and its almost cavalier, daring approach. Castro and his famous lieutenant Che Guevara were, for example, extremely correct and merciful in dealing with prisoners. The contrast with the murderous repression of Batista's men could not have been greater.

To the radicals Castro had broken the shackles of Yankee Imperialism. Not only had he led a successful revolution and instituted a socialist society but he had made himself independent of US approval and US subsidy, if only by eventually accepting Russian aid. It may seem rather a poor assertion of national independence to become the client of one superpower rather than another, but it was beguiling enough to the rest of the discontented in Latin America.

The US-organised coup against the radical government in Guatemala in 1954 had induced despair among the revolutionary movements of the continent. It seemed that no revolution could succeed if the US simply toppled the governments of which it disapproved. Castro's victory in 1959 changed despair to a dangerous euphoria. He had started with only a dozen men in the Sierra Maestra and overthrown a repressive dictatorship which had enjoyed US backing. After this he had maintained himself in a position of open defiance of the US and promised support to insurrections everywhere. It all seemed startlingly easy and the belief grew that there was no answer to guerrilla warfare; that socialist victory was inevitable. Dictators everywhere and particularly the three marked down by Castro – Anastasio Somoza in Nicaragua, Rafael Trujillo in the Dominican Republic and Alfredo Stroessner in Paraguay – had cause to tremble.

Exporting revolution

The year after Castro's victory saw a rash of hopefuls trying to imitate his example across the continent and at least some of them enjoyed Cuban

export their revolution to the mainland, offering both material backing and theoretical justification for guerrilla movements. Che and Castro developed a theory of revolution significantly different from traditional communist models. Both Soviet and Chinese revolutionaries emphasised the need for a mass movement which the party could lead as a 'vanguard'. Basing themselves on their own experience, the Cubans argued that a small band of guerrillas could defeat the regular army and seize power without the active involvement of the masses. After all, Castro had only some 1500 fighters when he took power; no political parties were involved in the actual struggle; and the expected working-class strike in the cities never materialised. Yet he had won.

One of the first places to bear the brunt of the new wave of guerrilla warfare was a country which offered an alternative example to reformers – Venezuela. A year before Castro's assumption of power in Cuba, a popular rising supported by elements of the armed forces overthrew the Venezuelan dictator Pérez Jiménez. Democratic elections were won by Rómulo Betancourt and his reforming Acción Democratica party. Betancourt was a lapsed communist of whom Castro once had great hopes, but the Venezuelan leader quickly provoked hostility amongst radicals by pursuing a moderate policy towards the US and expressing disapproval of Castro's intervention in other countries' affairs. In 1961 there were pro-Castro riots in the capital, Caracas, and guerrilla formations developed with Cuban backing.

They mounted a well-orchestrated guerrilla campaign, focussed on stopping the December 1963 presidential elections. American oil installations were sabotaged, a train was ambushed and an airliner was hijacked to drop propaganda leaflets. On 19-20 November 1963 fighting between guerrillas and government forces raged in the streets of Caracas. Yet the elections took place in good order and were won by Acción Democratica's new candidate, Raul Leoni. This was not the end of guerrilla activity in Venezuela. A resurgence occurred between 1965 and 1967, with repeated attacks on US property, kidnappings and assassinations. Operating from rural bases the guerrillas were difficult to repress, but after 1963 they never came near to toppling the government.

Military intervention

In other parts of Latin America, the Cuban example began to seem more and more desirable through the early 1960s as democracy was thwarted in one country after another if elected presidents espoused radical policies. The slightest whiff of major reform brought automatic military intervention: in 1962 the victory of Haya de la Torre in the Peruvian elections provoked an immediate coup; Argentina lost President Arturo Frondizi in 1962 and President Arturo Illia in 1966; and in 1964 President João Goulart of Brazil was overthrown by the military for trying to push through radical reforms. But by far the most interesting military intervention from the revolutionaries' point of view occurred in April 1965 in the Dominican Republic when a general insurrection was only put down after US Marines stormed ashore in Santo Domingo.

Some straightforward conclusions could be drawn from these events. Democratic government was unable to deliver reforms because conservative interests would call a halt through military intervention. More than this it seemed that, if the military were unable to

backing. Apart from the three dictatorships that Castro had castigated as particularly offensive, two other regimes – those of Panama and Haiti – faced invasion by armed bands of guerrillas. All these efforts were swiftly crushed, which should have served as some sort of warning that the extraordinary victory of the revolutionaries in Cuba would not be easily repeated. In fact Trujillo was assassinated in May 1961 but Somoza lasted a score more years and Stroessner seemed to be immortal.

Although, therefore, the immediate aftermath of the Cuban revolution was no more than a shake of the pepper pot in the face of entrenched Latin American regimes, the new Cuban government was to continue to pose a threat to their stability for some years. In the early 1960s the Cubans worked openly on projects to

Left: Typical Latin American hill country. The combination of dense impenetrable undergrowth commanded by areas of steep rocky hillside often gave guerrillas enormous tactical advantages over advancing government troops.

cope, the US would use its unmatchable military power to restore order (which generally meant the old, unequal order). Far from despairing at this analysis, the radicals saw signs of hope in it. This was rooted in events far from Latin America – the quagmire for US power in Vietnam.

The blueprint for action was still the Cuban revolution. Despite the failures of 1959-60 in Nicaragua, Haiti and Paraguay, there was great faith that repressive regimes would not be able to cope with guerrilla warfare. This hope was reinforced by Viet Cong successes in Southeast Asia, demonstrating as they did that US military force could be combated by guerrillas. By the end of 1965 it was far from clear that the US was headed for defeat in Vietnam but it was resoundingly obvious that irregular forces in a Third World country were maintaining a struggle against a superpower. In Latin America it seemed to the radicals that they should join the struggle by toppling their own governments and involving US forces against ever more armies of guerrillas. The end result, they hoped, would be to relieve the pressure on the communists in Vietnam and involve the US in a global defeat which would destroy US influence over Latin America for ever.

In 1966 Castro made an attempt to coordinate the international guerrilla struggle by convoking the Tricontinental Conference in Havana, with representatives from the Third World, China and the USSR. The Chinese were extremely radical, calling for 'revolutionary second fronts against American imperialism', while the Russians were extremely cautious, but neither were prepared to undertake any concrete action. Che Guevara then decided to reactivate the guerrilla struggle in person.

Che in Bolivia

In November 1966 Che slipped into Bolivia to join a small band of revolutionaries. One of the world's poorest countries, Bolivia had a strong revolutionary tradition. In 1952 a rising by militant tin miners had brought in a left-wing government which carried out a radical programme of nationalisation, democratisation and land reform. Elected-president Paz Estenssoro was overthrown by his vice-president, General René Barrientos, in 1964; Barrientos' policies provoked active opposition from miners and students which Che hoped to exploit. But the peasants, beneficiaries of previous land reforms, were not disposed to revolt. Lacking peasant recruits and shunned

Above, far left: Hugo Blanco the leader of an uprising in Peru and claimant to the title of 'the Castro of Peru'. Above left: The Marxist theorist Regis Debray in captivity. Debray had accompanied Che Guevara's men as an observer, and was captured after leaving them. He later became a foreign policy adviser to the French government of President Mitterand.

Above: The military court that tried the survivors of Guevara's Bolivian expedition. Below left: Bolivian tin miners, who had a tradition of revolutionary activity in the 20th century, prepare to meet oncoming government forces with their speciality – home-made dynamite grenades.

Below left: President Ydígoras (left) inspects his artillery in action outside Guatemala City during the attempted coup of 1962. Below: Brazilian government troops sweep an area with mine detectors in the search for hidden arms caches.

Below right: A Bolivian soldier wounded during the search for Guevara's guerrillas in 1967.

by both the Moscow-oriented and Peking-oriented Communist Parties in Bolivia, Che was doomed. After a few minor military successes, he was cornered by the army and shot.

White Hand terror

In retrospect, the idea of setting off a continent-wide revolt against US power from a small-scale guerrilla action in Bolivia may seem absurd, but in the mid-1960s it did not look so impossible. There were guerrillas active in Argentina – mainly leftist supporters of Perón. In Brazil, both urban and rural guerrilla groups opposed the newly-installed military regime and enjoyed considerable popular support. The famous Tupamaros urban guerrillas had begun to have an impact on Uruguay. Further north, land-hungry peasants threatened the Peruvian regime, the Venezuelan guerrilla movement was still active, a Colombian guerrilla campaign began in January 1965, and the Somoza regime in Nicaragua faced the beginnings of the Sandinista revolt from 1963.

But the most explosive situation in the mid-1960s was in Guatemala, scene of the US-backed coup of 1954. Despite massive US aid, the right-wing forces which dominated the country failed to ensure stability. In 1960, in the period of enthusiasm after the Cuban revolution, a group of young liberal army officers launched an unsuccessful insurrection. Defeated, they took to the hills. Known as the November 13 Movement or M.13, they financed themselves by kidnapping wealthy Guatemalans and demanding ransom. In 1965 a split in the movement produced the Fuerzas Rebeldas Armadas (FAR) led from 1966 by César Montes, a law student. The FAR established contact with Indian peasants as well as carrying on a campaign of assassination.

Opposed to the FAR were not only the army and police but also right-wing terror squads like the dreaded Mano Blanca (White Hand). The election of

a moderate to the presidency in 1966 placed both right and left in opposition to central authority; political killings reached about 1000 a year. While right-wingers murdered any left-wingers, guerrillas or not, the FAR liked to pick out leaders of the right-wing death squads, including those responsible for the 1954 coup. In January 1968 they gunned down two US military attachés from a passing car, and the following August the US ambassador was assassinated by the same method.

The US in Guatemala

The FAR attacks on US officials were provoked by direct US military involvement in the most brutal episode of the whole conflict. From 1966 to 1967 about 1000 US Green Berets accompanied Guatemalan army units commanded by Colonel Araña Osorio in a successful campaign against guerrillas in the countryside which cost an estimated 8000 lives, mostly of Indian peasants. By such methods the guerrilla movement was kept in check.

By the end of 1967 the tide had definitely turned against the Latin American rural guerrilla movements. Helped by US training and advice, governments had begun to find methods to combat irregular warfare. Right-wing death squads, torture and summary execution were proven resources which began to have their effect on the struggle. The death of Guevara was bound to cause some profound rethinking. César Montes was still active in Guatemala, as was Carlos Marighela in Brazil, while Uruguay and Argentina had still to see the peak of guerrilla activity. But the notion of a small guerrilla band toppling a Latin American regime in the Castro manner was dead. However, although the theory of revolutionary strategy had to be revised, there was to be no halt in revolutionary activity and no increase in stability in the sorely troubled countries of Latin America.

Graham Brewer

Death of a legend
Che Guevara's campaign in Bolivia

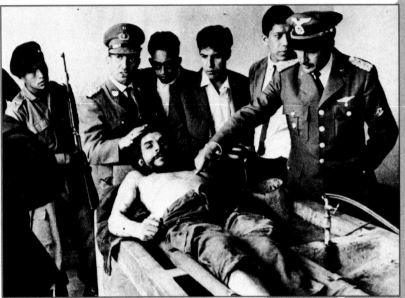

On 3 November 1966, disguised as a balding, middle-aged Uruguayan businessman 'Adolfo Mena Gonzalez', the Cuban revolutionary leader Ernesto 'Che' Guevara passed through immigration controls at the airport of La Paz, capital of Bolivia, and was whisked off by jeep to a distant jungle encampment, where he was to begin his last campaign.

Since the heady days of the successful Cuban revolution in the late 1950s, Che's progress had been uncertain. Uncomfortable in such posts as Cuban Minister for Industry and President of the National Bank, he had developed into a wandering advocate of revolution, expert at fiery public pronouncements. In 1965 he had returned to action, leading a small Cuban guerrilla force into the eastern Congo in support of the Simba rebels, but the experience was disillusioning and unsuccessful. Now, backed by President Fidel Castro, he was embarked on his most ambitious, and final, adventure – to lead a guerrilla campaign intended to provoke a revolt against American power throughout Latin America.

Che and Castro believed that a small guerrilla band operating in a remote area of one country could act as a *foco insurrecional* – an insurrectional focus – for revolutionary elements throughout the continent. Bolivia was chosen to be the field of battle because it has borders with so many other countries (Argentina, Brazil, Chile, Peru and Paraguay). Che believed that the failure of the Bolivian Army to cope with his guerrillas would lead to US military involvement, and that this 'South American Vietnam' would in turn provoke revolution in the neighbouring states. The desired conclusion was the total destruction of US power in Latin America.

The choice of Bolivia as the theatre of operations was a major mistake, however. To be sure, the government of President René Barrientos was authoritarian and experienced continuous, sometimes violent, difficulties with the workforce in the tin mines and with radical students; but it also claimed a degree of democratic support. Barrientos himself was a revolutionary nationalist who had won power in a military coup in 1964 but consolidated it by winning 62 per cent of the vote in reasonably free and fair elections held in July 1966. In addition to this he had continued agrarian reforms which made the peasants owners of their land – indeed in the Santa Cruz district of southeastern Bolivia where Che proposed to operate they were able to claim as much land as they could use. Che's slogans meant nothing to this newly liberated peasantry which regarded him as an invader and informed on him constantly.

So Che could expect no support in the rural areas of Bolivia – although he counted on it – and his position worsened when he lost the backing of the Bolivian Communist Party by asserting, in consequence of his experience in the Cuban campaign, that his military command of the revolution should take primacy over its political direction. This left him totally friendless and his guerrilla band received no reinforcement or

Above: A Bolivian Air Force chief proudly points to the rigid corpse of Che Guevara while press photographers take pictures. Left: Bolivian Rangers receive training from US instructors. The US supplied Bolivia with urgently needed expertise to meet the threat of revolutionary insurgency.

Eating mule meat...

Marching through difficult country preceded by *macheteros* clearing a path with their machetes, Che's men survived on a diet including horsemeat, tapirs, ant-eaters, monkeys, parrots and smaller birds. Che's diaries give a vivid sense of the privations endured.

'*August 28*...The little mare was finally slaughtered after accompanying us for two distressing months. I made every effort to save her but our hunger was getting worse and at least now we are only thirsty....

August 29. A difficult and frustrating day.... We camped at an altitude of 1600m in a relatively humid place which has a kind of cane whose pulp quenched our thirst. Some of the comrades ... are folding up for lack of water....

August 30. The situation was becoming desperate. The *macheteros* suffered fainting spells, Miguel and Dario were constantly dizzy ... with the unfortunate results of diarrhoea and cramps. Urbano, Benigno and Julio climbed down a canyon and found water.... I decided to stay with Nato but Inti came back up with water. The three of us sat there eating mule meat....'

supply after the beginning of its operations. However, he had learnt one lesson: the hardships and hunger experienced in the Cuban struggle persuaded him to set up a secure base and stockpile supplies before the campaign started. His supporters secretly bought and staffed a farm near Nancahuazú while he set up and stocked an extensive camp in nearby jungle. He had 17 picked Cuban guerrillas (including officers of the Cuban Army and members of the Communist Party central committee) so that, although he only managed to recruit 20 Bolivians and three Peruvians, he could be confident of the quality of much of his small force. The band also included Tamara Bunke, a young East German woman whom Che had recruited for guerrilla work, but who was spying on him for Soviet Intelligence.

With his ready-made camp and his entire force installed in it before any action began, Che was in a much better position than Castro at the beginning of the Cuban revolution; Castro had reached the Sierra Maestra with a mere dozen fugitives who were untried in battle. But Che immediately threw the advantage away in his first battle with Bolivian forces. This was an unplanned encounter on 23 March 1967. Deserters from Che's band had alerted the army to the presence of guerrillas and the camp had been reconnoitred by soldiers while Che's band was absent on a training march. Instead of moving the camp with its valuable stores before the perplexed Bolivian Army made up its mind to act, Che sanctioned the ambush of a strong follow-up patrol. The ambush was a tactical success in that the 32-man patrol lost seven dead, six wounded and 11 captured, but it provoked the occupation of the camp in force with a consequent loss of valuable stores. From that moment onwards the guerrillas led a nomadic existence and surviving documents record their continuous preoccupation with hunger.

Hit and run

Until August, the guerrillas fought a number of actions in which they proved themselves superior to the Bolivian Army. This was hardly surprising since Che and many of his men had spent years as guerrilla fighters and knew their business very well. The basic small change of jungle warfare was familiar to them: the siting of lookout points, the organisation of the column to make it difficult to ambush and other tactical procedures were carefully followed. On the other hand the Bolivian Army was ill-equipped and had largely been used to construct roads and bridges rather than as a trained fighting force. This unwarlike occupation had at least, however, made the army relatively popular. In addition, many of the soldiers were drawn from the local people, while half of Che's men were foreigners and none of the Bolivians in his band could speak the language of the peasants in the zone of operations. Small wonder that it was the army that received the cooperation of the people, rather than the foreign invaders.

As the campaign progressed the abilities of the guerrillas degenerated while that of the army improved. Che marched around aimlessly with no clear objective in view: the high point of his campaign – the brief occupation of the tiny town of Samaipata – seems to have been planned in an effort to find drugs at the pharmacy to treat Che's asthma. In their wanderings the guerrillas suffered greatly from lack of food and water while Che himself was so debilitated that, from the end of June, he was unable to keep up with

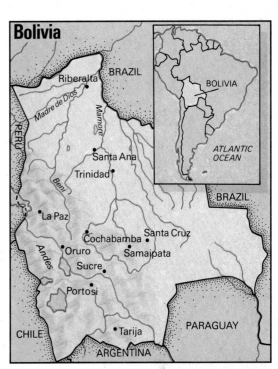

Below: A rare photograph of Che Guevara in the Bolivian countryside shortly before he was killed by government troops.

the march and was forced to ride a mule or horse. By then he had already lost his rearguard and the two groups never found each other again.

Still, the activities of Che's guerrillas were followed with concern and even a degree of panic by the Bolivian government and the United States. The loss of a small number of troops and quantities of arms in limited encounters provoked an urgent response. A battalion of Bolivian Rangers was given an intensive four months training course by US personnel. When these better quality troops began to be deployed at the end of July the fate of the guerrillas was sealed. In August the separated rearguard was hounded to destruction and the main body was taking losses in brushes with the army. Because of the steady flow of information from peasants the army could track Che but he, on the other hand, knew nothing of army movements. A series of clashes ended on 8 October 1967 at El Yuro, when the guerrillas awoke to find themselves surrounded by soldiers. After two hours' fighting, the bulk of Che's men were killed while the rest surrendered or fled. Che himself, wounded in the fighting, was taken prisoner. The following day he was killed. So the ill-starred, badly-planned guerrilla war ended.

P.J. Banyard

Above: Before returning to Bolivia to begin his own revolution, Che Guevara had been a prominent figure in the Third World. Here he meets with Nasser in his capacity as head of the Cuban economics mission.

Lore of the jungle

Survival techniques in tropical bush and forest

Above: The strain of hours in the jungle in tremendous heat and humidity is clearly written on the face of this British soldier in Malaya.

Left: Liquids are one of the most important factors for survival in jungle conditions. These can be obtained from many sources but one of the safest is from plants. Here John Glenn the astronaut drinks coconut juice while training at the US tropical survival school.

Survival methods in the British Army owe much to jungle-training courses in Malaya and especially the experiences of the SAS during the Malayan Emergency of the 1950s. The success of the SAS in this conflict in a hostile environment was due to their weapons and navigational skills, good communications and prowess with the humble machete. Navigation was a major problem, for in the Malayan jungle trees grow 60m (200ft) tall and densely packed foliage overhead blurs the daylight and blots out the stars at night. The maps used by the SAS consisted of white sheets displaying only grid lines and rivers for aerial reconnaissance; there were no landmarks to follow.

American elite units in Vietnam also encountered a wide variety of tropical hazards. The early US advisers in Vietnam learned much from the French experience of jungle fighting but it was some time before the Special Forces School adopted the army's SERE (Survival, Evasion, Resistance and Escape) training. The course was based on the experiences of Lieutenant-Colonel James N. Rowe, who survived over five years in a POW camp in Vietnam before escaping on his fourth attempt.

Mud and mosquitoes

The SERE course consisted of 24 consecutive, action-packed days from 0500 hours to 2200 hours each day. Instruction was given in survival, fieldcraft, tools, water and food procurement, and evading capture by the enemy. Evasion techniques included penetration of minefields and sensor barriers, eluding trackers, and silent killing techniques. Nowadays the US Army training school in Panama specialises in survival training with reference to conditions in Central and South America.

These courses are vital, because in the jungle the odds are against survival. A downed pilot, a fugitive from a POW camp or a Special Forces man must be tough and prepared to improvise, turning to good use every resource the jungle offers. For example, one of his worst enemies is the malaria-carrying mosquito, but luckily a form of protection is close at hand. Mud makes an effective insect repellent, and should be rubbed onto all exposed skin (not forgetting the eyelids) before going to sleep.

Other insects that may bother or even threaten the life of the would-be survivor are ticks, fleas and mites, and clothing should be inspected every day for signs of these pests. Ticks may be numerous, especially in grassy places, and can be removed by applying heat. Fleas are often found in dry, dusty buildings and are extremely dangerous as they transmit typhus and, in some parts of the Far East, bubonic plague. They should be removed with a sterilised knife. Another typhus-carrier is the tiny red mite, found in tall grass and on banks of streams.

The British Army's 22 SAS, who gained their survival experience in the Malayan jungle, named the leech as public enemy number one. Lurking in shallow water, they get in over the tops of boots and through the eyelets. Once embedded in the skin they must be removed by applying heat or mud. Hornets, centipedes, scorpions, wasps and wild bees can also be harmful, and their stings are best remedied by applying a cold compress, mud or coconut meat.

A potential hazard that can be turned to advantage is the prevalence of snakes in the jungle. They make good eating if you can kill them before they bite you. If the survivalist has the misfortune to be bitten by a poisonous snake, a tourniquet should be applied above the wound and an incision made to clean the wound thoroughly of venom.

Foraging is perhaps the most important skill for the would-be survivor to acquire. Although the average survival period on a purely liquid diet is over ten days, energy for mobility requires solid nutrients. All sources of food in the jungle must be exploited and the survivalist will look out for snails, ant-eaters, mice and guinea fowl as well as larger prey such as wild pigs on the forest floor. Edible species of bats, squirrels, rats, monkeys and various types of birds inhabit the trees above. There are various ways of catching wild animals, ranging from an accurate shot with a stone or an improvised bow and arrow to more complex trapping and netting techniques. Great care must always be taken in setting snares in order to avoid self-injury and, just as important, detection by the enemy.

Snares are best placed along well-used animal tracks (which can be identified by the presence of fresh droppings) and should be simply constructed. They should be positioned at narrow points along the tracks, with obstacles arranged so as to force the animal to pass through the snare. Two main types are used, the 'stop' snare and the 'twitch-up' snare. The first type must be watched constantly as the animal is trapped on the ground and may be taken by another predator. The second type lifts the prey clear of the ground and can safely be left unattended. The 'dead-fall' method should be used for larger animals. This involves digging a pit, filling it with sharpened stakes and camouflaging it. As long as the pit is deep enough, this trap can also be left unattended, leaving

Right: While shortage of nutrients and liquids is one danger in the jungle, a supplementary hazard is presented by the wildlife. These French legionnaires are being instructed in the recognition and handling of various tropical snakes.

the hunter free to indulge in other activities necessary for survival.

Catching fish in the streams and rivers of the tropical jungle can be a rather hazardous business. Apart from the obvious dangers from alligators or crocodiles, water-snakes, piranha fish and large land-based animals that go down to the water to drink, there are also many types of fish that are poisonous to humans. The toxins are tasteless and the flesh of poisonous fish appears palatable. Poisonous fish do, however, have some common characteristics: they usually live in shallow water; their bodies are round or box-like with hard, bony or spiny skins; their gill openings are small and they generally have undershot jaws. The only really safe solution, however, is to have prior knowledge of the types of edible fish indigenous to the area.

The raw and the cooked

Edible plant foods such as wild vegetables and fruit abound in the tropics. A coconut is a meal in itself but it is important to remember that the milk of those found lying on the ground may not be drinkable. Many fruits and vegetables have the added advantage that they can be eaten raw, which avoids the danger of lighting a fire. Not all vegetation, however, is edible, and before eating the whole of a questionable plant a small portion of it should be cooked, chewed and held in the mouth for five minutes. If it still tastes pleasant then it is likely to be non-toxic. A burning, nauseating or bitter taste can be taken as a sign of danger. This guideline, however, does not apply to poisonous mushrooms, and all fungi are best avoided.

Water is essential to survival and is relatively easy to obtain in the tropics. Natural sources of water can be traced by following animal tracks, though it is obviously wise to keep an eye open for the more dangerous beasts who may also be looking for a meal. Water should be both boiled and filtered (through a piece of parachute cloth, for example) before drinking. Rain and dew on leaf surfaces provide a cleaner supply of water, and as a last resort pure water can be obtained from the stems of vines.

Moving about in the jungle has its hazards and is generally impracticable at night. Travelling unde-

Below: Deep in the heart of the South-American jungle, legionnaires demonstrate their survival skills by capturing a wild boar. There is plenty of wild game in the jungle – the problem is how to catch it.

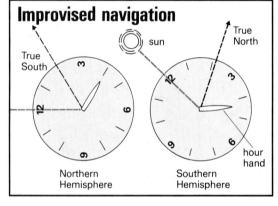

ground. An east/west line, for example, can be established by placing a 1m (3ft) stick in the ground, in a flat area which is clear of growth. Mark the tip of the shadow and again ten minutes later. The line joining the two points indicates the east/west line.

Similarly, a north/south line can be obtained using shadows at midday. This time, place a 0.6m (2ft) stick in suitable ground and just before noon mark the shadow. Using a piece of string, draw an arc around the base of the stick the same radius as the shadow. When the shadow again touches the arc (after noon) mark it again. Then divide the angle found by the base of the stick and the two markers, and this indicates south in the northern hemisphere and north in the southern hemisphere.

Shelters should be selected on a high spot if possible and well away from swamps if mosquitoes are to be avoided. Comfortable billets can be built improvising with branches and bamboo cane, raised above the ground and with palm leaves as a mattress. Such accommodation, however, is conspicuous and bad for security. A poncho or similar improvised garment is invaluable, combining the functions of groundsheet, raincoat, and roof over your head; it is an essential item of equipment.

Making fires is an unavoidable risk. Matches should be conserved and kept dry at all times. When they run out fires can be lit with the burning-glass,

Improvised navigation

True South — Northern Hemisphere

sun

True North — Southern Hemisphere

hour hand

bow and drill, or flint and steel methods. Dry fuel is plentiful in the tropics but may be a problem in the wet season – dry wood can then be cut from inside the hollow trunks of trees. Tinder can be obtained from the shavings of seasoned bamboo, the fibres at the bases of palm trees and the insides of dry termite nests. Green leaves thrown on a fire make a smudge that discourages mosquitoes. Green bamboo and plants that are skin irritants produce smoke that is toxic and should not be used as fuel. Platform fires can be made from stones or logs, which can also form the lining of an oven dug into the ground. An effective oven can also be made from a tin can, using flat slabs of rock for the bed of the fire and a narrow chimney.

All in all, survival in the worst kinds of tropical conditions and with the enemy all around you is only for the fittest. The most harrowing accounts of soldiers trapped behind enemy lines in the jungle have come from Vietnam. Those who survived were mostly fortunate enough to be picked up by helicopter or to stumble upon a friendly village. Courage alone is no antidote for festering wounds, fatigue, lack of food and water. It is as well to remember that the jungle is not neutral. It has a habit of turning its unfortunate guests into permanent residents. **Barry Gregory**

Top: The US survival training programme has been employed by civilians and military alike. These astronauts are being shown how to make a trap for large game. Above: The first woman to complete the jungle survival course in Panama, Theresa Pharms, staggers back to base.

tected is even more difficult if there are experienced trackers looking (and listening) for you. Trackers both look for and leave the following signs in tropical terrain: crushed and bent grass and vegetation; broken twigs and overturned leaves; displaced mud in streams; broken cobwebs; and mud and scratches on rocks and logs. Footprints in mud and soft ground can show whether the hunter or hunted is walking in boots or bare feet, and whether he is travelling light or carrying weapons and equipment. Needless to say, all signs of encampment should be erased and all discarded equipment carefully concealed.

When on the move the body should always be fully clothed to prevent insect bites, scratches and sunburn. Clothing should be loose-fitting but the face, ankles and feet well-protected. Trousers should be tucked into socks and boots and tightly bound with puttees, or, failing that, strips of any other material available. Even the most stoutly made boots have a habit of wearing out after only a few days on the march. Sandals made from rubber tyres, or, more likely, the bark of trees, are the last resort for walking in the jungle.

Heat casualties often occur in tropical conditions and are caused by heat stroke and exhaustion. Apart from unsuitable clothing (too little or too much) these maladies may also be due to lack of salt, nourishment or sleep. The best remedy is to move into the shade and rest for as long as possible.

Survival navigation in the northern hemisphere may be improvised without a proper compass by pointing the hour hand of a watch at the sun. An imaginary line is then drawn from the centre of the watch through the 12. True south is midway between the hour hand and the 12. In the southern hemisphere the imaginary line through the 12 is pointed at the sun but the midpoint between the 12 and the hour hand this time indicates true north. Other primitive methods of navigation involve measuring shadows on the

Key Weapons

KIEV-CLASS V/STOL CARRIERS

Previous page: An overhead view of the *Kiev* with four Ka-25 helicopters parked on the flight deck. Left: The superstructure of the *Kiev* – larger, in proportion, than the 'island' of a conventional carrier it contains a multiplicity of electronic devices.

Below: The separate divisions of the *Kiev* into superstructure, flight deck and weapons platform are clearly visible in this photograph. Bottom: The Kiev-class V/STOL carrier *Novorossiysk*, photographed northwest of Ireland in June 1983 on her maiden voyage in 'Western' waters.

The emergence of the Soviet carrier/cruiser *Kiev* in 1976 caused considerable consternation to Western defence commentators, not only because she was the largest warship to have been launched by the Soviet Union but because there was great confusion as to her true role and capabilities. What mystified observers was that the ship appeared to be a hybrid, with a cruiser's armament forward, but also carrying the classic island superstructure and angled flight deck of an aircraft carrier. She was described by the Russians as a large anti-submarine ship, but many Western commentators saw her as an attack carrier, intended to challenge the US Navy's carrier battle groups for mastery of the oceans.

This Western perception was a glaring error. The *Kiev* is certainly not a 38,000-tonne attack carrier. Whereas a typical carrier in the US Navy has four squadrons of fighters and strike aircraft, backed up by reconnaissance, electronic warfare and anti-submarine detachments totalling some 90 aircraft, the *Kiev* only has two squadrons of Ka-25 Hormone anti-submarine helicopters and one squadron of Yak-36 Forger VTOL (vertical take-off and landing) support aircraft. The Hormone is a small helicopter, obsolescent by Western standards, and the Forgers would be committing suicide if they tried to engage the F-14 Tomcats of an American carrier. In fact the air component of the *Kiev* accounts for only 50 per cent of the hull, the entire forward half of the ship being devoted to a surface cruiser's armament of anti-ship, anti-aircraft and anti-submarine weapons.

This enigma is more apparent than real, for the truth now seems that the *Kiev* and her sister ships *Minsk*, *Kharkov* and *Novorossiysk* really are hybrids, and that the Russians do regard them as large ASW (anti-submarine warfare) ships. The most rational explanation for the design is that the ships are successors to the helicopter cruisers *Leningrad* and *Moskva* which appeared in the late 1960s. But whereas these seem to operate mainly in the Black Sea and the Mediterranean, the Kiev-class ships range much further afield, from the Northern Fleet to the Pacific. This indicates that they are designed to take the offensive against Western submarines, particularly the SSBN strategic missile-firing submarines, and that the heavy surface armament and the Forger aircraft are intended to provide a measure of self-defence against Western forces. There is also the need for the Soviet Navy to establish defensive barriers to protect its own SSBNs from Nato attack, a point often lost on Western experts.

The Kiev-class ships are generally considered to be superior to previous Soviet designs. They differ from Western carriers in having a much longer superstructure, or island, and unlike any other Western air-capable ship they have a long forecastle studded with major weapons. They also lack the freeboard (the distance from the waterline to the upper deck) of comparable Western ships: 13m (40ft) aft as against the 19m (62ft) of an American carrier. The very beamy hull does, however, give a greater stability than is usual in carriers. On the other hand, the lack of freeboard means that side lifts (for winching aircraft directly up the outside of the vessel) cannot be installed, and the consequent centreline lifts encroach on hangar space. Another drawback of low freeboard is that many gun positions are subject to weather damage if the ship is driven at high speed in rough seas; and it is significant that the beam torpedo tubes seen in the *Kiev* have been omitted from her sister *Minsk*.

When the *Kiev* appeared the Western press speculated wildly about how many aircraft could be embarked. Initially it was claimed that as many as 50 helicopters and planes were carried, though the US Navy claimed a complement of only half the number. It was even suggested that the ship had two hangars; this is most unlikely, however, as the lower hangar would be below the waterline, where it would be a massive hazard to the ship's chances of surviving battle damage. As the Russian Navy's practice is to keep all aircraft in the hangar when not flying (a reasonable policy if the ships are operating in the rough seas of the North Atlantic and Northwest Pacific) a maximum of 12 Forgers and 24 Hormones seems credible.

The forward lift is on the centreline opposite the island, while the second lift is further aft and offset to starboard at the after end of the island, which because of its size is itself a limiting factor on the size of the hangar. The Forger differs from its British and American counterparts, the Sea Harrier and Harrier/AV-

Above: The *Minsk* steams through the Mediterranean just south of Crete. Right: Yak-36 Forger aircraft parked on the *Kiev* – the single-seat Forger 'A's can be compared with the two-seat Forger 'B' training aircraft.

Below: A view of the *Kiev* taken from the port side. The SS-12-N missile launchers are sited forward of the vessel's superstructure.

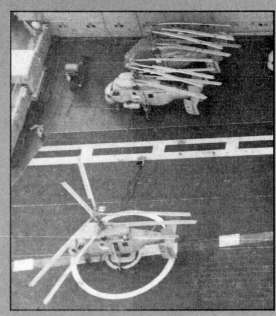

Left: A Swedish Viggen interceptor flies past the *Kiev* during a Warsaw Pact Naval exercise on the Baltic Sea. Inset: Beside the forward SS-12-N missile launcher tubes is the 76mm twin-gun turret, and offset from the fore-deck is a platform for two of the *Kiev's* eight 30mm 'Gatling' guns. Below: The *Kiev* in the Mediterranean.

Left: The mobile element in the *Kiev's* ASW capability is its complement of Kamov Ka-25 Hormone helicopters. Far left: The chin-mounted ASW radar is visible in this shot of a Ka-25 hovering alongside a US Navy vessel.

8B, in being restricted solely to vertical take-off and landing. There is therefore no 'rolling take-off' and so unless a STOVL (short take-off/vertical landing) aircraft replaces the Yak-36 we will not see a ski jump in the Kiev class.

What might be called the 'cruiser element' of the ship is represented by four paired cylindrical launchers on the foredeck. They are believed to contain a long-range anti-ship missile, designated SS-N-12 by Nato. As many as 16 reloads are carried, and they can be transferred from magazines below decks via a narrow elevating hoist on the centreline between the launchers. Two twin SA-N-3 Goblet area-defence missile launchers are carried, and are credited with a slant range of 30,000m (32,790yd). One of the twin-launchers is positioned on a forecastle deckhouse and the other at the after end of the island, thereby covering the widest possible arc of fire. Two SA-N-4 SAMs are responsible for intermediate-range defence and are housed in cylindrical weatherproof bins, one on the port side of the forecastle and the other outboard of the island. Backing them up are two twin-76mm gun mountings, one forward and one at the after end of the island. Close-in or point defence against aircraft and missiles is provided by four pairs of 30mm 'Gatling' guns, positioned at the corners of the ship.

Apart from the Hormone helicopters the anti-submarine armament comprises two auto-

Above: A Yak-36 prepares to land on the flight deck of the *Kiev*. Left: Yak-36s – with wings folded – and Ka-25s await maintenance crews to prepare them for flight duties.

Below: *Kiev* crewmen lounge by the ship's rails beside a tarpaulin-covered Yak-36.

matic 12-barrelled rocket launchers known as MBU-2500As. Beside the second rocket launcher is a twin-arm launcher for an anti-submarine rocket system known to Nato as FRAS-1. The data for both weapons is provided by a large low-frequency sonar mounted in the bow and a variable-depth sonar at the stern. The two sonars are able to provide the necessary tracking information so that the helicopters can pursue contacts.

The *Kiev* and her sister ships have no equal in the navies of the West, simply because Soviet perceptions of naval warfare are quite different from those of the US and her allies. We can only appreciate the thinking behind the Kiev class if we drop the habit of seeing the Soviet Navy as a mirror-image of the US Navy. Although they are not in any sense attack carriers their capabilities should not be underestimated. Any naval unit with their blend of weapons, aircraft and size can be expected to have considerable flexibility.

The most obvious secondary use for the Kiev class is in amphibious operations. In such a role her Forgers would prove extremely useful, and her SS-N-12 missiles could, presumably, be used against high-value targets ashore. There is a troop-carrying variant of the Ka-25 helicopter already at sea in the assault ship *Ivan Rogov*, so that a modification of the present Ka-25s to act as troop carriers – admittedly at the expense of their ASW role – would provide the *Kiev* with a genuine amphibious capability. Just where such amphibious operations might be carried out is, of course, a matter for conjecture. Clearly a wide range of options are open, and the writings of the Soviet naval commander-in-chief Admiral Gorshkov suggest that the Soviet Navy's interest in combined operations will expand over the next few years. The building of the Alligator and Polnocny class landing ships has been followed by the introduction of the Ivan Rogov class of assault ship, and there is no reason to suppose that the Kiev class does not feature in these plans to make the Soviet Navy capable of reinforcing national policy in a distant sea.

The *Kiev*, *Minsk*, *Kharkov* and *Novorossiysk* were built at the naval yards in Nikolayev on the Black Sea. Whether these ships will prove to be highly successful hybrids or merely a poor compromise of too many

separate naval elements is impossible to estimate with any accuracy in peacetime. But without doubt the Kiev class is an important step in the realisation of Admiral Gorshkov's plan for a 'balanced fleet', and from the evidence presented it would seem that the class has the ability to help further the Soviet Union's new, extended global foreign policy interests where adequate naval support would be essential for the conduct of sustained military operations.

Below: The stern section of the *Kiev*, revealing corner-mounted 30mm 'Gatling' guns and Yak-36s under wraps.

The Kiev

Type V/STOL carrier
Dimensions Length 275m (900ft); beam 28m (92ft); flight deck width 48m (152ft) maximum
Main engines Four sets of steam turbines; 40,000shp on four shafts
Speed 32 knots maximum
Aircraft 43 maximum

Armament Four twin SS-N-12 missile launchers; two twin SA-N-3 Goblet SAMS; two twin SA-N-4 SAMs; two twin 76mm guns; four twin 30mm 'Gatling' guns

Typical air complement 12 Forger V/STOL aircraft; 24 Hormone helicopters

Left: The *Minsk* and the guided-missile destroyer *Kara* are refuelled by the replenishment tanker *Boris Butoma* (centre) while on exercises in the western Pacific in November 1982.

The doomed republic

Revolt and repression in Diem's South Vietnam

On 8 May 1954, the first day of the international conference meeting at Geneva to attempt to settle the war raging in Indochina, French Foreign Minister Georges Bidault rose to address the assembled diplomats: 'The French delegation cannot conceal here its deep emotion and its pride in the face of the heroism of the combatants of France, of Vietnam, and of all of the French Union who had resisted beyond human endurance....' The foreign minister was referring to the long and bloody battle for the French fortress of Dien Bien Phu, which had ended one day before in a crushing defeat for the French forces in Vietnam. With the fall of Dien Bien Phu went the last realistic chance for France to maintain its hold on Indochina. Bidault went on to announce the French government's willingness to discuss a ceasefire and a negotiated settlement of the war.

After more than two months of tortuous and complex negotiations, the French and the Viet Minh government of Ho Chi Minh concluded a military agreement which partitioned Vietnam along the 17th parallel. Armed forces of the Viet Minh were to regroup north of the parallel, while French forces were withdrawn to the south. Civilians wishing to move from one zone to another were also permitted to

Following the crushing defeat of the French at Dien Bien Phu, the international conference at Geneva (above) was convened on 8 May 1954, and lasted two months during which time protracted negotiations over the future of Indochina took place. It was eventually agreed that North and South Vietnam would be divided along the 17th parallel. Top: By the late 1950s guerrilla war had once more broken out in the South, as Viet Cong insurgents tried to topple the regime of Ngo Dinh Diem. Here a French officer, attached to the Franco-American Training Relations and Instruction Mission, and South Vietnamese troops uncover a communist arms cache.

do so before May 1955. No new troops or equipment were to be introduced into Vietnam except as replacements, a proviso to be supervised by an International Control Commission (ICC) composed of representatives from Canada, India and Poland.

A separate 'Final Declaration', adopted but never signed by the delegates, confirmed the military agreements and added a provision that general elections, supervised by the ICC, were to be held in July 1956. The United States refused to associate itself in any way with the Geneva agreements but pledged to 'refrain from the threat or use of force to disturb them', while warning that 'it would view any violation of the aforesaid agreements with grave concern'.

In the midst of the Geneva negotiations, the French had concluded a treaty with the non-communist government of Emperor Bao Dai, recognising his 'State of Vietnam' as a fully independent, sovereign state. There were thus two Vietnams at the time of the conclusion of the Geneva accords and the non-communist State of Vietnam, soon to be referred to as South Vietnam, vehemently announced its non-concurrence in those agreements.

South Vietnam's dissent seemed, at first, of little consequence, for few people expected the shaky new

Left: Soldiers of the Cao Dai army present arms to their leader Pham Cong Tac. Below left: After the termination of negotiations at Geneva, part of the massive amount of reorganisation necessary to both sides was the exchange of huge numbers of POWs. These Viet Minh have just been exchanged for French prisoners and are on their way north.

state to last very long. Bao Dai had appointed as his new prime minister, with broad powers, Ngo Dinh Diem, a nationalist who was both anti-French and anti-communist and had a reputation for patriotism and honesty. Yet Diem was a northerner and a Catholic and had spent most of the war years outside Vietnam. He was largely out of touch with the people, politics and social developments in his country and was to remain so throughout his career.

In addition to the communists, Diem faced opposition from two powerful religious sects, the Cao Dai and the Hoa Hoa, which had their own private armies, and a gangster syndicate called the Binh Xuyen, who controlled the Saigon police force as well as most of the city's gambling and underworld activities. The South Vietnamese Army was smaller than the communist forces, ill-trained, demoralised and lacking in experienced leaders. For Diem that was probably just as well, since the loyalty of many of the army's generals was questionable, especially chief of staff General Nguyen Van Hinh, a former French air force officer, who openly talked of a coup.

Despite the dim prospects for the Diem government, US Secretary of State John Foster Dulles and other American leaders decided to aid the government of South Vietnam as the only hope, albeit a slim one, of staving off communist control of all Vietnam. Dulles persuaded the National Security Council and the Joint Chiefs of Staff to agree to a crash programme of assistance and aid to Diem, including American participation in the training of the South Vietnamese Army. To direct this programme, President Dwight D. Eisenhower appointed General J. Lawton Collins, a former army chief of staff and a close associate of the president, as his special representative to Vietnam with the rank of ambassador.

With American assistance the Diem regime began to find its feet. An immediate problem was the need to deal with the massive influx of refugees from the North. In the months following the Geneva settlement over 900,000 Vietnamese, most of them Catholics, took advantage of the provisions of the Geneva agreement to leave communist-controlled areas in the North and move to the South. The spectacle of thousands of its potential citizens fleeing to the South

Left: Victorious Viet Minh troops march into Hanoi. Opposite above: A 1963 photograph of President Diem's family. Standing from left are Ngo Dinh Nhu (who led the persecution of the Buddhists), Diem himself, Ngo Dinh Thuc (Archbishop of Hue), Mrs Nguyen Van Am (Diem's sister), Mrs Ngo Dinh Nhu (Diem's sister-in-law, known to the world's press as 'Madame Nhu'), Ngo Dinh Can (who was given control of central Vietnam), Ngo Dinh Luyen (ambassador to Britain), and Diem's brother-in-law Nguyen Van Am. Opposite below: Men of the Binh Xuyen gangster syndicate assault government forces during the trial of strength in 1955.

was a considerable propaganda defeat for North Vietnam but it also posed practical problems for the South, where massive American assistance was required to resettle the refugees. General Collins, backed by Washington, took a firm line with General Hinh, making it clear that the US would withdraw its support in the event of a coup, and eventually forced Hinh to leave the country. Collins also worked out an agreement with the French for a joint Franco-American training organisation called TRIM (Training Relations and Instruction Mission) headed by an American, Lieutenant-General John W. 'Iron Mike' O'Daniel.

Before much training could be accomplished, however, a crisis, developing out of a three-way clash between the religious sects, the Binh Xuyen and President Diem, called the entire American aid effort into question. Diem had skilfully used his American aid funds and equipment, along with the prestige they brought him, to win away factions of the sect forces to his side. He also put pressure on the Binh Xuyen by refusing to renew their licence to operate Saigon's largest gambling casino. At the end of March 1955 when Diem moved to replace the Binh Xuyen-controlled police chief with one of his own appointees, the Binh Xuyen attacked Vietnamese Army troops and shelled the presidential palace.

Underworld war

The fighting was quickly stopped but both the French and Americans were angry. French leaders believed that Diem's confrontation with the sects and Binh Xuyen courted the danger of precipitating civil war. Most Americans in Vietnam, on the contrary, believed that Diem and the army had a right to establish the authority of the national government against 'a bunch of gangsters'. They also suspected that some elements among the French were secretly aiding Diem's rivals.

General Collins, however, tended to blame Diem for most of the trouble. He saw the characteristics in the Vietnamese president that would later bring about his downfall – his rigidity, stubbornness, paranoia, and inability to work with other able men. In April Collins returned to Washington personally to persuade the president and the National Security Council that Diem should no longer be supported. Even while Collins was in Washington, however, fighting between the Binh Xuyen and the army broke out anew. The army speedily routed the Binh Xuyen, and sect forces which had sided with them, and drove them from the capital.

Washington leaders, surprised and delighted by Diem's unexpected victory, now reaffirmed their complete support for his regime while the French, angry and weary, agreed to close down most of their remaining military and assistance programmes in

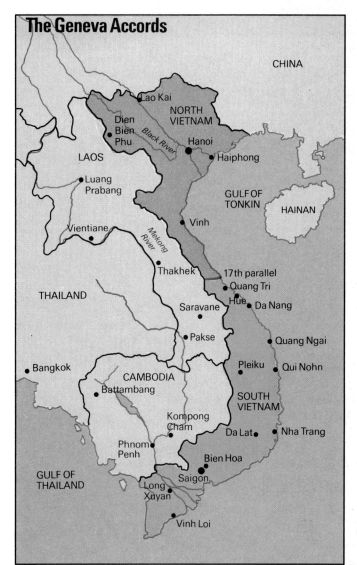

The Geneva Accords

Vietnam. By the summer of 1955 the US had assumed the entire burden of advising and supporting South Vietnam. In October 1955 Diem held a national referendum in which the people of South Vietnam voted to abolish the monarchy and elect Diem the president of a new Republic of Vietnam. Soon after, he announced that there would be no vote on reunification in 1956 because the people of North Vietnam would not be free to vote as they wished.

In retrospect it is clear that Collins and the French leaders were not far wrong in fearing that Diem's clash with the sects might precipitate civil war. Communist documents contain expressions of regret and disappointment that the party made the mistake of failing to intervene in the sect clashes. But in 1955 the communists were confused and divided. While they may not have expected nation-wide elections actually to take place in 1956 as they loudly insisted they must, they nevertheless believed that South Vietnam would soon be reduced to near-anarchy and was ripe for a communist political coup. Diem's success was thus as much of a surprise to his communist opponents as to his American supporters.

For the moment there was little the communist leadership could do to alter the course of events. Russia and China, for their own reasons, had clearly indicated that they would not then support a renewed war in the South and the government of Ho Chi Minh in the North was preoccupied with measures to consolidate its rule and reorganise the economy. These measures included the establishment of industrial facilities and a ruthless and doctrinaire 'land reform' programme which resulted in the execution or imprisonment of thousands of small farmers and a disastrous drop in agricultural production.

Over the next four years, however, Diem was to throw away whatever opportunity the disarray of the communists and massive American aid may have given him to build a strong, stable South Vietnam. The Diem regime was narrow, corrupt and inefficient. Many key officials were Diem's relatives.

Diem and his brothers Ngo Dinh Nhu and Ngo Dinh Can controlled a clandestine party known as the Can Lao, composed of relatives, Catholic refugees and government officials. The Can Lao had members in all key government agencies and levied an unofficial, but inescapable, tax on all persons seeking business or favours from the government. The party also maintained the equivalent of political commissars in various army units to keep an eye on commanders.

Although Vietnam received more US aid per capita than any other nation in Asia except Laos, few effective programmes of real benefit to the great majority of the people were ever undertaken. An ambitious land reform project proved too slow-moving, conservative and complicated to win the regime any friends among the peasants, while the minority of educated urban Vietnamese chafed under Diem's increasingly dictatorial rule.

While the Diem regime was grappling unsuccessfully with its economic and political problems, the US Military Assistance Advisory Group, headed successively by General O'Daniel and General Samuel T. 'Hangin' Sam' Williams, was attempting to train and reorganise the Vietnamese Army. In later years the Advisory Group would come in for considerable criticism. It was accused of having created a miniature version of the US Army, ill-suited to warfare in Southeast Asia, and of having neglected training for counter-guerrilla warfare in favour of preparing a conventional army to resist a North Vietnamese invasion on the lines of Korea. The latter criticism became less justified in the light of the massive North Vietnamese conventional attacks of 1972 and 1975. Yet both criticisms are equally irrelevant. The problem was not that the South Vietnamese Army was the wrong sort of army or had the wrong sort of training, but that it was an ineffective army with too little training of any sort.

Much of the blame for this situation was attributable to President Diem, who valued loyalty in his military commanders far above military competence

In 1957, communist activities against the government of South Vietnam resulted in harsh retaliation; suspected sympathisers could be tried by roving military tribunals and suspected terrorist hideouts were often bombed and shelled (below left) by troops without warning. The villages and towns of South Vietnam became battlegrounds (below) as the Diem government struggled to maintain its authority – a process not helped by the unpopularity of the anti-Buddhist policies that were pursued in some areas.

Religion in Vietnam

The religious question was one of the main difficulties confronting the Diem regime, and Diem's failure to resolve the issue was a major cause of his eventual failure. Most Vietnamese were Buddhist, with a strongly Chinese, Confucian influence, in that the social system was based on the clan, with all members of the clan claiming a common ancestor. Christianity had, however, made many converts under French rule, and in the south of the country were two powerful syncretic sects, the Hoa Hoa and the Cao Dai, combining elements of Catholicism with many other beliefs.

After the partition in 1954, about 900,000 refugees, mainly Catholics, fled to the South. Diem's family were staunch Catholics: his elder brother was Archbishop of Hue and his younger brother, Ngo Dinh Nhu, was a Catholic scholar. Diem was not himself opposed to the Confucian tradition but his attempts to establish a more centralised state inevitably brought him into conflict with many of the traditional elements in Vietnamese society. He came more and more to rely on Catholics and increasingly he entrusted power to his

A Buddhist suicide

brother Nhu, whose anti-Buddhism and personal ambitions were obvious by 1958.

By the early 1960s Diem had estranged himself from the majority of the Vietnamese population by his reliance on a religious minority whose most prominent representative, Ngo Dinh Nhu, was pursuing a venal and cruel policy towards the majority religion; and the public self-immolation of Buddhist monks brought this starkly to the attention of the rest of the world.

petence and heavy-handedness of many South Vietnamese government officials, together with the arbitrary and often unjust arrests of the anti-communist campaigns served to alienate ordinary citizens and made them more vulnerable to the communists' carefully orchestrated combination of intimidation, propaganda, blackmail and appeals to patriotism.

By early 1959 communist leaders in Hanoi felt confident enough to launch a new insurrection in the South. By May new directives endorsing armed overthrow of the Diem regime were on their way to party leaders in the South, and specially trained southerners, regrouped to the North after the Geneva conference of 1954, were infiltrated back into the South. A new Central Committee directorate for the South, popularly called COSVN, was established and communication routes into the South through Laos were improved and expanded. In July 1959 came an attack by South Vietnamese communists (now known as the Viet Cong) on the quarters of a US advisory detachment near Bien Hoa, north of Saigon, which produced the first American casualties of the new war.

Insurrection and terrorism

Throughout 1959 and 1960 the guerrilla war in South Vietnam grew in intensity. The communists stepped up their campaign of insurrection and terrorism. Armed bands of Viet Cong attacked government security posts and occasionally Vietnamese Army units, while party cadres organised mass demonstrations. The Diem regime responded with stepped-up security measures, including the establishment of rural development centres, commonly known as 'strategic hamlets', in an attempt to control and protect the people of the widely scattered villages of rural Vietnam. A new special security decree called 'Law 10-59' was introduced, which allowed suspected terrorists to be summarily tried by roving military tribunals and, if convicted, sentenced to death. Yet these measures failed to stem the rising tide of communist insurgency in the countryside.

American officials were slow to recognise the danger posed by the renewed communist agitation. Most of the incidents took place far from large cities, and Diem's officials often tried to cover up reverses in their areas of responsibility. A serious Viet Cong defeat of the South Vietnamese 32nd Regiment at Trang Sup, northeast of Saigon, in January 1960 finally alerted American leaders in Washington and Saigon to the danger. Washington requested the American embassy to make a special report on internal security in Vietnam. This was followed by more studies and a special National Intelligence Estimate which predicted that if current trends in the countryside continued, the Diem government would fall.

By the end of 1960, with the communists still unchecked, the US Mission in Saigon was directed to develop a comprehensive plan for countering the insurgent threat. The new 'Counter-insurgency Plan', approved by President John F. Kennedy soon after his inauguration, expanded support for Vietnam's security forces and increased the size of the army by 20,000 men. US advisers had already received permission to accompany Vietnamese units on combat missions and the first armed American helicopters had arrived in Vietnam. A new and more dangerous phase of the long struggle for Vietnam was about to begin. **Ronald Spector**

and was prepared to tolerate and even encourage rampant corruption, nepotism and favouritism in the assignment and promotion of officers. Aware that his chance of staying in power depended on keeping his rivals divided and indebted to him, Diem preferred to play off his generals against each other while keeping all real authority in his own hands. The president maintained his own radio net and often sent out orders to his field commanders directly, bypassing the army general staff and higher commanders.

By late 1956 Vietnamese communist leaders had concluded that the South Vietnamese government was not headed for an early collapse and that the Diem regime would have to be destroyed. How to do it was a question that was apparently vigorously debated in party councils. A new uprising was out of the question for the moment; the communist forces in the South were too weak and were constantly harried by Diem's security forces. An invasion might bring on US retaliation. Instead, the party, at the suggestion of Le Duan, a leading Southern activist, embarked on a campaign of selective terrorism and propaganda featuring assassinations and abductions of government officials and functionaries. This campaign was in full swing in 1957.

The Diem government struck back hard against the new communist campaign of terror, stepping up arrests of suspected communists and sympathisers and despatching troops to penetrate suspected communist base areas in remote corners of the country. Yet the very measures taken by the regime to protect itself against the communists served, in the long run, to strengthen its adversaries. The corruption, incom-

Vietnam:

the Americans move in

From Kennedy's commitment to Johnson's war

The position in South Vietnam by 1961 was that Prime Minister Ngo Dinh Diem, with all his faults, had the strong support of the United States, partly because there was no clear alternative to him. The start of the Kennedy administration, however, saw a growing divergence of views as to how that support should be manifested.

Diem's position in the countryside was weakening. His attack on the local village leadership, and the increasing exploitation of the peasants, fuelled opposition to his regime. The National Liberation Front (NLF), the political wing of the Viet Cong formed in 1960, was growing in power, and was capable of wiping out and replacing Diem's agents in the villages and the rural regions. The 'strategic hamlet' programme suggested by William Colby of the CIA and intended to protect the loyal population, was being transformed by Diem's brother Ngo Dinh Nhu and the Vietnamese Army into a policy of disguised concentration camps, as commentators in the administration in Washington, as well as in North Vietnam, were aware.

The US view over this period was divided as to whether the problem was a political or a military one. Colby, for example, saw the NLF as a symptom of North Vietnamese infiltration, but operating at a political level, which could be combated by political reforms. On the other hand, the military view was that the unrest in the countryside was the product of North Vietnamese aggression.

Overlaying this, of course, was the concern, particularly felt by Kennedy, that the outcome of events in Vietnam had a wide importance for the US position in world affairs, as well as reflecting on the political fortunes of the administration. Diem, despite his increasingly difficult position, did not want to see a large escalation in US forces. Yet it was clear that something had to be done.

In May 1961 Vice-President Johnson was sent on a fact-finding mission to Vietnam. On his return, he likened Diem to a Vietnamese Churchill, and put US support for the South Vietnamese in a global context.

Above: South Vietnamese troops scramble towards a US helicopter after a rapid deployment operation against a Viet Cong base. The provision of US equipment and support to the ARVN was the beginning of the direct involvement of US troops.

His words defined the US position for the rest of the war: 'The basic decision in Southeast Asia is here; we must decide whether to help those countries to the best of our ability or throw in the towel in the area and pull back our defenses to San Francisco, and a fortress America concept.'

At this time Kennedy was receiving military advice that guerrilla strength had risen to 17,000 men. For some months he remained indecisive. Conflicting advice was coming from the military, the CIA and his own personal advisers such as J.K. Galbraith or his aide and official observer in Saigon, Roger Hilsmore. Then, in October, Diem declared a state of emergency and requested further military aid. General Maxwell Taylor was sent to Saigon to consult with Diem, and the agreement reached was that 10,000 troops were to be sent to South Vietnam in a combat role. As a quid pro quo there would be political reforms on the part of Diem. Kennedy did not accept this immediately, but did send 300 helicopter pilots to lead South Vietnamese troops into combat. Throughout 1962 the number of military advisers increased until by the end of the year there were 12,000 in the country.

This build-up caused problems for the CIA. The military tended to follow its own decisions and its own chain of command. The dispute over the use of military or political tactics in Vietnam was therefore exacerbated. The military view was that, in the words of Hilsmore, 'winning hearts and minds was some-body else's job.'

As a further complication, Diem, surrounded as he was by the structures of his own privilege and nepotism, was incapable of initiating reforms. In fact, the brutality of his regime increased, especially in the persecution of the Buddhists. This marked the beginning of the split between Diem and the US. The first self-immolation by a Buddhist monk, protesting against the repression of the Buddhist religion, shocked public opinion in the US, and crystallised doubts in Washington about the value of supporting the Diem regime. Further acts of violence against monasteries and priests reaffirmed the view that Diem was beyond redemption. This view, however, posed a new problem. As Maxwell Taylor, by then chairman of the Joint Chiefs of Staff, expressed it: 'There was a strong group that picked up on the slogan, you can't win with Diem. The other group, to which I belonged, argued maybe you can't win with Diem, but if not Diem, who? And the answer was complete silence.'

In August 1963, Ambassador Nolting was suddenly replaced in Saigon by Henry Cabot Lodge. Kennedy instructed Lodge to get the South Vietnamese government to behave in a way more acceptable to US

Below left: A South Vietnamese Ranger follows an old woman and her family as they flee their burning village, burnt to the ground by government troops in search of Viet Cong. Below: A typical hill tribesman armed with a sub-machine gun. The US Special Forces teams armed and trained the hill tribesmen, who were traditionally anti-Vietnamese, in order to have local forces capable of denying the communists large areas of the sparsely inhabited central highlands.

public opinion. Upon his arrival, he was approached by a number of Vietnamese generals, who according to Lodge were worried about being purged, and were thinking of a coup. Lodge cabled to Washington for instructions. Hilsmore interprets the reply as follows: 'The overall gist of that cable was to say that we would prefer a government continuing under Diem, but if they felt they had no choice, then we would examine the government that they established on its own merits. Now of course there is no question that this, with all of its hedges, did encourage them.'

The question of responsibility for the downfall of Diem is still in dispute. William Colby may be near the truth when he says: 'This was a Vietnamese generals' coup, yes, but I think the fundamentals of it were decided in our White House.' In any event, discussions started with the generals, who at first were very dubious about the whole idea. But the pressure from Lodge, and probably Hilsmore, had a strong momentum. By the end of August, Lodge had sent a cable to Washington stating, among other things, that the US should make an all-out effort to get the generals to move promptly. Kennedy's reply was perhaps typical. 'We will do all that we can to help you conclude this operation successfully,' but then: 'I must reserve a contingent right to change course and reverse previous instructions.'

The generals, however, were worried about two things, firstly that Diem would move against them if a plot was discovered, and secondly that they had no firm guarantee of US support. While Washington debated over Diem's shortcomings, the Vietnamese generals ended discussions with Lodge and his CIA proxy. Then at the end of October, Lodge was informed that a coup was imminent. On 1 November 1963, Lodge kept Diem in a meeting all morning, in an attempt, it has been alleged, to keep him from his aides, who had become suspicious. At 1330 hours the coup was launched. Later that day Diem and his brother were arrested and shot in the back of the neck.

The murder of Ngo Dinh Diem

Kennedy, it is reported, was shocked by the murder of Diem – he had, after all, known and supported him for many years. Yet with the removal of Diem, Maxwell Taylor's question still remained unanswered. As Colby says: 'It really sounds incredible today that we made those decisions about getting rid of Diem without really careful consideration about what kind of government would replace him.' After the killing of Diem CIA opinion was that the situation was deteriorating rapidly, and that the communists would win the war by 1966.

Three weeks after the assassination of Diem, Kennedy suffered the same fate. Johnson's elevation to the White House was to mark another change in US policy in Vietnam. As vice-president, Johnson had seen Vietnam as a crucial battle against communism. But this was compounded by a more personal view. He was not going to be the 'president who saw Southeast Asia go the way that China went'.

With the fall of Diem the NLF started to make peace overtures to General Duong Van Minh ('Big Minh'), the dominant force in the new military triumvirate. Prince Sihanouk, president of Cambodia, and U Thant, the UN Secretary-General, also called for peace negotiations, and Johnson received messages from Ho Chi Minh calling for talks. The line in Washington, however, was hardening remorselessly, and Big Minh, who was not unfavourable to talks and was prepared to adopt a neutralist line, was labelled as drifting and indecisive by Secretary of Defense Robert McNamara.

Below: Four of the most important individuals responsible for the execution of US foreign policy in Vietnam. William Colby, director of the CIA (below) was instrumental in the adoption of the 'strategic hamlet' programme; General Maxwell Taylor (below right) was sent to Vietnam in late 1961 to consult with Diem over the number of US combat troops to be sent in; General William Westmoreland (bottom) became commander of all ground forces in mid-1964 and Henry Cabot Lodge (bottom right) was US ambassador in Saigon from August 1963 and was present at the time of the coup which overthrew Diem's regime.

In November 1963 Johnson ordered that military support for Saigon should continue. In March 1964 McNamara visited Saigon to assess the situation. His report recommended escalation of the war. He argued for total mobilisation of South Vietnam, for additional covert action against the North, and planning for taking the war to the North. By May Johnson had in his hands a list of strategic targets in North Vietnam which, if attacked by US bombers and bombarded by the Seventh Fleet, would leave the country crippled. Already Johnson had authorised the stepping-up of clandestine activity against North Vietnam such as U-2 reconnaissance flights and sabotage teams sent in by parachute and boat.

The military planning had begun to take on a momentum of its own. But Johnson does not seem to have realised the inevitable consequences of his policies. According to his biographer, he thought: 'he could finesse it somehow. He would send in a few people here and there. He would send a few bombs here and there.' The problems of getting the support of Congress for the major escalation of the war that McNamara proposed had been considered. According to William P. Bundy, Johnson 'felt that if we wanted to stabilize the situation, establish a clear-cut policy, we should get a congressional resolution'. This had been discussed in May. But nothing was to be done, according to Bundy, until after the elections in November.

Events were, however, to outpace everyone. On 30 July 1964, a raid by South Vietnamese boats was staged against the North, with direct shelling. Following this, a US destroyer, the *Maddox*, was sent into the area, entering well into the 19km (12-mile) limit. It returned to the Gulf on 2 August, where it came under attack by three Vietnamese torpedo

US military commitment South Vietnam 1960-64					
	1960	1961	1962	1963	1964
Military personnel	875	3164	11,326	16,263	23,310
Deaths in action		1	31	77	137
USAF sorties flown			2334	6929	5362

boats, which were later attacked by US air support. Two days later, the *Maddox* again returned, this time in the company of another destroyer. In the night, in the middle of a storm, *Maddox* radioed that she was under attack from torpedoes.

Receipt of this message in Washington initiated moves to change the course of the war for good. The countdown was started for retaliatory bombing raids against North Vietnam. This continued even after the commander of *Maddox* radioed that freak weather effects threw doubt on any reports of torpedo attack.

At 1800 hours on 4 August the Department of Defense in Washington issued the following announcement: 'A second deliberate attack was made during darkness by an undetermined number of North Vietnamese patrol boats on the USS *Maddox* and *C. Turner Joy* while the two destroyers were cruising in company on routine patrol in the Tonkin Gulf in International Waters about 65 miles from the nearest mainland.' At 1100 hours on 5 August US bombers attacked the North Vietnamese mainland. The air war proper had started.

Mike Rossiter

Below: South Vietnamese troops in the presidential palace hold back civilians at the perimeter fence shortly after the fall of Diem. Inset: The new military government poses for the press. General Duong Van Minh ('Big Minh') is front row left.

Chronology 1956-60

EUROPE & NORTH AMERICA

1956
January
18 **East Germany** announces creation of defence ministry and army.
February
14-25 **Soviet Union** 20th Congress of Soviet Communist Party ends with speech by Khrushchev exposing some of Stalin's worst crimes and so initiating the process of 'de-Stalinisation'.
April
19 **Britain** Commander Crabb lost in secret spying mission on Russian cruiser in Portsmouth harbour: diplomatic incident.
June
Cyprus Operation Pepperpot: British sweep against terrorists in Troodos Mountains.
28-29 **Poland** Popular uprising in Poznań suppressed by force, including use of Soviet troops.
October
11 **Britain** First test-drop of an atomic bomb from a British aircraft at Maralinga (Australia).
15 **Yugoslavia** President Eisenhower authorises further economic aid.
23 **Hungary** Demonstrations in Budapest.
24 **Hungary** Nagy reappointed prime minister.
29 **Hungary** Withdrawal of Soviet troops from Budapest.
November
1 **Hungary** Nagy renounces Hungarian membership of Warsaw Pact; declares neutrality.
4 **Hungary** Soviet troops re-enter Budapest; Nagy overthrown. Kadar forms new, pro-Soviet, government.

1957
January
1 **Northern Ireland** IRA attack on Brookeborough barracks.
5 **United States** Use of US forces 'to secure and protect the territorial integrity and political independence of nations requesting such aid against overt armed aggression from any nation controlled by international communism.' (Eisenhower Doctrine).
April
4 **Britain** Sandys White Paper revises defence policy, switching to reliance on nuclear deterrence and reducing size of armed forces. National Service to end after 1960.
May
15 **Britain** explodes first hydrogen bomb.
August
26 **Soviet Union** First ICBM tested.
October
Cyprus Sir Hugh Foot arrives as new governor.
3 **Poland** Rioting in Warsaw suppressed by force.
4 **Soviet Union** launches first space satellite *Sputnik I*.

1958
January
31 **United States** Army launches first space satellite *Explorer I*.
March
27 **Soviet Union** Khrushchev replaces Bulganin as prime minister while remaining first secretary of the Communist Party.
May
13 **Algeria** Unrest in Algiers: French officers under General Massu take control, join a Committee of Public Safety and protest against French political leadership in the war against the FLN. They call for return of de Gaulle to power in France.
20 **United States** establishes Strategic Army Corps to deal with emergencies in any part of the world.

June
1 **France** De Gaulle returns to power.
December
31 **Cyprus** EOKA activities cease.

1959
February
19 **Cyprus** London conference agrees form of independence.
March
13 **France** withdraws fleet from Nato.
May
7 **France** De Gaulle calls for French control of all Nato nuclear weapons on French soil: leads to withdrawal of US fighters and fighter bombers from France to UK (complete by August).
September
15-23 **United States** Khrushchev pays official visit.
December
4 **Cyprus** State of emergency ends.
14 **Cyprus** Archbishop Makarios becomes president.
30 **United States** First Polaris nuclear submarine USS *George Washington* commissioned.

1960
January
20 **Soviet Union** Long-range ballistic missile tested.
February
13 **France** explodes nuclear weapon in Sahara and becomes world's fourth nuclear power.
March
23 **France** Khrushchev pays official visit.
April
13 **Britain** decides to abandon development of ballistic missiles. Blue Streak cancelled.
May
1 **Soviet Union** US U-2 reconnaissance plane shot down over Soviet territory and pilot Gary Powers captured.
17 **France** Khrushchev uses U-2 incident to wreck Paris summit meeting.
21 **Turkey** Military coup.
July
20 **United States** First test-firing of Polaris SLBM.
November
1 **Britain** agrees to basing of US nuclear submarines in Scotland.
8 **United States** John F. Kennedy elected president.
December
6 **France** De Gaulle announces plan for independent French nuclear strike force.

SOUTHEAST ASIA

1956
March
31 **Laos** Prince Souvanna Phouma becomes prime minister.
April
28 **Vietnam** US Military Assistance Advisory Group takes over training of South Vietnamese Army; French withdraw.
July
31 **Burma** Chinese troops seize territory in northeast Burma.

1957
Vietnam Communist campaign launched against officials of South Vietnamese government.
August
31 **Malaya** receives independence from UK.

September
16 **Thailand** Military coup.
Vietnam Ngo Dinh Diem wins general election in South Vietnam.

1958
September
26 **Burma** General Ne Win seizes power in military coup.
October
20 **Thailand** Field-Marshal Sarit takes control.

1959
May
Vietnam US CINCPAC begins to send in US military advisers as requested by Saigon.
July
8 **Vietnam** First US casualties inflicted by Viet Cong in attack on US advisory detachment living quarters at Bien Hoa.
December
31 **Laos** General Phoumi Nosavan seizes power.

1960
January
Vietnam Viet Cong defeat South Vietnamese 32nd Regiment at Trang Sup.
July
31 **Malaya** Government announces communist revolt crushed and emergency officially over.
August
9 **Laos** Military rebellion under Kong Lae makes Prince Souvanna Phouma prime minister.
November
11-12 **Vietnam** Military revolt against Diem's administration repressed.
December
12 **Laos** General Phoumi Nosavan ousts Souvanna Phouma.
Vietnam Communist National Liberation Front (NLF) of South Vietnam formed.

SOUTH ASIA

1956
August-October
Afghanistan Soviet Union delivers weapons and planes to government.

1957
January
26 **Kashmir** incorporated into India despite protests by Pakistan.

1958
October
7-27 **Pakistan** General Ayub Khan seizes power and becomes president.

1959
February
25 **Pakistan** accepts arms aid from US.
August
28 **India** accuses China of violating India's frontiers with China and Tibet.

1960
June
10 **India** accuses China of occupying Indian territory in Himalayas.
December
15 **Nepal** King Mahendra Bir Bikram seizes power with army support.

EAST ASIA
1956
October
19 **Japan** agrees with Soviet Union that no further state of war exists.

1958
August
6 **China** Nationalists declare state of emergency on offshore islands of Quemoy and Matsu.
23 **China** Communists begin intense bombardment of islands in the Quemoy group.
September
6 **China** Communists declare an end to bombardment of Matsu and Quemoy.

1959
March
10-27 **Tibet** National revolt against Chinese domination is suppressed by Chinese Army and Dalai Lama flees to India.

1960
January
19 **Japan** renews defence treaty with US.

MIDDLE EAST
1956
June
13 **Egypt** Britain completes withdrawal ending 74 years of presence.
18 **Egypt** Soviet Union renews offer to finance building of Aswan Dam.
July
18 **Egypt** US withdraws offer to finance Aswan Dam.
26 **Egypt** President Nasser announces nationalisation of Suez Canal Company.
October
24 **Egypt** British, French and Israelis agree on joint military action.
29 **Egypt** Israeli paratroops drop near Mitla Pass and take El Kuntilla.
30 **Egypt** British and French issue ultimatum to Egypt demanding cessation of hostilities and Anglo-French occupation of Port Said, Ismailiya and Suez.
31 **Egypt** British and French bomb Egypt's airbases; Egyptians withdraw from Sinai.
November
5 **Egypt** Anglo-French paratroopers dropped near Port Said.
6 **Egypt** Anglo-French amphibious landing at Port Said. Ceasefire at midnight.
15 **Egypt** UN emergency force of 6000 men arrives in Sinai to supervise cessation of hostilities.

1957
March
7 **Egypt** Suez Canal is reopened to navigation.
9 **Middle East** US President Eisenhower authorises use of US troops in Middle East if necessary.
23 **Middle East** US accedes to Baghdad Pact as associate member.
July-August
Oman British and SAF troops contain revolt against Sultan.

1958
February
1 Egypt unites with Syria to form the United Arab Republic (UAR). Yemen becomes an associate from March 1958.
April
14-July 14 **Lebanon** Fighting between Druze and Christians.

July
14 **Lebanon** President Chamoun appeals to US, Britain and France for military aid.
14 **Iraq** Army revolt led by General Abdul Karim el Kassim overthrows monarchy. King Faisal II and Premier Nuri es Said murdered.
15 **Lebanon** US Marines and Army troops arrive.
17 **Jordan** British troops arrive to defend King Hussein's regime.
August
21 **Lebanon** US begins withdrawal of troops, completed by October.
October
Iraq Mullah Mustafa Barzani, president of the Kurdish Democratic Party (KDP) returns to Iraq.

1959
January
27 **Oman** Rebels finally defeated by British Army and SAF.
March
24 **Iraq** withdraws from Baghdad Pact, which is renamed Cento on 19 August.

CENTRAL AMERICA
1956
September
21 **Nicaragua** President Somoza assassinated.
October
21 **Honduras** Military seize power.
December
2 **Cuba** Fidel Castro arrives from Mexico. His force of 81 men is dispersed by government troops three days later.

1957
May
2-3 **Honduras** Border clashes with Nicaragua.
28 **Cuba** The battle of El Uvero, the first victory for Castro's army.
October
25 **Guatemala** Military coup.

1959
January
1 **Cuba** Revolutionaries led by Fidel Castro capture Havana; General Batista flees the country.
7 **Cuba** Castro government recognised by US government.
April
24-30 **Panama** Cuban-based insurgent invasion defeated.
November
3 **Panama** Anti-US riots.

1960
October
26 **El Salvador** Military junta led by Colonel Urias overthrows government of President Lemus.
November
11-15 **Nicaragua** insurgent invasion from Costa Rica defeated.

SOUTH AMERICA
1956
June
10-14 **Argentina** Peronist revolt suppressed.

1957
May
10 **Colombia** Military junta seizes power from Lieutenant-General Rojas Pinilla.

1959
December
Paraguay Rebel invasions from Argentina defeated.

AFRICA
1956
March
2 **Morocco** ceases to be French protectorate.
17 **Tunisia** gains independence from France; Habib Bourguiba made premier.
July
25 **Tunisia** proclaimed a republic; Bourguiba president.

1957
January
7 **Algeria** General Jacques Massu, commanding 10th Colonial Parachute Division, ordered to assume responsibility for public order in city of Algiers.
March
6 **Ghana** gains independence, remaining a republic within the British Commonwealth; Kwame Nkrumah made president.
May
26-June 7 **Tunisia** Clashes between French and Tunisian troops on Algerian border.
September
Algeria Completion of defensive anti-terrorist Morice Line on Tunisian border.

1958
October
2 **Guinea** demands and gains independence from France. Prime Minister Sekou Toure becomes president.
November
17 **Sudan** General Ibrahim Abboud takes power in bloodless military coup.
28 **Chad** gains independence from France to become the Republic of Chad.

1959
February
Algeria General Maurice Challe launches an all-out offensive against the FLN.

1960
January
1 **Cameroon** gains independence.
12 **Kenya** State of emergency ends.
22-February 1 **Algeria** 'The Week of the Barricades': French troops under General Challe suppress uprising of French Rightists opposed to self-determination.
February
3 **South Africa** Macmillan's 'Winds of Change' speech in Cape Town: 'The wind of change is blowing through this continent and whether we like it or not this growth of national consciousness is a political fact.'
March
21 **South Africa** Sharpeville: 60 black demonstrators killed by South African police; worldwide condemnation of white regime.
April
27 **Togo** obtains independence from France.
June
20 **Senegal, Upper Volta, Dahomey and Soudan** (later renamed Mali) obtain independence from France.
25 **Madagascar** gains independence as Malagasy Republic within French community.
30 **Congo** Belgium grants independence.
July
11 **Congo** Katanga proclaims independence under Moise Tshombe who resists control by Congo central government.
14 **Congo** UN sends security force to restore order.
August
1 **Dahomey** gains independence from France.
3 **Niger** granted independence by France.
October
1 **Nigeria** becomes republic within British Commonwealth.
November
28 **Mauritania** gains independence from France.
December
13-17 **Ethiopia** Military revolt against Emperor Haile Selassie is suppressed by loyal troops.

The night belongs to Charlie

Psychology and guerrilla warfare

It has been very rare in the history of war for one side to win by killing or wounding all the enemy. Usually, at some point in the war one side recognises that continued resistance is hopeless and surrenders. Frequently, the main objective of military commanders is to mislead and mystify the enemy to such an extent that the morale of his forces will collapse.

Psychological warfare is war on the mind, an attack on the enemy's morale to mislead him, frighten him, surprise him, outguess and demoralise him. These aspects of psychological warfare can sometimes make up for inferiority in men and weapons, less military experience and lack of allies. And if psychological warfare is about deception and attacking the morale of the enemy, it is also about sustaining the morale of one's own side.

There are several reasons why psychological warfare has become so important since 1945, but most stem from the basic fact that guerrilla campaigns have become the most common form of warfare. Fighting long, protracted campaigns where there are no clearly defined front lines, and where all the technology in the world will not compensate for a lack of will to win (as the Americans found in Vietnam), there is a great premium on the morale of the troops involved – both one's own and the enemy's. And this is where psychological warfare comes into play with a vengeance.

For the insurgent leaders, maintaining the morale and loyalty of their own forces is a basic need. And although they may feel that a belief in the rightness of their cause is a sufficient basis, this ideological tie is usually reinforced in various ways. In most communist movements there is intense indoctrination of recruits, with hours of 'political education' every day. Some terrorist groups, such as the FLN in Algeria, made sure that recruits burnt their boats by killing a member of the security forces before they were fully inducted; the Mau Mau in Kenya tried to impress would-be insurgents by the power of the oathing ceremony. And these methods of enforcing solidarity are usually accompanied by threats of reprisal against turncoats – in Northern Ireland, the IRA's barbarous punishment, 'knee-capping', is well known.

Once in the field, the insurgent forces, with the advantage of holding the initiative (at least at first) may often succeed in keeping the enemy pinned down by threat as much as by actual force. The Viet Minh and later the Viet Cong were past masters at this. Both French and American troops were confined to a passive role at night, peering out from defensive positions, desperately wondering what could be happening just out of vision...The American phrase 'The night belongs to Charlie' (from 'Victor Charlie', the initials VC) expressed a major advantage that the Viet Cong had won.

For regular forces, merely looking for insurgents can be made a dangerous process that saps morale. As one American in Vietnam explained: 'We had a constant attrition from booby traps, seven out of ten casualties a month were traumatic amputees. On a

Left: An RAF Vickers Valetta drops leaflets over suspected communist hideouts in the Malayan jungle. Offering security to terrorists who surrendered proved very successful.

Above: One of the most efficient methods for reaching guerrilla enclaves with propaganda material is through aerial distribution. Here US troops drop leaflets over Vietnam. Right: A British Dakota C-4, with loudspeakers slung under the fuselage, flies over the Malayan jungle broadcasting to terrorists below.

LAISSEZ·PASSER

SOLDATS DE l'ARMÉE FRANÇAISE Conduisez le porteur à votre Officier ET TRAITEZ LE BIEN

賞 金 $500/- HADIAH

sweep you all get in a long line and walk in. You're watching every place you step wondering who's going to hit it. You know someone is going to. Sweep and sweep and sweep, halfway through the day and nothing's happened. Are we going to hit a booby trap today? Who will it be? It was mentally draining.

'Boom! Just like that and a guy is missing a leg, somebody is missing a foot . . .'

A further aspect of this psychological warfare is the use of suicide squads, or the demonstration of fanaticism on behalf of the insurgents' cause. This has been particularly important in those struggles where the enemy's main force is foreign, and almost by definition less fanatically determined. The British decision to abandon Palestine in 1948 was greatly influenced by the determination of the Jewish terrorist groups.

Where the enemy forces are not foreign, but come from the same country, then other methods can be used to discomfit them. Selective assassination of the police, as practised by the IRA in Northern Ireland and also by EOKA in Cyprus may be very effective. The most obvious method of hitting the morale of regular forces is to threaten their families. In predominantly rural societies, such as South Vietnam, this can be a very potent threat, but it can also rebound. In Algeria, the *harkas* who fought for the French against the FLN knew what their probable fate would be if they surrendered or went over to the insurgents; the FLN had little reputation for clemency. The *harkas*, therefore, stayed loyal to the end – an end which for many (including their families) was a brutal death at the hands of the victorious FLN.

Indeed, the whole question of terror as a form of psychological warfare is a confusing issue. In both China and Cuba, the rebels impressed both populace and the enemy forces by their regard for human life. In these countries, the fact that the rebel forces upheld certain values, which the respective governments certainly did not, gave them a moral advantage that was of great psychological value.

Above: Three different leaflets (two French from Algeria and one from Malaya), typical of the sort often dropped over rebel-held areas: one promising safe-conduct to the bearer, one offering money to surrendered guerrillas and the other contrasting the life-style of the government-in-exile with the insurgents themselves.

JAMIAT.I.ISLAMI AFGHANISTAN

The insurgents then, have certain advantages in psychological warfare that they can employ to good effect. But so do the forces that they are opposed to. Often badly supplied and badly armed, knowing he is outnumbered and usually fighting in difficult terrain, the rural guerrilla, be he hiding out on a Greek mountain side in mid-winter or crouching in a pool of stagnant water while a helicopter gunship flies overhead in Vietnam, has rarely been in an enviable position. For the urban guerrilla, the ordeal of living a double life 24 hours a day, always waiting for the knock at the door from the security forces, is an appalling strain. If the counter-insurgent units can capitalise on this, then they can exert a considerable psychological pressure.

The problem is how to do it. Sometimes sheer unbridled force may provide a short-term answer; but the French found after the 'Battle of Algiers' in 1957 that unrestricted torture made the French stand in Algeria untenable in that large sections of the population in France henceforth found the war immoral. Where standards of conduct are kept high, however, the security forces may well claim that the insurgents are being dealt with too softly for efficient counter-insurgency, and that such tactics are playing into the hands of the guerrillas.

Gangs and counter-gangs

In the most successful counter-insurgency campaigns – such as those waged by the British in Malaya and Kenya – one element stands out above all others in the application of psychological warfare: the offer of complete security to guerrillas who have surrendered, especially to those prepared to join 'counter-gangs' and go back to fight against their former comrades. Once this is sufficiently well known among the insurgents, it tends to generate its own momentum; increasingly severe discipline within guerrilla bands to discourage desertion may make government pledges seem even more attractive.

Yet what may work in one environment may not be effective in another; the application of techniques of psychological warfare by counter-insurgency forces must always take account of the specific characteristics of each war.

There is one area of psychological warfare, however, that security forces all over the world have honed to a fine art since 1970, by the application of broadly similar techniques; and this is in the treatment of terrorists who take hostages. The sieges, of embassies or of aircraft, that have taken place in the 1970s and 1980s are prime examples of psychological warfare, with threat, bluff and fear playing as important a role as the final use of force. After the first years of PLO hijackings, it appeared that modern society was extremely vulnerable to such terrorism; but now, security forces understand how to leave the terrorists to build up a relationship with their hostages (making them less likely to slaughter them); how to apply a gradual increase in tension (low-flying aircraft, searchlights glaring day and night), until the terrorists became less capable of assessing what is happening around them; how to negotiate through any deadlines the terrorists may make; and finally, to recognise when it is time to send in a specially trained squad, such as the British SAS, who can storm a building and overcome the terrorists inside within seconds. Such tactics are supreme examples of psychological warfare. **Ashley Brown**

Above: A Russian soldier captured by Afghan insurgents is forced to pose for the camera below an anti-Soviet poster.

As the sun goes down ....

The nerves, tension and fear of the night in Vietnam were something most American soldiers found a terrifying experience as this extract from an interview with a G.I. makes clear.

I hear a thump. I look and I see somebody's throwing rocks. I think, 'Oh, shit, they're probing to see who's asleep.' I got really scared and I took it personal, too. I says, 'Man, why are they probing this side.' You don't want to open up if nothing is there, because then you're so embarrassed. Not only that, but they're going to take all your ammo. . . . They don't fool around. I was really starting to get nervous. It happened again, a pebble hit me. I thought, 'Fuck, man, I'll just make like I'm sleeping and I'll blow away whoever comes up.'

This thing rushes up to me in the dark. It had a leather face. I didn't have time to be scared. I just opened up on it. . . . The next thing I know, I'm out of rounds . . . .

We stood up all night . . . . everybody trembling . . . . We started calling all sorts of people to back us up. They told us they can't do nothing until daylight.

As the sun comes up, there's maybe six or seven monkeys laying around. We had been attacked by rock apes. I didn't know, I thought they were NVA guerrillas or something. So to speak, they were gorillas.

The
A-10 THUNDERBOLT II

The single-seat Fairchild A-10A is the United States Air Force's (USAF's) standard close air-support aircraft and surprisingly, it is the first post-World War II American warplane specifically designed for this role to enter service. In the Vietnam War a wide variety of aircraft were used for close air support, ranging from the piston-engined A-1 Skyraider to the Mach 2 F-4 Phantom. The lessons learnt in this war strongly influenced the USAF in its decision to deploy a low-cost attack aircraft with good handling qualities, accurate weapon delivery capability and the ability to withstand a high degree of battle damage. In 1970 the Northrop and Fairchild companies were chosen to build competitive aircraft to fulfil this need and the first A-10 prototype flew on 10 May 1972. After winning the fly-off competition against Northrop's A-9, the A-10 went into production and entered service with the USAF in 1975.

Officially the A-10A is named Thunderbolt II after the great World War II ground attack fighter, but among its pilots the angular and pugnacious A-10A is universally dubbed the 'Warthog'. One of the fundamental considerations in its design is simplicity. The A-10A's straight wing has a simple aerofoil section optimized to give high lift at low airspeeds and the fuselage, built in three main sections, is of aluminium alloy construction. The twin General Electric TF34 turbofans are mounted high on the rear fuselage to reduce the problem of foreign objects being sucked in during operations from rough, semi-prepared airstrips and also to provide a degree of shielding from hostile ground fire. Fuel is concentrated in the centre fuselage and wing centre section near the aircraft's

Previous page: Painted in standard Tactical Air Command 'lizard' camouflage, three A-10 Thunderbolts fly in echelon formation. Above: The versatile A-10 can be serviced and flown from elementary airfields in a variety of adverse weather conditions. Opposite page top: An A-10 armed with a Hobos television-guided bomb and a Paveway laser-guided bomb (starboard wing).

Right: An A-10 pilot prepares for flight, his aircraft protected by a reinforced blast wall. Below: Two A-10s taxi out onto the runway.

Above: A-10s make a
flying pass over a Soviet
T-62 while on a training
mission. Right: The A-10
in flight (above) and
operating from a grass
strip in Britain
(below).

centre of gravity, so that as it is burned off there are no significant effects on the aircraft's trim and handling. The twin fin and rudder tail assembly provides good control response at low altitude and a degree of masking for the engines' infra-red emissions. The design also ensures that if one surface is damaged a degree of control is retained through the other.

One of the most crucial considerations in the design of close-support and tank-killing aircraft is survivability. In this respect much of the A-10A's structure is redundant. Fuselage longerons and skin panels for example, can be severely damaged without the structure failing and the hydraulically-actuated control systems are duplicated. Should both fail the aircraft can still be flown by a manual back-up system. Vital systems are heavily protected against battle damage.

A titanium-armoured shield protects the pilot's cockpit and is capable of withstanding hits from 37mm high-explosive rounds. The fuel tanks and fuel system are self-sealing and a damaged tank can be isolated. The gun's ammunition tank is located deep within the fuselage and protected with armour plate to reduce the risk of groundfire igniting the ammunition load. A good deal of ingenuity has been applied to the A-10A's design to enhance its resistance to battle damage and it has been claimed, though not yet proven, that the aircraft can remain airborne after the loss of one engine, half a tail and two thirds of a wing.

The A-10A's main armament consists of the massive 30mm GAU-8A cannon, which with its ammunition drum fills a large proportion of the forward fuselage. The seven-barrel, Gatling-type rapid-fire

Top: An A-10 blasts away with its powerful 30mm anti-tank cannon, a weapon notable not only for its high volume of fire but also for its accuracy. The A-10 is a highly stable weapons platform and as such is able to pinpoint small ground targets to considerable effect.

Left: Split ailerons are opened above and below the wing as this A-10 air-breaks over the target and fires a Maverick air-to-ground missile.

Above: Fully bombed-up an A-10 banks over to starboard on a training mission over desert terrain.

Above: An unusual view of four A-10s flying in line ahead. Despite its seeming clumsiness the A-10 has been carefully designed to maximise its ability to absorb enemy ground fire.

cannon can be fired at rates of either 2100 or 4200 rounds per minute. The ammunition drum holds a total of 1350 rounds and a cockpit counter allows the pilot to check on his ammunition expenditure. The 30mm rounds can be either armour-piercing/incendiary, capable of penetrating a tank's side armour and engine compartment, or high explosive for use against soft-skinned vehicles. Because these high energy rounds follow a flat trajectory and the aircraft itself provides a very stable gun platform, the GAU-8A has proved to be a highly accurate weapon and experienced pilots have achieved 100 per cent scores during firing practice. The gun's ammunition can be replenished in about 10 minutes while the aircraft can be refuelled at the same time. Consequently, the turn-around times between sorties is short. Even when wearing restrictive NBC suits an armament crew can load an A-10A with ammunition and full underwing ordnance in 35 minutes.

The A-10A is provided with eleven weapons pylons capable of lifting a maximum ordnance load of 7257kg (16,000lb). Stores carried include free-fall bombs, cluster-bomb units and laser-guided bombs,

although the A-10A itself cannot designate targets for laser-guided weapons. A favoured weapon in Europe is the AGM-65B Maverick TV-guided ASM (air-to-surface missile), up to six of which can be carried. Maverick has a maximum range against conspicuous targets of approximately 19km (12 miles). Its TV-seeker head is locked onto the target by the A-10A pilot before launch and then automatically guides onto the image at the centre of the aiming reticle.

The A-10A's principal aid to weapon aiming is the pilot's wide-angle HUD (head-up display) onto which is projected an aiming reticle in addition to primary flight data. A Pave Penny laser-spot tracker can pick up laser-designated targets and indicate their position on the HUD, while a cockpit-mounted TV monitor is used to designate targets for the Maverick ASMs. Navigation aids are simple, comprising TACAN (tactical air navigation), an instrument that indicates distance and bearing from a coded ground beacon, and a heading and altitude reference system. Generally the A-10A's pilot relies on map reading, although later aircraft are being fitted with an inertial navigation set and a radio altimeter. Communications

Fairchild A-10A Thunderbolt II

Type Single-seat, close-support aircraft
Dimensions Span 17.53m (57ft 6in); length 16.26m
(53ft 4in); height 4.47m (14ft 8in)
Weight Empty 9433kg (20,796lb); maximum
take-off 21,500kg (47,400lb)
Powerplant Two 4112kg (9065lb) General Electric
TF34-GE-100 turbofans

Performance Maximum speed at sea level
722km/h (449mph); cruising speed 623km/h
(387mph) at 1500m (5000ft)
Range Combat radius 463km (288 miles)

Armament One 30mm GAU-8A cannon; 11 pylons
for up to 7257kg (16,000lb) external stores including
bombs, cluster bombs, laser-guided bombs and
AGM-65B Maverick ASMs

Above: Although not
embodying the advanced
electronics of the modern
fighter the A-10
nevertheless is by no
means a simple aircraft, as
these cockpit side-views
reveal.

Below: The size of the
30mm GAU-8 cannon can
be seen when compared
with a Volkswagen. The
massive ammunition drum
at the rear holds 1350
armour-piercing
incendiary rounds.

are vitally important in the close air support mission and the A-10A has both UHF and VHF sets, enabling the pilot to talk to ground forces and forward air controllers, as well as other aircraft and anti-tank helicopters.

The A-10A pilot's main defence against enemy anti-aircraft systems is his elusiveness. Flying at zero altitude and making maximum use of any ground cover to mask his approach, the A-10A offers only a fleeting target to anti-aircraft guns or surface-to-air missiles. In addition the A-10A deploys ECM (electronic counter measures) equipment to jam enemy target-acquisition systems. The aircraft has a built-in ALR-46V radar warning receiver to alert the pilot to the presence of hostile radar transmitters. Radars can be dealt with either by means of the ALQ-119 jamming pod, which can be fitted to an underwing pylon, or by releasing chaff. Infra-red flares can also be ejected to divert heat-seeking missiles.

In operations against enemy armoured forces, the A-10A attacks will be closely coordinated with those of friendly artillery and anti-tank helicopters. Artillery will be especially valuable in dealing with hostile anti-aircraft fire, while the helicopters will make initial contact with the enemy and brief the USAF FAC (forward air controller) on the position. The FAC, circling the battle zone in an OV-10 Bronco, will then advise the A-10As of the location of enemy and friendly forces and suggest an initial heading for their attack, so that the A-10As' pop-up manoeuvre from tree-top height to acquire their targets will not bring them under heavy anti-aircraft fire. The A-10As will remain under cover until the last possible moment and once in the open will only maintain a steady course long enough for them to aim and fire their weapons. Only when they turn away from an attacking pass will the A-10As present their vulnerable underside to the enemy but this will offer only a fleeting high-deflection target.

In 1978 the A-10A became fully-operational with the 354th Tactical Fighter Wing (TFW) at Myrtle Beach, South Carolina and only one other operational active-duty A-10A wing is based in the United States. However, A-10As serve with both Air National Guard and Air Force Reserve squadrons. In Europe the A-10A currently equips the 81st TFW based at Bentwaters and Woodbridge in the United Kingdom, but also deploys to FOLs (forward operating locations) in West Germany. The 81st TFW has a strength of 108 A-10As distributed between six squadrons while an eight-aircraft detachment usually operates from each of the FOLs at Sembach, Ahlhorn, Nörvenich and Leipheim. A-10As also serve in Alaska with the 18th Tactical Fighter Squadron at Eielson air force base and in South Korea with the 25th Tactical Fighter Squadron at Suwon.

Production of the A-10A is scheduled to end in 1985, after the delivery of 733 aircraft to the USAF. One of the aircraft's major shortcomings, its lack of all-weather capability, will be improved by the retrofitting of LANTIRN (low altitude navigation and targeting infra-red systems for night) to existing aircraft. LANTIRN consists of pod-mounted radar and forward-looking infra red for all-weather navigation and target acquisition. With this enhanced capability, enabling it to fly through the worst of Europe's weather, the A-10A is likely to provide a potent defence against hostile armoured forces for many years to come.

Decline and fall

The death throes of Portugal's overseas empire

Of all the European colonial powers the Portuguese clung most tenaciously to empire. The Dutch had evacuated their major overseas possession by 1949, the Belgians followed suit in 1960 and Britain and France had ceded the greater part of their empires by the early 1960s. Even the Spanish began to decolonise in 1968. But Portugal long refused to follow the trend set by the other colonial powers. The first European nation to establish an overseas empire, the Portuguese were the last to decide upon imperial withdrawal.

Paradoxically, Portugal's reluctance to withdraw from empire was a result of weakness rather than of strength. As one of Europe's poorest and most backward countries, Portugal was in no position to maintain effective control over ex-colonies through economic dominance and occasional military intervention, as the French for example were able to do; for Portugal, it was direct rule or nothing. Some of the overseas territories, notably Angola, were net contributors to the Portuguese economy – a contribution

Above: A typical map used in schools during Salazar's regime to illustrate the nationalist slogan 'Portugal is not a small country', showing how the addition of her colonies made this small nation one of the largest in Europe.

Below: A Portuguese instructor trains ex-Angolan guerrillas in the use of smallarms. The success of the combined Portuguese policies of counter-insurgency and 'hearts and minds' led a number of nationalists to support the Portuguese regime. The instructor shown here claims to have killed over 100 guerrillas.

Portugal naturally wished to maintain. But more important were political considerations. The continued possession of vast overseas territories was a solace to national pride, conferring on Portugal an international status which a small and impoverished country could not otherwise have attained. The authoritarian regimes of prime ministers António Salazar (1932-68) and Marcello Caetano (1968-74) exploited to the full the ideology of empire. Every Portuguese schoolchild was taught to believe in the greatness of Portugal's 'civilising mission' in Africa.

The Portuguese did not so much defend colonialism as deny it. They claimed that their overseas possessions formed an integral part of the Portuguese state, a claim given formal status in 1951 when these possessions were declared 'overseas provinces' of Portugal. Moreover, the Portuguese claimed that the aim of their policy in the so-called *ultramar* was not to suppress or exploit the natives but to turn all of them eventually into Portuguese citizens. This policy was enshrined in the constitution of 1933. The population of the African territories was divided into two distinct categories, the *indígenas* (natives) and the *não-indígenas* (non-natives). But the 'non-native' category included not only whites but *mestiços* (half-castes) and *assimilados* ('civilised' blacks). In theory there was nothing to stop a 'native' achieving 'civilised' status and thereby attaining full Portuguese citizenship. But in practice it was appallingly difficult. Educational qualifications were a fundamental requirement before the Portuguese authorities would grant an African *assimilado* status. Since there was a chronic lack of educational facilities, by 1961 barely one per cent of the 'native' population of the African territories had become *assimilados*.

Cheap labour

Compared with other African colonies, the Portuguese African territories were remarkably free of racial discrimination, but the Africans still had many grievances. Especially resented was the system of contract labour, whereby the government forced Africans to work on plantations producing cash crops such as coffee and cotton. The number of contract labourers was greatly increased during the 1950s, and this adversely affected traditional subsistence farming. In addition, wages for Africans were low and increased immigration of poor whites from mainland Portugal displaced blacks from even menial employment. The development of industry and social services was painfully slow; Portugal found it impossible to achieve adequate development at home, let alone in its colonies.

The 1950s and early 1960s saw the foundation of nationalist movements in all the Portuguese African territories, movements which tended to be led, ironically, by *mestiços* and *assimilados*. In Guinea and the Cape Verde Islands the Partido Africano da Independência da Guiné e Cabo Verde (PAIGC) was set up in 1956 under the leadership of the Cape Verdean *mestiço* Amílcar Cabral. In the same year in Angola Agostinho Neto and others founded the leftist Movimento Popular de Libertação de Angola (MPLA),

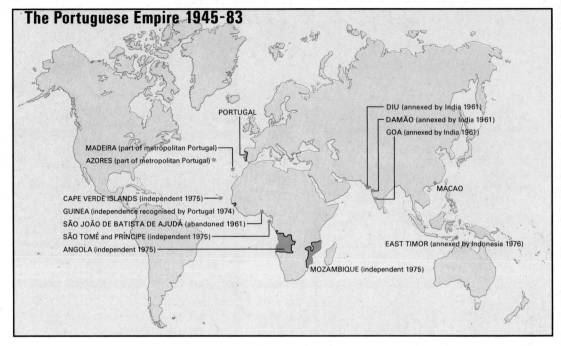

The Portuguese Empire 1945-83

PORTUGAL

MADEIRA (part of metropolitan Portugal)
AZORES (part of metropolitan Portugal)

DIU (annexed by India 1961)
DAMÃO (annexed by India 1961)
GOA (annexed by India 1961)

MACAO

CAPE VERDE ISLANDS (independent 1975)
GUINEA (independence recognised by Portugal 1974)
SÃO JOÃO DE BATISTA DE AJUDÁ (abandoned 1961)
SÃO TOMÉ and PRÍNCIPE (independent 1975)
ANGOLA (independent 1975)

EAST TIMOR (annexed by Indonesia 1976)

MOZAMBIQUE (independent 1975)

Below: General António de Spínola, the Portuguese commander-in-chief in Guinea. Although his campaign was relatively successful, he became convinced of the need to rethink policy in Africa. He became head of the government in Portugal after the military coup of 1974 – though he was forced to resign six months later by the left-wing government.

and two years later another nationalist group, the União das Populações de Angola (UPA), later to become the Frente Nacional de Libertação de Angola (FNLA), was established by Holden Roberto. Mozambique's main nationalist movement was the Frente de Libertação de Moçambique (FRE-LIMO), led initially by Eduardo Mondlane. Each of these nationalist movements became increasingly militant and turned to armed conflict in order to oust the Portuguese.

During the early 1960s Portuguese imperial power came under widespread attack. First to succumb were the small enclaves. In August 1961 the Portuguese 'fort' at São João de Batista de Ajudá on the coast of Dahomey (now Benin) was burnt down by troops from that newly independent state, and its sole European occupant, the Portuguese 'governor', was sent back to Lisbon. Later that year, in December 1961, 30,000 Indian troops invaded the enclaves of Goa, Diu and Damão, which comprised Portuguese India, overwhelming the 3500 Portuguese defenders.

In the three major African territories, Angola, Guinea and Mozambique, guerrilla wars began between 1961 and 1964. Angola was the first of the three to experience warfare when in March 1961 UPA guerrillas massacred several hundred whites and thousands of blacks. Later attacks were launched by the MPLA and also by

another guerrilla movement, the União Nacional para a Independência Total de Angola (UNITA), an offshoot of the FNLA led by Jonas Savimbi. Meanwhile the nationalists had also begun guerrilla operations in Portuguese Guinea, in January 1963, and in Mozambique in September 1964.

Portugal's response to all these attacks was defiant and uncompromising. The seizure of the enclaves by Dahomey and India was not recognised. Portugal continued officially to claim that these enclaves formed part of the Portuguese state. In the case of the African territories Portugal's response was equally intransigent but far more practical: large numbers of troops were sent in to fight the guerrillas. During the 1960s the Portuguese engaged in a systematic build-up of their forces overseas. Troop levels were raised from a few thousand in 1961 to some 130,000 by 1964. Guinea received 30,000 troops and Angola and Mozambique 50,000 apiece. Aircraft and helicopters were despatched and counter-insurgency operations begun. Large numbers of Africans were moved into 'strategic villages' where they could be isolated from contact with the guerrillas.

Stabilisation and stalemate
At the same time, the Portuguese instituted reforms aimed at winning support away from the guerrillas. The distinction between *indigenas* and *não-indigenas* was abolished in 1961; henceforth all blacks were officially classified as Portuguese citizens. The system of contract labour was officially prohibited. Social services expanded rapidly, schools and clinics often being built by the army. Industry and communications were also developed, particularly in Angola.

These policies – counter-insurgency accompanied by a 'hearts and minds' campaign – met with considerable success. The guerrilla movements gained support and recognition from the Organization of African Unity (OAU), but within the Portuguese African territories they were seldom able to penetrate far beyond border areas. By 1974 the Portuguese still appeared to have the military situation under control. In Angola all three nationalist groups had been con-

Above: Dr António de Oliveira Salazar who was unchallenged as Portuguese head of state from 1932 until 1968 when illness forced his retirement from leadership.

tained. The situation in Guinea, the scene of initial guerrilla successes, had been stabilised for the Portuguese between 1968 and 1972 by their monocled commander-in-chief, General António de Spínola. Even in Mozambique, where the situation was deteriorating, the Portuguese were still able to cope with the guerrillas. The Portuguese could also boast that by 1974 almost 60 per cent of their forces in Africa were black and that white emigration to the *ultramar* had doubled during the course of the wars.

Despite these successes, however, the Portuguese became increasingly disenchanted. The guerrillas had been checked but they could not be beaten, and the prospect was one of endless warfare. And the wars were very costly – in political, economic and human terms. Portugal's international standing was badly tarnished, and within Portugal itself the wars became increasingly unpopular. Defence expenditure, as a proportion of the national budget, rose from 25 per cent in 1960 to over 40 per cent by the early 1970s, a heavy burden for a relatively poor country. The African commitments were also a drain on manpower, despite the increasing Africanisation of the armies in the field. In the late 1960s the age of conscription

After the military coup in 1974, Portugal swiftly abandoned her African Empire. In September 1974, Guinea was granted independence (left, the Portuguese flag is lowered). In Angola rule was handed over to a 'government of national unity' in November 1975 (below, scenes of jubilation in Luanda).

had to be lowered and the length of service extended. On top of all this there was the cost in lives: by 1974 Portugal had sustained 11,000 dead and 30,000 wounded, a proportionally far higher loss rate than that of the US in Vietnam. After 13 years of conflict, the Portuguese were war-weary.

It was neither popular disaffection nor military defeat which brought the wars to a close, however, but a coup in Lisbon launched by the Armed Forces Movement (MFA). This movement emerged originally in 1973 not as an anti-war group but as a protest by young regular officers over their professional status, but it soon took on a more political tone. When General Spínola, now the deputy chief of staff, was dismissed by the government in March 1974 for criticising the regime's African policies, the MFA decided to act. On 25 April 1974 they launched a coup in Lisbon, toppled the Caetano regime and installed Spínola as the new head of government.

Spínola's solution to the African wars was to federate the *ultramar* with metropolitan Portugal but this scheme never got off the ground. The MFA became increasingly radical and within six months of the coup Spínola had been forced to resign. A policy of total withdrawal was then adopted, to be carried out as swiftly as possible. Without consulting the people of the *ultramar*, Portugal's left-wing government handed over power to the PAIGC in Guinea in September 1974, to FRELIMO in Mozambique in June 1975, and to a joint MPLA-FNLA-UNITA regime in Angola – though by the time independence came in November 1975, Angola was already in the throes of a war of succession between the three guerrilla movements. São Tomé and Príncipe and the Cape Verde Islands also received independence in 1975, while Timor was annexed by Indonesia in 1976. Only Macao, of the overseas territories, remained Portuguese. The 400-year-old Portuguese Empire had thus, over a two-year period, ceased to exist. **Francis Toase**

The divided revolt

Angola

Angola was the first of the Portuguese African colonies to experience the trauma of insurgency and counter-insurgency. In January 1961 Africans centred on a dissident Christian sect led by Antonio Mariano launched a campaign against the forced cultivation of cotton in the central plateau. They destroyed crops and European property; the Portuguese counter-attacked swiftly and brutally. By February this so-called 'Guerra de Maria' (Maria's War) was over.

Little of this appeared in the world press. But on 22 January 1961 Captain Henrique Galvão, a former colonial administrator in Angola, hijacked a Portuguese liner in the Caribbean and proclaimed his intention of sailing to the Angolan capital, Luanda, where he would raise the standard of revolt against the Portuguese government. This spectacular action grabbed the attention of the news media. On 4 February, as the world's press gathered in Luanda in anticipation of Galvão's arrival (in fact he never got there), the city's prison and two police barracks were attacked by a few hundred Africans.

It has never been satisfactorily explained whether this incident and the rioting that followed were planned to coincide with the presence of the international press, but certainly the publicity received put Angola on the agenda of the United Nations and stimulated further anti-Portuguese actions. Organised by the Movimento Popular de Libertação de Angola (MPLA), the attacks in Luanda were a failure; the reaction of both the authorities and white vigilante groups was indiscriminate but severe, and nearly destroyed the African nationalist movement in the capital. But on 15 March another nationalist group, the União das Populações de Angola (UPA), based in the newly independent Congo (now Zaire), decided to take advantage of Portugal's international discomfiture by applying more pressure. UPA guerrilla attacks developed into a widespread rebellion throughout northern Angola.

The revolt centred on the Bakongo tribe who were the UPA's almost exclusive supporters. The Bakongo nursed a special sense of grievance in that their kingship had been assumed by a Portuguese nominee. To make matters worse, the Portuguese nominee was a Catholic tribesman, while most of the Bakongo, including the UPA leader Holden Roberto, had been educated by Baptist missionaries. The Bakongo rising showed strong elements of racism, fetishism and tribalism, with the massacre and mutilation of several

Above: Portuguese government troops use a heavy artillery piece to shell MPLA positions in northern Angola.

Left: A comprehensive collection of war material captured from guerrillas by Portuguese troops. This motley collection including carbines, grenades, mortar shells and a sten gun illustrates that the nationalists were by no means well enough equipped to maintain a conventional-type war against the Portuguese ground forces.

hundred whites and thousands of *mestiços* (half-castes), *assimilados* ('civilised' blacks) and blacks from other tribes, especially the Ovimbundu, southerners who generally stayed loyal to the Portuguese.

The MPLA, whose supporters suffered from UPA attacks, was dedicated to escaping tribalism and racism. Originally founded in Luanda in 1956, MPLA's leadership was dominated by *mestiços* like Viriato da Cruz and *assimilados* like the doctor and poet (in Portuguese) Agostinho Neto. Marxist in ideology, the MPLA aspired to win a national following amongst all races and tribes, although in practice it drew its rank and file largely from the Mbundu tribe in the area around the capital.

Massacre and counter-massacre

The revolt in the north took the Portuguese totally by surprise since the authorities had ignored intelligence warnings of its imminence. It was two months before they could organise a proper military response. In the meantime, white settlers and loyal blacks defended isolated farms and towns as best they could against the numerous but ill-armed Bakongo. When the opportunity arose, whites executed terrible counter-massacres, burning villages and killing any Africans who had not joined their side. Africans were attacked far from the scene of the revolt: members of the Mbundu tribe were massacred in the Cuanza valley, for example, and large numbers of *assimilados* were arrested throughout Angola – many disappearing for good.

From May to October 1961 the Portuguese Army re-established control over most of the north of Angola. The Bakongo fled *en masse* into the bush or towards the Congolese border, and tens of thousands died in military action, reprisals, or through hardship and disease. Weak and leaderless, most eventually drifted back into Portuguese-controlled villages and plantations.

Yet from the time of the 1961 revolt onwards, Angola was never at peace. Inevitably there were, as in the other colonies, further splits within the nationalist movement. Neto ousted his rivals to become the MPLA's undisputed leader in 1963, while Roberto's 'foreign minister', Jonas Savimbi, broke

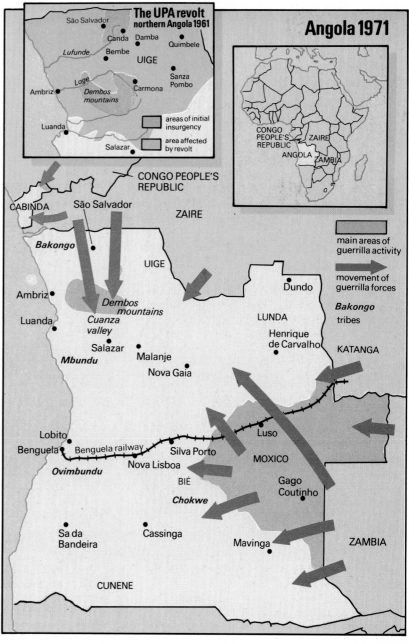

The UPA revolt
northern Angola 1961

São Salvador
Canda Damba
Lufunde Bembe Quimbele
UIGE
Loge Sanza Pombo
Ambriz Carmona
Dembos mountains
Luanda
Salazar

areas of initial insurgency

area affected by revolt

Angola 1971

CONGO PEOPLE'S REPUBLIC ZAIRE
ANGOLA ZAMBIA

CONGO PEOPLE'S REPUBLIC
ZAIRE
CABINDA
São Salvador
Bakongo
UIGE
Ambriz
Luanda
Dembos mountains
Cuanza valley
Salazar
Mbundu Malanje
Nova Gaia
Lobito
Benguela Benguela railway
Ovimbundu
Nova Lisboa Silva Porto
BIÉ
Chokwe
Sa da Bandeira Cassinga
CUNENE

Dundo
LUNDA
Henrique de Carvalho
KATANGA
Luso
MOXICO
Gago Coutinho
Mavinga ZAMBIA

main areas of guerrilla activity

movement of guerrilla forces

Bakongo tribes

Left: Portuguese and black civilians stand side by side, armed and ready to defend their north Angolan town against possible guerrilla incursions.

Below: The cause of most casualties to Portuguese troops was booby-trapped roads. Here troops uncover, with the aid of a mine detector, one such device. Below right: A lorry swerves off the road to avoid a simple but probably effective obstacle dug by nationalist guerrillas.

away in 1964 and formed the União Nacional para a Independência Total de Angola (UNITA) two years later. UNITA was dependent on the Ovimbundu and Chokwe tribes of the south for its support. The UPA became the Frente Nacional de Libertação de Angola (FNLA) in 1962 and the following year set up a government-in-exile which was recognised by the Organization of African Unity (OAU).

It is difficult to determine the exact number of guerrillas operating against the Portuguese at any given time. Although the FNLA claimed some 10,000 men by 1972, it is unlikely that more than 6000 at most were really at Roberto's disposal. In fact after the initial uprising had been contained in the north, the FNLA was only sporadically active from its refuges inside Zaire (the former Belgian Congo), although pockets of FNLA guerrillas continued to infest the heavily wooded Dembos mountains for many years. The FNLA attempted to create a kind of mini 'Ho Chi Minh Trail' to the Dembos through coastal swamplands but was not noticeably successful. Roberto's movement gradually lost the support of the OAU, which finally dropped its recognition of the FNLA government-in-exile in 1968. Roberto was then forced back on the support of Zaire and the Chinese. The United States also appear to have channelled some assistance to the FNLA, probably as an attempt to hedge their bets against possible Portuguese defeat, but this was not to become of significance until the build-up to independence in 1975.

At one time the MPLA claimed to control 50 per cent of the colony but again it is doubtful if more than a small proportion of its estimated 3000 – 5000 guerrillas were ever operating permanently inside Angola. Having begun its campaign by trying to infiltrate into the Cabinda enclave from the Congo People's Republic (the former French Congo) in 1963-64, the MPLA was forced, through failure to raise local support, to move its principal bases to Zambia, which became independent in 1964. The MPLA then opened an

'eastern front' in the Moxico and Bié regions in 1966 and 1967, but by 1974 its forces there had been badly defeated by the Portuguese. The movement was thrown back once more on the Congo People's Republic for its refuge and base. The MPLA's original nucleus of 350 guerrillas had been trained in Algeria and MPLA recruits continued to receive training not only in their host countries but also in Bulgaria, Czechoslovakia and the Soviet Union.

UNITA alone operated permanently inside Portuguese territory, having been expelled from Zambia following attacks on the Benguela railway which was vital to the latter's economy. But UNITA does not appear to have numbered more than 300 or so guerrillas by 1970 and was always concerned more with political than military action. Its reliance on Chinese advice led its members to be known as the 'Black Chinese'.

The Portuguese themselves rapidly built up their Angolan garrison from 3000 men in 1961 to approximately 60,000 (30-40 per cent of whom were black troops) by the 1970s. This total excludes large numbers of white volunteers and the black militias raised for local defence.

Operations in the savannah

In many respects the Portuguese were fortunate both in their opponents and the terrain in which those opponents operated. Although Angola had over 4800km (3000 miles) of frontier to defend, it was also one of the most sparsely populated countries in the world. The eastern regions, for example, were mostly flat without vegetation. The sandy soil prevented the construction of roads but this proved an advantage in that Portuguese truck drivers chose their own routes across the savannah, thereby reducing the likely effectiveness of guerrilla mines. Despite this, mines accounted for over 50 per cent of Portuguese casualties in 1970, which indicates a marked absence of contact between security forces and guerrillas.

Guerrilla ambush

'Our forces were placed at eight to ten metres from the road except for the bazooka man; his task being to stop the enemy column, he was placed at about two metres from the road. A field of anti-personnel mines was sown on the side of the road opposed to the bulk of the ambush force so as to prevent the enemy from taking up positions there.... Two 60mm mortars completed the circle of fire, their task also being to protect our forces if enemy reinforcements should appear. Two protective positions were also mounted at either end of the ambush with the same object in mind....

'Everything went as planned. The column entered the ambush. The truck in front braked hard to go over a deep pot-hole, and when its back wheels were over, and in the fraction of a second when it halted as the driver changed gear, our bazooka-man jumped on to the road and opened fire, hitting the middle of his target....

'Two trucks, meanwhile, had not crossed the bridge into the ambush. Their men had no time to organise, however, because our northern protective position opened up at once, as did the two mortars, causing those men to abandon their trucks.... We then passed to the assault.... This action killed 25 of the enemy, a number that was confirmed, 12 being identified. We also took valuable secret documents, various materials of war, and a good quantity of crates of beer.'

Jaime Morais, MPLA commandant.

From 1966 onwards when Alouette helicopters became available for the security forces (some 60 being deployed in Angola by 1971), the Portuguese were able to mount major dry-season operations in the east. In 1966, 1968 and 1972 a combination of light bombers, helicopter support and reinforced ground patrols by elite units brought major successes in an area devoid of cover for the guerrillas. The MPLA suffered badly by trying to push columns across the eastern savannah towards their 'natural' supporters around Luanda and the Dembos in 1968 and 1970, and there was always the problem of having to carry all the supplies required to mount the long-range but short-term incursions they favoured.

The Portuguese forces derived enormous advantage from their monopoly of airpower, their Nato membership enabling them to obtain and deploy relatively modern aircraft in Angola. The Fiat G-91, the F-84 Thunderjet and the Lockheed PV-2 were used for offensive air support while the North American T-6 and Dornier DO-27 trainer served as light ground-attack aircraft. Portuguese airpower was not challenged as it was in the other colonies and proved useful in supplying the garrisons in the Dembos as well as operations in the east. The advent of the rainy season, producing low cloud and the growth of vegetation on the eastern savannah, gave the guerrillas some respite, but Portuguese airpower could also be used to attack the woodland *kimbos* that grew much-needed food for the guerrillas. The war was not, however, always one of high technology as far as the Portuguese were concerned. Cavalry also proved useful in difficult terrain, particularly for covering the flanks of operations, and some three mounted squadrons were deployed by the war's end.

The Portuguese sought to curb the influence of the guerrillas by resettling the sparse population into 'strategic villages' or *aldeamentos*. These had originally been implemented in the Uige region after the 1961 revolt but were greatly expanded upon the introduction of a resettlement programme in the east in 1967. The policy was not always implemented with the necessary care, however, more resources being devoted to road-building than to 'winning hearts and

Above: Jonas Savimbi, flanked by bodyguards, addresses a crowd of supporters. Savimbi broke away from the UPA in 1964 to form UNITA.

Left: A typical MPLA guerrilla carrying a Soviet-made 7.62mm light machine gun and link-belt ammunition.

minds' in the *aldeamentos*, despite the fact that 70 per cent of the Portuguese troops were employed on a 'psycho-social programme' or 'social promotion'. There was some division among the Portuguese authorities on the merits of extending resettlement in the form of civilian-run *reordamentos* to zones well away from the fighting. It was suggested that the introduction of these resettlement schemes in the centre and south of the colony owed more to a desire to release land for further white settlement than to controlling the extent of insurgency. In all, over a million people or roughly 20 per cent of the native population were resettled, but this probably engendered more hostility than confidence and certainly damaged agricultural production.

Rocket attacks

Despite Portuguese failings, however, the guerrillas were always confined to areas remote from the population, and by the end of the war the MPLA was restricted to long-range bombardment of Portuguese targets with 82mm mortars and 122mm rockets. Vital economic concerns, such as Gulf Oil's installations in the Cabinda enclave (exploited from 1966 onwards), the important Cassinga iron-ore mines and the plantations of the north were never seriously threatened. There is some evidence that the large-scale Cunene hydro-electric power project in the south of Angola may have been defended by South African troops while the Diamang diamond mines of Lunda were defended by a mercenary force of Katangese gendarmes.

The Portuguese claimed that less than two per cent of the colony was under guerrilla control by 1973 and certainly when the coup in Portugal occurred the guerrillas in Angola were far from success in a war that had degenerated into a low-intensity stalemate. The existence of three guerrilla groups in the field, however, made agreement on Portuguese withdrawal difficult to achieve and civil war broke out in Angola long before the date of 11 November 1975 set for its independence. **Ian Beckett**

Left: A rebel mans his anti-aircraft gun in anticipation of a sortie by Portuguese ground attack planes.

Guinea
Cabral's revolution

Guinea was by far the smallest and least productive of the Portuguese colonies in Africa. With some 40 per cent of its total area of 36,000 square km (13,900 square miles) either covered in water or completely uninhabited, it had never enjoyed much Portuguese investment. It had also failed to attract settlers and much of the land remained in African ownership, although the economy was manipulated by large Portuguese concerns such as CUF (Companhia União Fabril). Yet the colony spawned the most sophisticated of the guerrilla groups that fought the Portuguese – the PAIGC (Partido Africano de Independência da Guiné e Cabo Verde) – and Portuguese casualties were proportionally higher there than in either Angola or Mozambique. The cost of maintaining Portuguese control was high, but became symbolic of Portugal's resolve to remain in Africa. Had Guinea been easily surrendered, then guerrillas elsewhere would have derived enormous encouragement. The Portuguese also believed that the Cape Verde Islands, administratively linked to Guinea, were of great strategic importance for the West's control of the Atlantic trade routes.

The PAIGC was founded in 1956 by Amílcar Cabral, a Cape Verdean *mestiço* (half-caste) and Portuguese-trained agronomist. Initially, the movement recruited among the urban *assimilados* ('civilised' blacks) and waterfront workers of the capital, Bissau, and among the many rootless young people drifting into the city from the countryside. Many of the latter were from the Balante tribe, which comprised 31 per cent of Guinea's total population of about 800,000; the PAIGC suffered from an often

Right: Amílcar Cabral, founder of the PAIGC and one of the most successful modern guerrilla leaders. He was an influential theorist who attempted to deal with the central problem of African politics: how to knit the aspirations of the educated urban elite into the needs of the rural masses.

The Bissau waterfront massacre

'On 3 August (1959) we all gathered at Pidjiguiti, about 500 men. Nobody worked, neither on the dock nor on the boats.... At about 4.30 in the afternoon several trucks of armed police arrived. First they sealed off the gate to the street, then they ordered us back to work. When no one obeyed, they began moving slowly down the pier, now packed with striking workers.

'This old friend of mine, Ocante Atobo, was leaning against the wall of the office shed. When the line of police reached the spot where he was, an officer suddenly raised his gun and shot him point blank in the chest. Ocante collapsed in a pool of blood. For a split second everyone froze – it was as if time stood still. Then hell broke loose. The police moved down the pier, shooting like crazy into the crowd....

'The tide was out so all the boats and canoes were resting on the beach. To hide there, however, was impossible since the police, standing high up on the dock, were shooting right into them. One officer was kneeling on the edge, firing at those trying to get away in the water....

'When the massacre finally ended, I saw dead and wounded all over: on the dock, on the beach, in the boats, everywhere.... Afterwards we were taken to the police for interrogation. For three days I had to report to the administrator, Guerra Ribeiro, who wanted to know who had organised the strike. My answer was always the same: "We all organised it; our wages are so bad we had no choice." Later, when Ribeiro had finished his inquiry, the wage went up to 14 escudos a day.

'Soon after the massacre a message from Amílcar Cabral was secretly circulated among us. It said that 3 August would never be forgotten and that we now had to organise to win our independence from Portuguese colonialism. Since then we never looked back.'

João Emilio Costa, a Guinean dockworker.

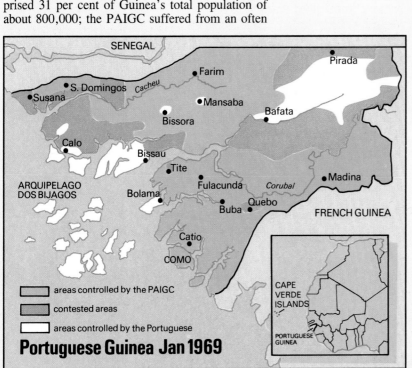

SENEGAL

Pirada

Farim

S. Domingos · Cacheu
Susana
· Mansaba
Bissora · Bafata

Calo
Bissau
· Tite
ARQUIPELAGO
DOS BIJAGOS
Bolama · Fulacunda · Corubal · Madina
· Buba · Quebo
FRENCH GUINEA

Catio
COMO

▢ areas controlled by the PAIGC
▢ contested areas
▢ areas controlled by the Portuguese

Portuguese Guinea Jan 1969

CAPE
VERDE
ISLANDS

PORTUGUESE
GUINEA

uneasy relationship between its Balante rank and file and Cape Verdean leadership. Whereas an animist tribe like the Balante could be attracted by the PAIGC's egalitarianism and revolutionary programme, the more hierarchical tribes such as the Muslim Fula (12 per cent of the population) resisted it. Indeed, approximately half the 30,000 Portuguese troops eventually deployed in Guinea were local blacks.

After 1959 when a dock strike in Bissau was broken by the Portuguese, Cabral began preparing for a rural guerrilla campaign. He established his headquarters in Conakry, capital of the neighbouring newly-independent Republic of Guinea (often known as Guinea-Conakry to distinguish it from Portuguese Guinea, known as Guinea-Bissau), and won the backing of the Soviet Union and the Organization of African Unity (OAU). In fact, the first guerrilla activity in Portuguese Guinea (in July 1961) was carried out not by the PAIGC but by FLING, the Frente para a Libertação e Independência de Guiné Portuguesa, a coalition of African groups with a particular hatred for Cape Verdeans. However, FLING's activity proved short-lived. In January 1963, PAIGC launched its campaign with attacks on Buba, Tite and Fulacunda. With only two infantry companies in the colony, the Portuguese were immediately forced on the defensive and by the end of 1963 the PAIGC controlled 15 per cent of the colony.

The pattern of the war was largely dictated by the nature of the terrain, the tidal inlets, rivers and extensive swamps denying both sides easy movement. The guerrillas made considerable use of dug-out canoes and even had a 'naval' branch, while the Portuguese employed marines and naval fusiliers in rubber patrol boats and assault craft to a much greater extent than anywhere else in the colonies.

Early guerrilla targets were the Fula tribe, whom the Portuguese had armed, and the trading posts and CUF warehouses on which the economy was based. The PAIGC also concentrated on the political aspects of insurgency, establishing 'liberated zones' which they claimed amounted to 80 per cent of the colony by 1971. In these they organised primary schools and clinics, as well as village committees, village courts and 'people's shops'. Guerrilla activity spread from the southeast to the east in 1966 and to the north when Senegal reached an accommodation with the PAIGC in 1967. At first it was mostly conducted by small groups of 17-25 men, but by 1971, when the guerrillas numbered between 6000 and 7000, the PAIGC was using larger groups of up to 120 men, operating mostly by night (sometimes with Guinean artillery support) and then withdrawing to sanctuary in the Guinea Republic or Senegal. Only small, highly mobile commando units remained in the colony on a more permanent basis.

Although claim and counter-claim are invariably difficult to reconcile in insurgency, figures released for 1967 by the PAIGC at least give an indication of the kind of activity undertaken, with claims of 142 attacks on camps or barracks, 22 raids on airfields or ports and 476 ambushes. Increasingly, PAIGC attacks were in the form of minelaying or long-range bombardment, 122mm rockets being employed for this purpose from 1971 onwards. As time went on, more foreign advisers became involved. A Cuban was captured by the Portuguese in 1969 and a further four killed in 1970, and Nigerians flew MiG-17 reconnaissance flights over Guinea from 1971.

After the failure of a determined Portuguese assault on the island of Como in February 1964, the Portuguese forces undoubtedly surrendered the initiative to the PAIGC – tending to remain within firebases protected by 140mm howitzers. However, the Portuguese commander-in-chief from May 1964 onwards, Arnaldo Schultz, managed to stabilise the situation and began a resettlement programme which eventually relocated 120,000 people in strategic villages or *aldeamentos*. Schultz's successor, António de Spínola, arrived in May 1968 with the full powers over civil and military administration effectively denied Schultz. Instantly recognisable by his characteristic monocle and riding crop, Spínola improved the situation in Guinea, not least by raising the morale of the Portuguese forces.

A 'Better Guinea'

Under the slogan of *Guiné Melhor* ('Better Guinea'), Spínola initiated an energetic programme of 'social counter-revolution' to win over the population. The army, as the instrument of this policy, built over 15,000 houses, 164 schools and 40 hospitals, while also attempting to raise the standards of cattle-breeding. Spinola claimed to be winning back 3000 refugees a year from neighbouring countries. He also withdrew isolated garrisons and began a road-tarring programme to eliminate the threat from guerrilla mines. The effectiveness of Portuguese counter-insurgency was considerably boosted by the deployment of 12 Alouette helicopters. Three or four were always available for tactical support operations and this was a great help in a country the remotest areas of which were only 30 minutes' flying time from Bissau. The army could do little against guerrilla sanctuaries across international frontiers and the Portuguese rarely crossed them even 'in hot pursuit'. They were, however, involved in an abortive landing of armed exiles in the Republic of Guinea in November 1970. They may also have been implicated in the assassination of Amílcar Cabral by his naval commander in January 1973, although the plot possibly owed rather more to internal rivalries between mainlanders and Cape Verdeans. In 1974 leadership of the PAIGC passed to Amílcar's brother, Luiz Cabral.

More sophisticated equipment was reaching the PAIGC all the time, and Portuguese airpower was challenged for the first time in March 1973 by SAM-7 missiles; three aircraft were lost within two months. Spínola returned to Portugal convinced that a radical change in his country's African policy was essential, and unwittingly precipitated events that would bring down the Portuguese regime. But in Guinea itself, despite the proclamation of an 'independent republic' by the PAIGC in September 1973, the military situation remained tenable.

After the coup in Portugal in April 1974, fighting in Guinea rapidly ceased. Negotiations began in May 1974 and the Portuguese completed their withdrawal by mid-October. A PAIGC government took power, led by Luiz Cabral, and the country became independent as Guinea-Bissau.

The Portuguese have admitted to 1875 troops killed in action in Guinea although this figure does not take into account black troops. By 1973, the financial cost of the campaign had reached almost 200 million escudos. No accurate figures are available for guerrilla losses: estimates range from 6000 to 12,000 dead.

Ian Beckett

Right and below: Portuguese troops advance cautiously towards and through a village suspected of harbouring guerrillas in June 1972. This was a period when the Portuguese had managed to stabilise the situation and when Spínola's programme of 'social counter-revolution' was in full swing. Nevertheless, the fighting was still hard: the guerrillas were building up considerable stocks of war material, including ground-to-air missiles, in the areas they controlled and the Portuguese conscripts were still condemned to fight a vicious war in swamp and jungle.

Mozambique

Holding the dam

Following the outbreak of insurgency in both Angola (1961) and Guinea (1963), the Portuguese prepared to meet its likely spread to Mozambique. By the time FRELIMO (the Frente de Libertação de Moçambique) launched its first foray into the colony on 25 September 1964, there were already 16,000 government troops deployed to confront them.

The main guerrilla bases were in Tanzania, divided from Mozambique by a major natural barrier, the Rovuma river. At first the guerrillas confined their activities to the Cabo Delgado region of northeast Mozambique. It was here that the Makonde tribe, their first main source of support, lived on the Meuda plateau. The Makonde, however, represented barely two per cent of the total population of Mozambique and any attempt to progress further south brought FRELIMO into contact with the tribal areas of the largely Muslim Macua. The Macua, who made up 40 per cent of Mozambique's population, were bitterly hostile to their traditional Makonde enemies. They were extensively recruited into the Portuguese forces,

Above: A unit of the 16,000 Portuguese troops which were deployed in Mozambique to meet the threat posed by FRELIMO infiltration. These troops are armed with standard Nato 7.62mm semi-automatic weapons. Right: Samora Machel, who emerged as the leader of FRELIMO in 1974 and became President of Mozambique in 1975.

as were the Muslim Yao of the Niassa region.

FRELIMO enjoyed little success in its early campaigns, although in 1967 its operations were extended into the Niassa region, where the Nyanja tribe proved cooperative. Guerrilla activity consisted largely of hit and run attacks, although the size of units increased from 1966 onwards as FRELIMO approached its maximum strength of between 6000 and 8000 men. The majority of Portuguese casualties, as in other colonies, resulted from mines. At first the Portuguese tried sending troops ahead of patrols to probe the ground with sticks, or running Berliet trucks with water-filled tyres and heavily-sandbagged floors in front of convoys. But the long-term answer lay in road-tarring, since it was dirt roads that made mine concealment so easy. At the peak of their programme, the Portuguese tarred 1400km (870 miles) of road a year, more than was ever achieved by the British in Malaya or the US in Vietnam.

Operation Gordian Knot

FRELIMO infiltration of Niassa and Cabo Delgado posed worrying problems for the Portuguese. When the forceful Kaulza de Arriaga took over command of the Portuguese war effort in 1969, he determined on a large-scale assault. Operation Gordian Knot in the summer of 1970 initially employed 10,000 troops in an attempt to clear the whole northern area of guerrillas. Achieving initial surprise, the Portuguese used artillery bombardment followed by heliborne assault, mine clearance and consolidation on foot. Arriaga claimed to have killed 651 guerrillas and captured 1840 in the seven months the operation lasted. Certainly, Gordian Knot seriously interrupted guerrilla infiltration and destroyed much of FRELIMO's infrastructure in the north, although Arriaga's critics maintained that his predecessors had enjoyed equal success without the cost and effort of so major an operation.

Linked to the offensive in the north was the further extension of a network of *aldeamentos* ('strategic villages') which were to contain almost a million inhabitants or some 15 per cent of the native population by 1973. Arriaga planned to create a 'human border' along the Rovuma river with frequent settlements, such as the model *aldeamento* constructed at Nangade to house 2500 people, linked by all-weather roads which widened every few kilometres into an airstrip. The *aldeamento* programme was not a wholehearted success. Too many of the villages were badly prepared and lacked adequate facilities. Guerrilla sympathisers within the *aldeamentos* passed on food grown there to FRELIMO activists. Many blacks were not happy to be moved from their homes into military-controlled camps, and the whole scheme probably generated support for the guerrillas in the long run.

Meanwhile, FRELIMO switched its main effort to the west. In 1968 guerrilla attacks began in the Tete region, site of the vital Cabora Bassa dam project. Designed to be completed in 1975, Cabora Bassa would irrigate 1.5 million hectares and be the largest single source of hydro-electric power in Africa. FRELIMO operated from bases in Zambia, infiltrating through Malawi; having no natural friends amongst the tribes of the Tete area, the guerrillas frequently extorted cooperation through selective terrorism.

The move took the Portuguese totally by surprise since Tete had seemed a peaceful area under no

obvious threat. Small-scale guerrilla operations by a splinter group from FRELIMO in the region since 1964 had been of little account. The Portuguese set about repairing the damage done by years of administrative neglect; the dam itself was ringed with defences and a force of 15,000 troops. FRELIMO had an ambivalent attitude to the dam: on the one hand they regarded it as a suitable target for sabotage since most of the hydro-electric power was to serve the industries of racialist South Africa, but on the other hand they were mindful of the value of the completed project to an independent Mozambique. Unsure of their objectives and in any case unable to penetrate the Portuguese defences, FRELIMO resorted to long-range bombardment and attacks on the dam's supply routes, but they failed to prevent work continuing on schedule.

As the fighting progressed, FRELIMO went through internal changes. The organisation's first leader, the American-educated anthropologist Dr Eduardo Mondlane, was killed by a book-bomb in February 1969, possibly as a result of internal dissension within FRELIMO. After Mondlane's death, the movement leant more towards the Soviet Union, notably after the emergence of Samora Machel, a former male nurse, as leader in 1970.

The Portuguese countered FRELIMO on the political as well as the military front. Arriaga mounted a major 'social promotion' campaign to build farms, medical centres, cattle dips and schools. Over five million propaganda leaflets were dropped in 1972 alone. Arriaga claimed a 90 per cent success rate in inducing captured guerrillas to fight for the Portuguese against their former colleagues and some 40,000 of the 60,000 troops deployed in Mozambique by the end of the war were black. Many Africans served in the army's elite Grupos Especiais (GE) or

Below: General Kaulza de Arriaga who took over command of the Portuguese war effort in 1969. His Operation Gordian Knot seriously interrupted guerrilla activities in the north, although his detractors claimed that by denuding other areas of troops he achieved very little in the long run.

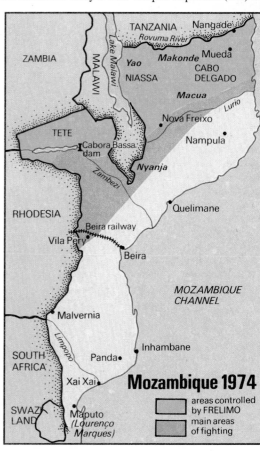

Mozambique 1974

areas controlled by FRELIMO

main areas of fighting

Above: Portuguese troops move through the jungle after a successful action against a guerrilla camp in Mozambique as part of a sweep against nationalist strongholds.

Below: A heavily-armed machine gunner advances with caution during a search and destroy operation by government forces.

airborne Grupos Especiais de Paraquedistas (GEP), while the Portuguese security police (DGS) also recruited its own black intelligence-gathering units or *flechas* ('arrows').

But morale in the Portuguese forces was shaky, despite Arriaga's policy of giving his troops extended political instruction. In Tete, the Portuguese adopted a largely passive defensive role, to such an extent that the region was utilised by FRELIMO and ZANU (Zimbabwe African National Union) guerrillas as a springboard into northeastern Rhodesia in December 1972. The Rhodesians complained bitterly that the attacks had come through a 'back door' they had believed firmly closed and they committed troops to assist the Portuguese under a 'gentleman's agreement'. Some Rhodesians claimed that Portuguese

troops made sufficient noise in their operations to ensure little contact was made with the guerrillas. It was ironic that the clearest evidence of disintegration in the Portuguese Army's will to fight should come from the colony in which most had been done to give the troops a political education.

At the end of 1972 FRELIMO changed strategy again and, having failed to damage Cabora Bassa, began to infiltrate south and east from Tete. They had penetrated into Vila Pery and even the Beira region by the end of 1973. The Beira railway came under increasing attack, especially after FRELIMO's Zambian backers had ceased to use it for the export of copper (when the Rhodesians closed the Zambian frontier). The first murder of a white farmer sparked off settler riots in Beira in January 1974; the settlers demanded more army protection. This, in turn, enabled the security police, the DGS, to exploit the army's growing unpopularity in a power struggle between army and police which had never been far from the surface in Mozambique.

By July 1974 guerrillas had penetrated into the Zambezia region for the first time. A further indication of growing security problems was the appearance of SAM-7s in March 1974 to challenge the air supremacy of Portugal's eight Fiat G-91s, 15 Harvard T-6s, 14 Alouettes and two Pumas. In the last months of the war Portuguese casualties, which had numbered only approximately 18 dead per month in 1972, had risen to double those in either Angola or Guinea. Guerrilla losses averaged about 1250 annually (or roughly an 18 per cent casualty rate).

Despite their growing problems, the Portuguese had still not lost the battle for Mozambique when agreement was reached with FRELIMO in September 1974 which led to independence in June 1975.

Ian Beckett

Key Weapons

The FN FAL

Fabrique Nationale Herstal SA, the well-known Belgian gunmakers, began experimenting with automatic military rifles well before World War II, the idea being to replace the conventional bolt-action rifle with a gas-operated model. The German invasion of Belgium in 1940 put a temporary halt to this programme but after the end of hostilities a new rifle was designed and was put into production as the ABL (Arme Belgique Légère). It was supplied to the Belgian, Venezuelan, Egyptian and other armies in various calibres.

As the ABL began its manufacturing run, FN then began contemplating the idea of producing an assault rifle of modern type, and built a prototype using the wartime German 7.92mm 'Kurz' cartridge. By the late 1940s the British were busy developing weapons for their experimental .280 (7mm) round in the hope of seeing it adopted by Nato, and FN rebuilt their new rifle to suit this calibre. But although the .280 was a good cartridge, the Americans refused to accept it, at that time having little interest in the 'assault rifle' concept of short-range light weapons. FN realised that the Americans – as the senior partner in Nato – were going to push their .30 T65 cartridge into acceptance, and so they immediately began redesigning their assault rifle for the new round. When the American T65 was formally approved as the 7.62 × 51mm Nato cartridge, FN were ready with a working rifle, the FAL or Fusil Automatique Léger.

The FAL is one of the few military automatic rifles in use today which does not use a rotating bolt. It is gas-operated, and a portion of the gas following the bullet is vented through a port in the barrel to drive a gas piston backwards. The rear end of the piston rod strikes the bolt carrier, driving it backwards to compress a spring. Below and enclosed by the carrier, lies the bolt, its rear end pressed down in front of a transom in the rifle body which prevents it moving back during firing. As the bolt carrier moves back, so shaped cams on its side strike two lugs at the sides of the bolt and lift the rear end out of engagement with the transom. The bolt is then free to be pulled back by the carrier, extracting the spent case and ejecting it. The rearward movement also passes over the hammer and cocks it

Above and right: Both British and Argentinian troops were armed with FN rifles during the Falklands conflict. The Argentinian soldiers depicted here carry the post-1964 pattern rifle, very similar in appearance to the British-produced SLR (self-loading rifle).

Previous page: Few firearms have seen such widespread service as the FN FAL, and it was a popular weapon during the fighting in the former Belgian colony of the Congo, here being carried by these Katangan mercenaries.

Right: Armed with SLRs a patrol from the Rhodesian security forces carefully makes its way through the bush as part of a search and destroy mission against Patriotic Front guerrillas.

Right: A highly dramatic firing position is adopted by this SLR-armed trooper of the Rhodesian Greys Scouts. More a pose for the camera than anything else, an aimed shot of this type would have little chance of hitting anything smaller than the side of a barn. Below right: The other extreme – taking few chances FNLA guerrillas gun down a civilian at short range during fighting in Angola in 1975.

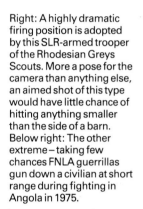

ready for the next shot. The spring then drives the carrier and bolt forward; the bolt face collects a fresh cartridge from the magazine and forces it into the chamber, and as the bolt carrier runs forward so the cams now force the rear end down into engagement with the transom once more. The firer pulls the trigger to release the hammer and the next shot is fired.

The gas is channelled to the gas piston through a regulator which is adjustable. The object of this is to ensure that there is always sufficient gas to operate the mechanism, even though it may be stiff from dust or lack of lubrication after prolonged firing. Adjustment of the early design of regulator was a long and tiresome business but a more simple design was later adopted. In addition, since the rifle can be used for launching grenades (by slipping their hollow tails over the rifle muzzle), the regulator permits the supply of gas to the piston to be completely shut off so that all the available gas is used to propel the grenade. When launching grenades a special blank cartridge is usually provided, though some new grenade designs permit the use of ordinary ball ammunition for this purpose. A number of sights can be fitted; besides the sniper's telescopic sight, the FAL can take the Trilux night sight. In service with the British Army since 1974, and designated SUIT (Sight Unit Infantry Trilux), it is self-energising and can be used to observe indistinct targets in daylight as well as at night.

Since the British 7mm rifle could not be redesigned to suit the 7.62mm cartridge, the British Army were among FNs first customers for the new weapon, adopting it as the SLR L1A1; the SLR's first service use was against the Mau Mau in Kenya in 1954. Production was begun in the Royal Small Arms

Factory, leaving the FN plant in Belgium available for other orders, which came in profusion. Licenses to manufacture also went to Argentina, Australia, Austria, Canada, India, South Africa and Norway, while exports were made to almost every country outside the communist bloc. A total of 90 countries have used the FN FAL as their standard rifle. Much of its popularity can be attributed to its robust design and overall reliability. This makes it virtually 'soldier proof', but at the same time gives the infantryman a reasonably accurate weapon with good stopping power.

As might be expected, not every army wanted the same specification, and therefore there are innumerable minor variations of the FN FAL in existence. The British L1A1, for example, fires only single shots and has had all its dimensions changed to suit British measurements and manufacturing techniques; it also has deep oblique cuts in the bolt carrier which collect dust and dirt that might otherwise jam the mechanism in battle conditions. The Canadian C1 version has a unique five-position sight and a two-piece firing pin; the Australian F1 model has a shorter barrel and butt than usual; the Netherlands Army has modified its FN to take a fixed 150m (165yd) sight, a metal handguard and a permanently-attached bipod. Although the standard FAL is capable of firing on automatic, problems of accuracy arose when long bursts were

Opposite page: British troops have employed the L1A1 SLR since the 1950s, both in training (above) and in earnest on the streets of Northern Ireland (below). Right: A member of the IRA takes aim with his FN; a possible target might be the similarly-armed British soldier at the scene of an incident in Northern Ireland (below). Bottom: Israeli soldiers set about cleaning their FN rifles during a break in fighting in the Negev Desert.

fired as the light-weight barrel tended to rise above the target. As a result, many countries followed the British and had the rifle fixed on semi-automatic, which nevertheless allows 30 well-aimed shots to be fired every minute. By contrast, FN has produced a number of heavy-barrelled models which, with bipods and full automatic fire capability, are used as squad light machine guns by some armies. Short-barrelled carbine versions are also made, as are models with folding butts for parachute troops.

The FN FAL is now reaching the end of its service life with several major armies. The British have indicated that they will soon go over to their own design in 5.56mm calibre; the Austrians are replacing it with their 5.56mm Steyr AUG, the South Africans with the R4, a locally-produced version of the 5.56mm Israeli Galil. As early as 1963 FN debated the possibility of scaling-down the FN to 5.56mm calibre so as to be ready for the new trend, but adopted a different method of bolt operation for their CAL – Carabine Automatique Légère – model. A particular feature of the CAL was its ability to fire three-shot bursts with one pull of the trigger, as well as operating on the standard automatic and semi-automatic modes. In the event the CAL was ahead of its time, largely because when it was introduced in 1966 few of the world's armies were ready to make the change to 5.56mm calibre. Subsequently the design was dropped in favour of another known as the FNC (Fabrique Nationale Carbine) which is now being considered by various armies as a possible replacement for their FAL models.

L1A1 SLR

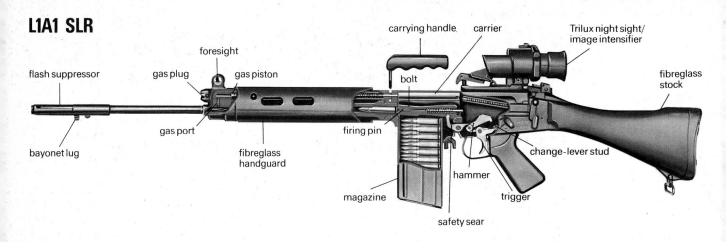

flash suppressor

gas plug

foresight

gas piston

carrying handle

carrier

bolt

Trilux night sight/
image intensifier

fibreglass
stock

bayonet lug

gas port

firing pin

fibreglass
handguard

magazine

hammer

safety sear

trigger

change-lever stud

FN FAL

Calibre 7.62mm
Length 105cm (41.5in)
Weight (loaded) 4.31kg (9.5lb)
Rate of fire Cyclic 650-700rpm; practical
semi-automatic 30rpm
Maximum sighted range 600m (650yds)
Ammunition Ball, tracer, armour piercing, blank,
grenade launching
Magazine 20-round box
Cartridge 7.62 x 51mm Nato round
Muzzle velocity 853mps (2800fps)

Right: The successor to the
FN FAL was the 5.56mm
FNC, available with either
the standard barrel as the
Model 2000 (above right)
or with the shorter barrel as
the Model 7000. Both
models have fold-away
stocks.

Right: The FNC is a leader
in the trend towards the
basic rifle being the central
element of a complete
weapons system. Below
the rifle is a clip-on bipod, a
magazine (interchangeable
with the M16A1 magazine)
and a compact cleaning kit
which slots into the pistol
grip. By the muzzle is the
blank round firing
attachment, and directly
above that are an M7 and a
standard tubular bayonet,
surmounted by a rifle
grenade. Two telescopic
sights are provided; the
smaller one, the basic
infantryman's scope and
the larger, a special
sniper's model. On the rifle
itself the change lever has
four possible positions:
S – safety; 1 – single shot/
semi-automatic;
3 – controlled burst of three
rounds; A – fully
automatic.

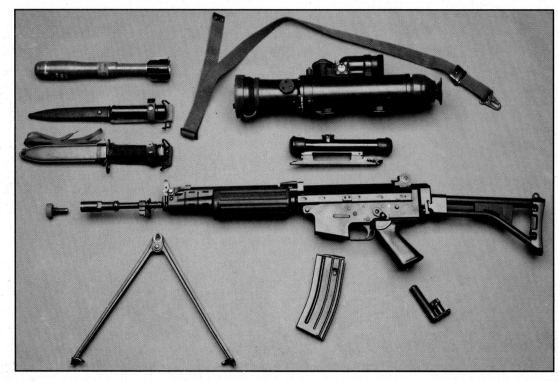

To John F. Kennedy the priorities were obvious. 'Domestic policy,' he used to say, 'can only defeat us; foreign policy can kill us.' His inaugural address as president was devoted entirely to foreign affairs; at a time of international tension it seemed to radiate a certain level-headed optimism appropriate to 'a new generation of Americans – born in this century, tempered by war, disciplined by a hard and bitter peace'. In this respect the election of 1960 had witnessed the changing of the guard, the ageing former Supreme Commander Eisenhower replaced by the youngest-ever elected president, a mere junior officer in World War II. Later, critics were to wonder whether the youthfulness might at times lead to excess: 'Let every nation know, whether it wishes us well or ill, that we shall pay any price, bear any burden, meet any hardship, support any friend, oppose any foe to assure the survival and success of liberty.' Even his closest adviser, Ted Sorensen, was later to refer to 'inaugural rhetoric'.

Still, in early 1961 two facts seemed to stand out: that the communist cause was in the ascendant and that Kennedy had been narrowly elected to arrest American drift. In January that year, a bare fortnight before the inaugural, Khrushchev had exulted that 'there is no longer any force in the world capable of barring the road to socialism'. The challenge could not be avoided. 'What your government believes,' Kennedy wrote to the Russian leader later that year, 'is its own business, what it does in the world is the world's business.' Yet the challenge might take various forms, and appear at various levels. At its most overt, it might be direct confrontation over Berlin, which could lead through miscalculation to nuclear war; at the other extreme it could consist of small localised acts of aggression, linked as often as not with wars of national liberation, subversion or even guerrilla activity, each inconsequential in itself to a complacent public, but potentially deadly in its outcome. Cuba or Laos might be such instances. Thus Kennedy still had to be a Cold War warrior in the mould of the 1950s, yet be flexible to the changed conditions of his time.

There was always to be this ambiguity in the Kennedy approach to foreign policy. Since he had campaigned on the issue of increasing Soviet technological might – of which Sputnik was a formidable example – and the Democrats had made great play with the so-called 'missile gap', he would preside over the development of the most powerful military force the world had ever known, at an additional cost of some $17,000 million, when America was supposedly at peace. Yet as he himself admitted: 'We possess weapons of tremendous power, but they are least effective in combating the weapons most often used by freedom's foes: subversion, infiltration and civil disorder.' Aware that the Russians no more than the Americans deliberately wanted nuclear war, Kennedy sought where possible to accommodate; in times of crisis to keep in touch with Khrushchev and to make those minor

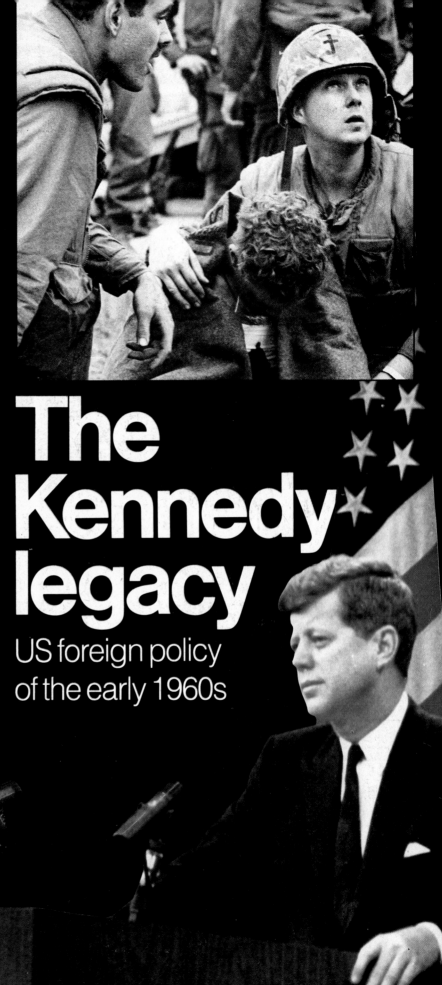

The Kennedy legacy
US foreign policy of the early 1960s

Left: As US Secretary of State the unobtrusive Dean Rusk was a staunch supporter of Kennedy's desire to control communism in Southeast Asia.

Below: Robert McNamara was appointed by Kennedy as Secretary of Defense. His advice was crucial in determining the level of US commitment in South Vietnam, particularly during the early months of Lyndon Johnson's presidency.

Previous page, above: During fierce fighting around Hue City in Vietnam in 1968, a US Marine, wounded in the chest, is comforted by a padre. Previous page, below: John F. Kennedy, newly elected as US president, was determined to bring a fresh approach to a complicated world, but found Southeast Asia an intractable problem.

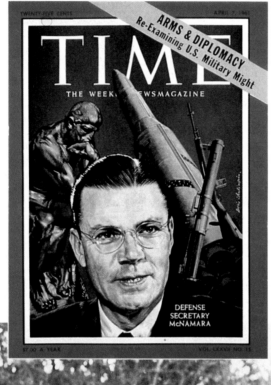

All the President's men

When Lyndon Johnson took over the presidency he was, of course, surrounded by Kennedy's foreign policy aides. One of his predecessor's last actions had been to order a withdrawal of some American advisers from Vietnam, but according to author Michael Maclear, this was soon reversed: 'Only one day into his presidency ...Johnson now heard from Secretary of Defense McNamara and Secretary of State Rusk that Kennedy's instructions were incompatible with his wider objectives .... McNamara was forceful with Johnson, declaring that Kennedy's orders would be a "death sentence" for South Vietnam .... Within 48 hours of taking office President Johnson announced that US Military support for the Saigon junta would continue ....

'Within nine months, without prior warning, Johnson would take America to war in Vietnam. He would eventually commit 543,000 combat troops to "draw a line" against communism ....'

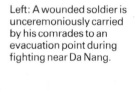

Left: A wounded soldier is unceremoniously carried by his comrades to an evacuation point during fighting near Da Nang.

Above: Lyndon Johnson, who became president after the assassination of Kennedy, meets US troops in Vietnam. The Vietnam War dominated Johnson's presidency, so that his ambitious programme of domestic reform was overshadowed by events in Southeast Asia.

concessions over trade, for example, where goodwill might be signalled. He would feel impelled to resume atmospheric nuclear testing but press forward to a test ban treaty; in his own words: 'On the Presidential coat of arms, the American eagle holds in his right talon the olive branch, while in his left he holds a bundle of arrows. We intended to give equal attention to both.' Hence the Peace Corps for the Underdeveloped Nations or the Alliance for Progress for Latin America were as much part of the repertoire of diplomacy as Seato or the Seventh Fleet.

For the real battle was frequently off-stage. More than ever it was necessary to move away from the monolithic assumptions of nuclear deterrence to a policy of flexible response geared to non-nuclear and even unorthodox forces. In principle this was only sensible: there had been an increasing unreality about America's defence posture in the closing years of the 1950s when massive retaliation had become virtually the only weapon in her armoury against any Soviet provocation. The Russians had increasingly come to see that the best chance to push the world in their direction lay in support, tacit or avowed, for 'wars of national liberation' – a phrase generously interpreted to include any form of anti-Western insurrection. In these situations, a policy of massive retaliation was useless. Yet in practice the diversification of forces to permit a series of graduated responses to differing situations encouraged precisely the kind of unorthodox military adventurism that could drag America into conflicts from which she might not easily disengage. Of course, the intention was to allow a broader range of choice, yet ironically the absence of a flexible response capacity imposed a greater sense of restraint; it was difficult to argue that any brush-fire war so impaired the West's security that it necessitated descent into a nuclear Armageddon. Conversely, once limited means were readily available to meet a limited attack, failure to react to any minor communist advance could be interpreted as a loss of Western will; in order to make America's commitment to Nato, or her stand over Berlin seem credible, a president might feel bound to commit forces in areas of marginal interest; it was this last argument that Lyndon Johnson was constantly to use over Vietnam.

Kennedy might warn that: 'we must face problems which do not lend themselves to easy, quick or permanent solutions. And we must face the fact that the United States is neither omnipotent nor omniscient, that we cannot always impose our will on the other 94 per cent of mankind – there cannot be an American solution for every world problem.' He could hardly have said otherwise. Yet in the same speech in November 1961, he could talk of being 'determined to defend the frontiers of freedom by an honourable peace, if peace is possible, but by arms if arms are used against us'. Where one drew those frontiers was not explained.

Kennedy was determined to assert civilian control over the military; in some ways his appointment of Robert McNamara as Secretary of Defense – the first proper Secretary of Defense, it was said, since the post was instituted after World War II, a man who controlled his department as opposed to arbitrating between contending factions – was more important for the shape of foreign policy than the nomination of the unobtrusive Dean Rusk as Secretary of State. In other ways, though, having muzzled the military and refused to endorse their wilder options, the civilians

were left with a predisposition to appear equally tough; to prevent the communists pushing their luck through miscalculation of American determination (and thereby blundering into war), it became important not to show the indecision that might encourage them so to do. Nor was this policy merely for foreign consumption; it was part of a political strategy in which a president who was widely regarded as a force for liberalisation and change in domestic politics was able to pre-empt attacks from the hawkish, and usually extremely conservative, right of the spectrum. A reformer could not risk being accused of softness on communism.

Problems with the Third World

These complications and pressures stemming from the US domestic political scene meant that the administration's response to any one problem was not always well founded, or based on a correct assessment of the situation in the particular area in question. For the change in US response to pressures all over the world was not just due to the fact that 'massive retaliation' seemed an outdated concept; it was also due to the difficulties of a changing world. By 1960, the empires of Britain and France were all but finished, and the newly independent nations of Africa and Asia posed a complex and intractable set of problems. A foreign policy towards the Third World that took account of individual differences and yet had a strong central thread was hard to find.

This need for a subtle and often flexible approach that would take account of the needs of individual countries was not necessarily met by the vigour and reformism of the young men who now ran the administration and who appeared so attractively different from Eisenhower's old guard. Dynamism and Harvard Business School methods might seem the answer to many domestic problems, but they were often out of place in dealing with the problems of a different society — say the situation of the Meo tribesmen in Laos.

America's approach to its situation in the world may, therefore, have seemed vigorous, idealistic and successful at certain levels: in his resolute stand on Berlin in 1961, and in his firm handling of the Cuban missile crisis a year later, Kennedy was a symbol of Western determination. But at a lower level there was less clarity of aim, and less sureness of touch. The Bay of Pigs fiasco in April 1961 was an early disaster; and attempts to find a low level response to the challenge of communism – such as in Laos and Vietnam in the early 1960s – were confused and in the latter case ultimately disastrous. Where a simple show of force could achieve the desired end, as in Thailand in 1962 or, under Lyndon Johnson, in the Dominican Republic in 1965, success was possible, albeit at a price in terms of public opinion. But otherwise, there were problems.

The early 1960s were, then, a confused period in American foreign policy attitudes. There was a tentative searching for new directions, an awareness that all was not well, but a difficulty in formulating an alternative. A sense of crisis, sometimes artificially generated; a groping after solutions; a tendency to strike postures; these were the characteristics of the period. Kennedy had described himself as 'an idealist without illusions'; soon even the idealism would become jaded, with momentous consequences, especially in Southeast Asia. **John Kentleton**

Defending the dominoes

US intervention in Laos and Thailand

Above: During the 1950s and early 1960s, the US made much use of Laotian hill tribes such as the Meo in an attempt to contain the communists. Here Meo tribeswomen are carrying supplies from a helicopter to their village.

Right: The bodyguard of Prince Souphanouvong, the leader of the communist Pathet Lao forces that dominated the north of Laos.

The Vietnam War dominated all events in Southeast Asia from 1965 onwards, but in the early 1960s the communist threat appeared to be general over much of the region, and the specific importance of Vietnam had not yet been established. Both Thailand and Laos were seen by the US as requiring help against communist insurgency, but the American response to the situation in the two countries was very different. In Thailand, a secure right-wing government was easily bolstered against small-scale insurgency, but in Laos the short-sightedness and crudeness of US policy ended in disaster.

Thailand had been a military dictatorship since 1932, albeit with a monarch as titular head of state. By 1960, although the Communist Party of Thailand (TCP) had embarked on armed revolt, communist numbers were small, and their influence restricted because of rivalries between the various strands of the TCP, that were backed by the Chinese, the Viet Cong and the Pathet Lao (the Laotian communists).

The influence of the Viet Cong and Pathet Lao was felt in the northeast and south, while the Chinese had a greater influence in the north. In the latter area the dissidence was centred around the Meo tribesmen, and there was a different policy adopted by the Thai government, mainly one of confrontation, to that followed in the other areas, where some attempt was made to alleviate conditions with the use of US development aid. There were no serious military clashes in Thailand between guerrillas and government forces until the middle of the decade. The government, therefore, looked very secure in the early 1960s and was, in the words of one commentator, 'more anti-communist . . . than the US'.

The Thai government had been receiving military aid for some time, but the military successes of the Pathet Lao on the other side of the Mekong in 1962 brought an abrupt change. In May of that year, after both Secretary of State Dean Rusk and Defense Secretary Robert McNamara had visited Bangkok, President Kennedy sent 5000 US Marines into northern Thailand, ostensibly to counter the threat of a Pathet Lao invasion.

From then on the US military presence mushroomed until by the end of the 1960s there were approximately 50,000 US troops stationed in Thailand, and U Tapao was the largest airbase in Southeast Asia. From Thailand, US bombers launched their attacks on North Vietnam and Laos with ever-increasing frequency. At the same time US helicopter pilots and advisers were assisting the Thai troops in their operations against the guerrillas in the north. There was never any disagreement between the Thai government and the US. Thai forces were sent to both

Laos and Vietnam, over 30,000 men being committed in these countries.

The situation in Laos was very different. After being granted autonomy by the French in 1949, the country was effectively ruled by half-brothers, both princes of the Royal Family, Souvanna Phouma and Souphanouvong. Souvanna Phouma was a neutralist, whereas Souphanouvong was sympathetic to the communist governments of North Vietnam and China. Splitting with his half-brother, he moved into the countryside and helped establish the Pathet Lao.

The Geneva Conference of 1954 attempted to find a solution for Laos, more or less divided geographically between the forces of the Pathet Lao in the north and the Royal Lao Forces. A peace treaty was signed, and Laos was designated a neutral, demilitarised area. However, two months after the Geneva accords were signed, US aid to the anti-communist forces was stepped up and the CIA intervened, trying to oust Souvanna Phouma from the government, largely, it would appear, because of his determination to negotiate with the Pathet Lao. For a brief period from November 1957, Souvanna Phouma successfully ran a coalition government in which both right-wing and Pathet Lao leaders participated. But in July 1958 right-wing military leaders took control of the government and the Pathet Lao withdrew once more.

Phouma replaces Phoumi
Two military men were dominant in government from 1958: firstly General Phoui Sananikone and then General Phoumi Nosavan. Both were backed by the CIA and their sponsored right-wing bloc in the Laotian National Assembly. In August 1960 Captain Kong Lae, a parachute battalion commander, overthrew General Nosavan and reinstated Souvanna Phouma as head of a neutralist government. Officially the US government supported Souvanna Phouma, but the CIA continued to back General Nosavan. In December 1960, Nosavan retook Vientiane and installed another prince, Boun Oum, as prime minister. Kong Lae fled to the Plain of Jars where he formed an alliance with the Pathet Lao, and Souvanna Phouma set up a neutralist government-in-exile. US policy was in disarray. The CIA had a heavy interest in establishing an overtly anti-communist regime, yet most of the dominant groups in Laos clearly opted for a neutralist stance.

To try to resolve the confusion, President Kennedy convened another Geneva Conference in 1961. Fighting continued in Laos – it is now widely believed that the CIA encouraged Nosavan to attack the Pathet Lao, provoking their very effective attack on Nam Tha in May 1962, in order to prevent agreement being reached. Nevertheless, in July 1962 it was agreed that a new neutralist coalition government would rule Laos. The government was to be composed of Souvanna Phouma as prime minister, with Souphanouvong and Nosavan as deputy prime ministers. Nosavan was not at all happy with this outcome. He still controlled large forces, and US ambassador Averell Harriman had to go to Vientiane and threaten to cut off military aid if Souvanna Phouma was not installed.

Although officially the coalition government was set up, in effect it was a dead letter. North Vietnamese support for the Pathet Lao continued, and from 1962 US involvement with anti-communist forces was stepped up. The problem was that whatever Kennedy,

Harriman or the politicians might decide, the intervention in Laos was an undercover operation run almost entirely by the CIA, and control was very difficult. Reading a digest of intelligence reports was no recipe for understanding exactly how the aristocratic warlords of southern Laos related to the Meo hill tribesmen, nor how the communist Pathet Lao came to be headed by a royal prince. Laos was increasingly seen as merely an adjunct to the deepening involvement in Vietnam whereas, in fact, it was a whole bundle of problems in its own right.

Arms and military personnel were all supplied to the Royal Lao Forces under the auspices of the Agency and its proprietory companies. Bombing missions, arms drops and incursion operations were all run by Air America, the CIA airline, and its staff. Operations were also mounted against the Viet Cong supply routes through Laos. So great was the CIA presence that the Meo stronghold in Long Cheng, supported and armed by the CIA, became the second-largest town in Laos, and the CIA maintained a force of 40,000 Meo tribesmen under arms. The CIA also gave supplies to the forces of Kong Lae, the leader of the coup in 1960, who had turned against the Pathet Lao. It is now estimated that the total aid poured into Laos under CIA auspices far exceeded the official US government aid of $80 million a year after 1963.

Of course, by the late 1960s, Laos became completely subordinate in American minds to the war in Vietnam. Then Laos and the Ho Chi Minh trail were subjected to a deluge of bombs from the bases in Thailand. The devastation was immense. Bombing of northern Laos and the trail started in 1964, and it is estimated that there were 1000 air strikes in 1966. However, in October 1968, there were 600 strikes a day. The effect was to produce 600,000 refugees, and massive recruitment to the Pathet Lao.

By the end of the 1960s, a small covert operation had escalated into a massive bombing campaign, the coalition government was tottering, and all that defended north and central Laos against the Pathet Lao were groups of CIA-backed Meo tribesmen. In ten years a country had been laid to waste, as US attempts to defend it against communism had failed utterly.

Mike Rossiter

Above: Part of the 5000-strong contingent of US Marines sent to Thailand in May 1962 march along a track during acclimatisation exercises. The Marines were sent into northern Thailand to counter Pathet Lao successes on the Laotian side of the Mekong. By the end of the 1960s there were some 50,000 US troops stationed in Thailand.

Descent on Santo Domingo

America moves into the Dominican Republic

In the four years following the assassination of dictator Rafael Trujillo in 1961, the Dominican Republic searched in vain for political stability. In December 1962 the first free elections for 38 years brought a moderate left-winger, Juan Bosch, to power, but seven months later a military coup deposed Bosch and replaced him by a three-man civilian junta. The Organization of American States (OAS), including the United States and Latin American countries, at first reacted with hostility to this anti-democratic military coup, but soon settled down to acceptance of the new regime.

In late April 1965, the junta itself was victim of a military revolt. Rebel forces eventually united under Colonel Francisco Caamaño overthrew the junta and invited Bosch to return from exile and lead a return to constitutional government. Opposition to Caamaño's revolt centred mainly on San Isidro airbase, commanded by Brigadier Elias Wessin y Wessin, a participant in the 1963 military rising and an officer of extreme right-wing views. San Isidro is some 20km (12 miles) east of the capital, Santo Domingo, which was largely in the hands of Caamaño's men. Wessin was able to defend the airbase with a small ground force and to launch token raids against the capital, but his resistance seemed bound to fail. In Santo Domingo, all semblance of law and order had vanished.

Ordinarily, the outbreak of another disturbance in the Dominican Republic would have been a matter of minor importance to the United States, which was poised on the threshold of a major commitment to the conflict in Vietnam. But reports from Santo Domingo indicated the presence of communist-oriented leaders in the rebel forces. President Lyndon B. Johnson was determined that there would not be another Cuba in the Caribbean. Under the guise of taking steps to protect the lives of American nationals located in the capital area, the president ordered the Caribbean Ready Amphibious Squadron of the Atlantic Fleet to move to Dominican waters on 25 April 1965 and alerted ground and air units in the US the following day.

During 27-28 April, the warring Dominican factions engaged in indecisive skirmishes and the number of civilian casualties increased. At the request of the US ambassador, Marines came ashore at the western edge of Santo Domingo on the 28th and deployed to protect American and other foreign nationals located in that part of the city. Their presence, however, failed to halt the growing momentum of the rebel Caamaño forces while opposition from pro-junta elements was dwindling.

Convinced that a victory for the rebels would

lead to the establishment of another communist-oriented regime in the sensitive Caribbean area, President Johnson took vigorous action. On the 29th, he ordered the remainder of the Marines offshore to join their sister units in the western suburbs of Santo Domingo, bringing the total involved to 1500 men. At the same time, he instructed two battalions of the alerted 82nd Airborne Division to emplane and move to Puerto Rico where they would be in a better position to react quickly if the situation continued to worsen.

On 30 April the president managed to persuade the OAS to pass a mild resolution requesting the opposing groups to arrange a ceasefire and to permit the establishment of an international neutral zone in the area surrounding the foreign embassies in Santo Domingo. He then used the resolution as a shield for a build-up of American military strength that would

enable the US to dominate the situation in the capital and forestall any possible communist take-over. To ensure success in the operation, Johnson ordered the commitment of the entire 4th Marine Expeditionary Brigade (four battalion-landing teams) and the remainder of the 82nd Airborne Division to the Dominican Republic; the 101st Airborne Division was alerted as a back-up force.

As the first two battalions of the 82nd were en route from Puerto Rico under the command of Major General Robert H. York, the division commander, they were ordered to fly directly to San Isidro airbase, where they airlanded. The last-minute decision not to stage an air drop turned out to be a very fortunate one for the American paratroopers, since the selected drop zone had a number of coral patches and casualties would doubtless have been suffered.

The paratroopers fanned out from the airfield, establishing a perimeter, and then began to work their way westward toward Santo Domingo. They met little resistance. When they reached the Ozama River, which bisected the eastern sector of the city, they halted and waited for reinforcements to arrive.

Sending in the troops

During the opening days of May, the build-up of American forces continued, limited only by the inability of San Isidro to handle more than 11 planes an hour. With over 150 C-130s and 70 C-124s committed to the movement of troops and supplies from the 82nd's home base in North Carolina, the US had diverted over 90 per cent of its air transport strength to support of the Dominican operation.

Although several truces were arranged between the factions in Santo Domingo, violations were frequent and roving rebel bands of commando-type units roamed freely throughout the city. Since there was no sign that the pro-junta forces were going to be able to curtail rebel activity, President Johnson consulted Lieutenant General Bruce Palmer, Jr, who had been

Left: Crowds of civilians protest at US intervention in Santo Domingo in April 1965. The large banner (far left) proclaims 'out with the invading Americans'.

Above: US troops fortify positions and build barricades using sandbags and barbed wire as part of the US plan to impose order on the city of Santo Domingo. Left: The rebel leader Colonel Francisco Caamaño whose forces overthrew the three-man junta that had gained power by military coup.

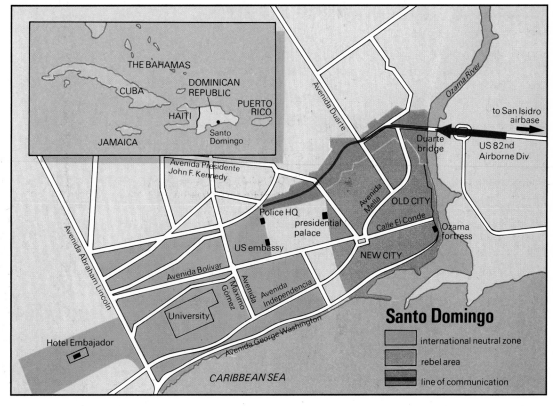

named commander of all US forces ashore, about positive American steps to bring the situation under control.

Palmer recommended the immediate despatch of two additional airborne battalions to bring his current strength to six and the mounting of a night operation on 2 May to establish a link-up between the 3000 Marines in the west and the army units in the east. The corridor would be manned by airborne troops who would thus place a cordon between the rebel forces and the remaining pro-junta units, effectively hemming the rebels into southeastern Santo Domingo.

To secure presidential consent for his daring scheme, Palmer had to obtain the approval of an OAS commission in Santo Domingo. The commission reluctantly agreed that, in view of the lack of any control in the city, the establishment of a line of communications was necessary to permit the further evacuation of foreign nationals and the distribution of food and medicines to the people.

In a television address to the nation on 2 May, President Johnson emphasised the humanitarian role of the US in intervening to save the lives of foreign nationals and alleviate the suffering of Dominican civilians. He also left little doubt that the US intended to prevent the establishment of another communist state in the western hemisphere.

Shortly after the president finished his speech, General Palmer launched Blue Chip, the key military operation of the intervention. Using three airborne battalions as ordinary infantry, with the lead battalion backed by two blocking battalions, the brigade left the Ozama bridgehead that night and cautiously pushed westward toward the US Marine positions. When the lead battalion was in place, the second battalion passed through its lines and manned the middle section of the planned corridor. As the third battalion moved through the lines of its sister units to establish the link-up with the Marines, the rebels finally realised what was happening. Some sniper fire began to

come in but was quickly silenced. The only US casualty in the hour-long operation was a paratrooper wounded in a case of mistaken identity. With the completion of Blue Chip, the rebels were effectively sealed off from their supporters in the rest of Santo Domingo and outside the city.

Although the setting up of a line of communications across the capital ended the critical phase of the intervention, additional reinforcements continued to pour in. The remainder of the 82nd Airborne and a fourth Marine battalion arrived by 4 May and support units gradually swelled the total of American personnel committed to the Dominican operation to about 32,000 later in the month, including 14,000 army personnel, 8000 Marines, 9000 seamen and 1000 airmen.

The separation of junta and rebel forces by the new American buffer zone produced a period of military stalemate and shifted the focus to the political arena where negotiations were being carried out on several fronts without much success. In the meantime, the major part of the American military effort was concentrated on maintaining the peace and providing food, water and medical assistance to the civilian population of Santo Domingo.

To give an international complexion to the American intervention, President Johnson also sought to gain moral support from other members of the OAS. Despite the opposition and deep misgivings of many of the OAS governments, a resolution requesting that military contingents be sent to form what would be the first Inter-American Peace Force was passed on 6 May. Contributions to the multi-national peacekeeping force proved to be disappointing – only Brazil, Honduras, Nicaragua, Paraguay and Costa Rica sent units. Since Brazil's was the largest contingent, a Brazilian lieutenant-general became the commander of the Inter-American Force on 23 May, with General Palmer serving as his second-in-command. The US had to provide logistic support, including transporta-

Above: Dr Joaquin Balaguer, who was elected president of the Dominican Republic in June 1966 and whose first major task was to arrange for the withdrawal of OAS troops.

Left: US troops and civilians clash in the streets as tempers fray over occupation. Right: US Marines, supported by an M48 medium tank and the aircraft carrier USS *Boxer* (background left), man defensive positions on George Washington Avenue in Santo Domingo.

Above: With bayonets fixed to their 7.62mm M14 rifles US troops take cover behind a low wall while under fire from rebel snipers.

Left: As part of the OAS peace force, Brazilian troops move cautiously towards the national palace in Santo Domingo. The soldier nearest the camera is carrying a US M1919 machine gun. Extra rounds for this weapon are carried by the soldier to the right.

tion, tentage and other equipment, for all of the Latin American contingents.

Once the Latin American units were in place, the US began to reduce its military strength. First to depart were the Marine battalions and by early June over 10,000 troops had left the Dominican Republic. Since intense political wrangling between the hostile factions showed little sign of abating, the withdrawals slowed until, after an abortive rebel attack on 82nd Airborne positions in eastern Santo Domingo had been repulsed in mid-June, the rebels adopted more conciliatory attitudes in the negotiations. Further reductions then took place and two airborne battalions returned home in July.

In August the opposing parties agreed to a compromise settlement and Hector García Godoy became provisional president until new elections could be held in early 1966. His main tasks were to maintain a neutral position during the transition period, prevent reprisals against the rebels, and allay the suspicions of junta leaders that he was favourably disposed toward leftist elements. With his assumption of office on 3 September, the revolt officially came to a close.

The inauguration of García Godoy opened the way for additional troop withdrawals. By November four more airborne battalions returned to North Carolina and the residual American force was one brigade of three battalions and support units, totalling about 6500 men. Together with the Latin American units, the Inter-American Peace Force, as it was then named, contained a little over 8000 troops.

An election and an exodus

Although there were sporadic incidents in Santo Domingo during the early part of 1966, the June elections were held without any major disturbances. The installation of the new president, Dr Joaquin Balaguer, in July was quickly followed by an increase in pressure from all political parties for the swift withdrawal of all foreign military forces from Dominican soil. The OAS supported the move and the final exodus took place during the summer. The closure of the Inter-American Peace Force headquarters on 20 September brought the intervention in the Dominican Republic to an end.

The human costs of the Dominican revolt can only be guessed at on the civilian side, but it is probable that about 2000 were killed and 3000 wounded during the critical first two months. Military casualties for the Dominican armed forces on both sides were estimated at about 1500, including 800 dead. US casualties totalled 24 killed and 164 wounded, while the other members of the peace force suffered only seven wounded.

The political costs of the intervention are even more difficult to measure. Besides the expenditure in lives, money and resources, there are also nagging questions about the legality and morality of the American action. The use of US military force on a unilateral basis was not in accordance with inter-American agreements and alarmed many Latin Americans. A failure to intervene, on the other hand, might have resulted in higher casualties, both military and civilian, further deterioration of law and order, and possibly, but only possibly, the establishment of a communist-oriented regime. President Johnson had decided at the outset that this possibility was strong enough to justify US intervention; he preferred to be safe rather than sorry.   **Walter G. Hermes**

Burning ghettos...

The US Army from Korea to Vietnam

President Dwight D. Eisenhower came to power in the United States in 1953 determined to take a 'New Look' at defence policy. The fighting in the Korean War was drawing to a close and Eisenhower's administration did not intend to repeat the experience. Limited wars, it seemed, were not only expensive in lives and money but inevitably indecisive. Government spending on rearmament during the Korean War had fuelled inflation and Eisenhower believed that this aided the spread of communism by weakening the American economy. Defence spending had to be cut, but without sacrificing American security. The solution to this apparent contradiction was provided by the strategy of massive retaliation (generally associated with Eisenhower's Secretary of State, John Foster Dulles).

Dulles made it clear that America intended to respond to aggression with nuclear weapons. 'The military were to plan to use nuclear weapons whenever their use was militarily desirable.' This, Dulles claimed, offered 'the maximum deterrent at a bearable cost'. Prospective aggressors would be deterred by the certainty that war would result in nuclear holocaust. There was no prospect of prolonged conventional fighting as in Korea or World War II.

The implications of this strategy for the US Army were far-reaching and discomforting. Dulles proposed to rely more on America's allies for local defence, cutting overseas garrisons in favour of a mobile strategic reserve based in the US. In the event

Above: US paratroopers move through the riot-torn streets of Washington D.C. during civil disturbances in 1968. Above right: A mushroom cloud rises after the world's first atomic artillery shell was fired from a 280mm cannon at Frenchman's Flat, Nevada, USA in 1953. Right: A night-firing tank uses a xenon searchlight (125 million candlepower) and an infra-red periscope during target exercises in the USA.

...and the nuclear battlefield

nisation of the ground forces would be required. The army was convinced that it would be impossible to hold continuous fronts as in past wars. Instead, units would have to be dispersed and deployed in greater depth than previously, with considerable intervals between them. This would reduce their vulnerability to nuclear strikes by making it impossible for one nuclear explosion to affect several units. This deployment was generally described as 'chequerboard defence'. A nuclear battle would involve locating the enemy, striking him with nuclear weapons and then exploiting the strikes with highly mobile forces, able to concentrate quickly for the attack and to disperse just as rapidly before the enemy retaliated.

The ground forces were therefore reorganised on the model of the 'pentomic division'. American divisions in World War II and Korea generally consisted of three brigades each of three battalions. The new division commanded five self-contained battle groups, with infantry, armour, artillery and logistic elements. The brigade level of command disappeared, although divisional headquarters could form smaller tactical headquarters to command one or more battle groups in a particular task. There were three types of pentomic division: infantry (with 13,748 men), armoured (with 14,617 men), and airborne (with 11,486 men). A typical infantry division's battle groups would consist of an infantry battalion, a tank company and a battery of 105mm howitzers. The division would also command an armoured reconnaissance unit and a general support composite artillery battalion, with two 155mm gun batteries, a battery of 8-inch howitzers, and a battery of Honest John rocket launchers. The 8-inch howitzer and the Honest John were the basic nuclear delivery means. Corps headquarters could provide additional support for the division, such as nuclear strikes by the Redstone missile.

Simulating a nuclear strike

In May 1955 the army's new tactical concepts were tested in the Nevada desert. A battle group built around a tank battalion was deployed 2750m (3000yds) from a nuclear explosion and then moved through the area of the explosion to simulate exploiting a nuclear strike. The test showed the value of armoured forces on the nuclear battlefield and provided the impetus for the development of new weapons such as the M60 tank and the M113 APC.

Pentomic divisions had less conventional artillery than their predecessors, but it was hoped to compensate for this by using nuclear weapons like the 280mm cannon and the Davy Crockett mortar. The 280mm cannon proved to be far too cumbersome and was dropped from the army's inventory. The Davy Crockett mortar was intended to provide a battalion-level nuclear weapon, but its range was far too short.

Eisenhower's defence policy was not without its critics, both civilian and military. The reliance on nuclear weapons was widely challenged. Once the Soviet Union developed the capability to strike the US itself with nuclear weapons the doctrine of massive retaliation was less credible. It was hard to believe that the US would deliberately risk the horrors of a nuclear war to achieve a limited political objective such as the defence of an ally. But if the nuclear deterrent was stalemated the US lacked the forces to fight a conventional war and might be faced with a choice between humiliation and annihilation. Two

of a war, nuclear firepower would make it possible to use smaller, more mobile formations. In 1953 the US Army totalled 1,534,000 men and 20 divisions (eight in the Far East, five in Europe, seven in the USA), and cost $13,000 million. This was to be cut by 1958 to 859,000 men, with 15 divisions and a budget of $9000 million.

These economies heralded a period of neglect for the US Army. The air force became the dominant service, absorbing the lion's share of the defence budget because it was responsible for the nuclear deterrent. The navy was also subject to cuts but not as seriously as the army, because its aircraft carriers also provided a nuclear capability. The army tried to maintain its budget share by developing nuclear missiles but in 1956 the air force was made responsible for long-range missiles. The army's only contribution to the strategic deterrent was the defensive one of providing air defence for America. The US Army Air Defence Command (USAADC) had its headquarters in Colorado Springs and controlled five regional commands. Its first suface-to-air missile, the Nike-Ajax, was deployed between 1953 and 1957, to be followed by the Nike-Hercules after 1958. As the threat shifted, however, from manned aircraft to missiles, air defence was down-graded, although the army made an unconvincing attempt to develop an anti-missile missile, the Nike-Zeus.

It was clear that if nuclear weapons were to be employed on the battlefield, a considerable reorga-

successive army chiefs of staff pointed out the military deficiencies in the 'New Look' strategy. General Ridgway, chief of staff from 1953 to 1955, not only doubted the effectiveness of massive retaliation but did not accept that nuclear firepower could compensate for manpower reductions. He argued that more men, not less, would be required on the nuclear battlefield, because nuclear weapons could quickly cause heavy casualties.

Ridgway's successor from 1955 to 1957 was General Maxwell Taylor who eventually resigned in order to make public his objections to a new series of cuts in spending and manpower. His book, *The Uncertain Trumpet*, argued for a strategy of flexible response. Nuclear weapons should be a shield but limited war forces were required as a 'flexible sword for parry, riposte and attack'. Taylor's ideas were sympathetically received by the Democratic candidate for the presidency in 1960, John F. Kennedy. When Kennedy came to power he started a complete overhaul of American defence policy. One of his objectives was to obtain usable military power which could provide a credible response to a wide range of threats to the US and its allies. The result was a reorganisation of America's forces for limited war and counter-insurgency roles as well as general war. Flexible response eventually became Nato's official strategy in 1967. As a result of these changes the American Army grew in size and the number of divisions was increased. Under-strength formations were fleshed out, increasing the number of combat-ready divisions from 11 to 16.

Trying new ROADS

The divisional structure was also reorganised to take account of criticisms of the pentomic concept. Two divisions were re-formed as Reorganization Objective Army Divisions (ROAD). After exhaustive trials all divisions were converted to the ROAD model by 1964. There were four types of new division: airborne, armoured, infantry and mechanised infantry. Each ROAD division had a common base, consisting of divisional headquarters, three brigade headquarters, artillery, engineers, aviation, signals, armoured reconnaissance and transport and logistic units. The division thus had much more artillery and more support elements than the pentomic division, which had been criticised for its inability to operate independently for any length of time. Furthermore, instead of the five pentomic battle groups, the new division commanded a flexible mix of battalions. The average strength of a division was 13,500 men for an airborne division and about 15,000 men for the others. Typical unit allocations were nine parachute and one armoured battalion for an airborne division, eight infantry and two armoured battalions for an infantry division, seven mechanised infantry and three armoured battalions for a mechanised division and for an armoured division, six armoured and five mechanised infantry battalions. The exact number of battalions in a division however, depended on the task it was given. The flexibility of the ROAD division was increased by its three brigade headquarters which could command any mix of battalions and support elements, according to its task.

Each type of ROAD division was suited to a particular role or area of operations. Thus the armoured and mechanised divisions were most suitable to a European battlefield, because of their tactical

Top: The West's first surface-to-air missiles, the Douglas Nike-Ajax. The photograph shows a typical small missile base consisting of four launchers. There would also be two underground magazines, a control area and associated radar. Above: Three Marines pose with the latest in US weapons and equipment in 1960. The man to the left carries an M14 assault rifle; the man in the centre is wearing NBC protective clothing and carries a lightweight portable flame-thrower; and the man to the right wears experimental body armour and helmet, and carries an M60 machine gun. Left: US M60 tanks on manoeuvres in Germany in 1961.

General Maxwell Taylor (above), chief of staff from 1955 to 1957 and his predecessor General Ridgway (below) argued strongly against army cuts.

Below: A US tank moves through East Berlin during the confrontation of August 1961.

mobility, firepower and protection. They could operate with conventional or nuclear weapons. The infantry division had a worldwide role in limited or guerrilla wars. It was lighter, and therefore strategically more mobile, than armoured and mechanised divisions, and could operate in more difficult terrain. Even greater mobility was found in the two airborne divisions, the 82nd and 101st. They could be used for traditional airborne operations in Europe or a quick-alert intervention force anywhere in the world. The search for tactical mobility eventually led to the formation of a fifth type of division, the air mobile division. The concept was tested between 1963 and 1965, and in the latter year the 1st Air Cavalry Division was formed and deployed to Vietnam. The air mobile division depended on nearly 450 helicopters for its mobility and much of its firepower. Units could be instantly deployed over considerable areas to respond to the rapidly changing tactical picture of a guerrilla war.

American doctrines for the nuclear battlefield were never put to the test and most of the army during the 1950s and early 1960s was employed on garrison duties or acting as a deterrent force in Europe and the Far East. Some parts of the army, however, did see action in this period.

American troops twice intervened to influence the outcome of civil conflicts in countries the US considered important. The first was Lebanon in July 1958. Marines from the American Sixth Fleet were the first to be deployed but they were quickly followed by airborne troops and later by two tank battalions from Germany. The action prevented a possible civil war and stabilised Lebanese domestic politics for a while. Together with similar British action in Jordan at the same time, it demonstrated the West's determination to see that pro-communist regimes were not established throughout the Middle East. The second intervention was in the Dominican Republic in 1965. Rebel military forces, whose supporters included communists, had overthrown a right-wing regime and seemed set to defeat their remaining opponents. Sensitive to the threat of a new Cuba, the American government decided to intervene. Marines and paratroops from the 82nd Airborne Division were landed on 28 April. They were quickly able to separate the two factions, isolate the rebel forces and impose a ceasefire. By mid-May the US had 32,000 personnel engaged in operations in the country, but by November only one brigade of the 82nd Airborne remained as part of a multi-national peacekeeping force. Final withdrawal took place in September 1966.

The deterrent role of American forces in Europe was emphasised by their part in the crisis sparked off by the building of the Berlin Wall in August 1961. One of President Kennedy's first steps was to order a 1500-man battle group to reinforce Berlin from West Germany. The arrival of the troops demonstrated the American commitment to West Berlin and raised morale in the city. Kennedy followed this with more general measures in September when two National Guard divisions and a large number of smaller reserve units were ordered to report for active duty. In all 120,000 reserves were called up and the draft increased to provide for an extra 80,000 men in the regular army establishment. Further to this, 40,000 reinforcements and 100,000 tonnes of equipment were sent to Europe.

The crisis never developed into a shooting war but there were several moments of high tension. In August 1961 an American tank prevented East German water cannon from attacking demonstrators in West Berlin. When East German border guards tried to restrict the movement of American forces in East Berlin contrary to the postwar Four Power Agreements, tanks and APCs were deployed to the border.

By the mid-1960s, the ability to wage a limited war had brought the army back into favour. Below: US troops work hard to construct gun emplacements for 105mm howitzers during the intervention in Santo Domingo. Bottom: Covering a general advance with an M60 machine gun during an action in Vietnam.

On 25 October, 10 American tanks were sent to Checkpoint Charlie to demonstrate American determination to enforce their right of unhindered access. This forced the Russians to back up the East Germans with their own tanks, and Soviet and American tanks confronted each other on 27 October. The Soviet deployment was in fact a defeat because it showed that they still considered themselves, rather than the East Germans, responsible for East Berlin. After a Soviet withdrawal on 28 October the crisis died down.

One of the most difficult duties facing the army in this period was within the US itself. As the government insisted on racial desegregation, the army had to be used several times to overcome local resistance by white racists. In 1957 troops of the 101st Airborne Division enforced the desegregation of schools in Little Rock, Arkansas. In 1962, 20,000 army troops and 10,000 National Guardsmen were sent to ensure the enrolment of a black American at the University of Mississippi. Troops were used again in 1963 and 1965 as the Civil Rights movement grew.

A growing concern of the American Army, particularly after 1960, was counter-insurgency. Teams of advisers were sent to many countries to assist governments in dealing with guerrilla wars. Kennedy was impressed by the potential of the Special Forces, which had originally been formed to lead guerrilla movements behind enemy lines in a conventional war but whose skills were also suited to organising local forces against insurgents. Fort Bragg became the base of the Special Warfare School and Kennedy gave the Special Forces their distinctive Green Beret and increased their complement from 1500 to 9000 men. This was a mixed blessing, however, because it was hardly possible to absorb such a rapid increase and maintain the same standards.

By the mid-1960s the American Army had achieved almost a complete reversal of fortune since the early Eisenhower days. Instead of being neglected and despised as irrelevant, the army had become the main cutting edge of American foreign policy. It was prepared for limited war and especially counter-insurgency roles when the occasion arose in South Vietnam. The American military commitment gradually grew from a handful of advisers based in Vietnam to 23,000 men in November 1963, working with every Vietnamese unit. Eventually American combat units were committed in March 1965. The wheel had come a full circle since the Korean War and the American Army was once again enmeshed in the complexities of a limited war. **Michael Orr**

Key Weapons

The
F-16 FIGHTING FALCON

The F-16 Fighting Falcon was designed in response to the United States Air Force's requirement – issued in January 1972 – for a lightweight fighter aircraft. The intention was to produce a highly manoeuvrable fighter at low cost, which could be produced in greater numbers than the highly-complex and expensive warplanes in the F-15 or F-111 categories. The low initial purchase price meant the lightweight fighter could be bought in far greater numbers than more complex multi-role aircraft, and with the Warsaw Pact air forces introducing high-performance warplanes in quantities larger than those deployed by Nato in Europe, the F-16 appeared to be an attractive proposition to the USAF in the early 1970s. Yet instead of an all lightweight fighter force, the USAF decided to buy a mix of the advanced F-15 Eagle and the F-16. Present plans call for the procurement of 969 F-15s and 2333 F-16s for the USAF.

The selection of the General Dynamics design to meet the lightweight fighter requirement was not a foregone conclusion, however, as the YF-16 prototype found itself in competition with Northrop's YF-17. Nor was it certain at the time of the YF-16's first flight on 20 January 1974 that the USAF would buy either fighter. However, the USAF's interest in the project was confirmed by Secretary of Defense James Schlesinger later that year and in January 1975 the YF-16 was announced as the winner of the lightweight fighter trials. A batch of eight development aircraft was ordered, comprising six single-seat F-16As and two F-16B conversion trainers. The USAF's decision to go ahead with the F-16 led to

deepening European interest in the fighter, as the nine Nato nations which operated the F-104 Starfighter began to look around for its replacement.

As light weight and low cost had to be combined with agility and high performance (Mach 2-plus maximum speed) in the F-16's design, the fighter incorporated advanced technology features where these contributed to keeping down the aircraft's size or achieving simplicity of operation. For example, composite materials were used instead of metals in the construction of the tailplane, fin and rudder, thus achieving a 30 per cent reduction in weight without compromising structural strength. The selection of a single powerplant, rather than the twin engines used in the rival YF-17 design, reduced weight and was

Previous page: An F-16 painted in low-visibility two-tone grey, the standard colour scheme for the US Air Force's Tactical Air Command squadrons. Above: The 'blended' wing and fuselage of the F-16 can be seen in this photograph.

Below: The first prototype F-16 takes-off from the airfield at Fort Worth in Texas.

Right: The different colour schemes of the prototype and production model F-16. Centre right: The second F-16 prototype undergoes flight trials over a desert area in Texas. Below right: An AIM-7F Sparrow missile is fired from an F-16. Sidewinder missiles are positioned alongside the wing tips. Bottom: The two-seat version of the F-16 comes into land after completing its maiden flight on 29 October 1980.

simpler to install. Furthermore, as the powerplant selected was the 11,340kg (25,000lb) thrust Pratt & Whitney F100-PW-100, which also powers the F-15 Eagle, there were further advantages in engine standardisation and maintenance support.

A number of very advanced aerodynamic features have contributed to the F-16's high performance and manoeuvrability. The wing and fuselage are 'blended', so that the latter contributes more lift than does a conventional design. The resultant thick wing-roots make it easier to position fuel tanks near the aircraft's centre of gravity, so that as fuel is burned-off the fighter does not have problems with changes in trim. In order to reduce landing speeds and to enhance manoeuvrability, the F-16 has a variable camber wing. Leading-edge flaps and trailing edge 'flaperons' (surfaces combining the function of flaps and ailerons) are automatically extended on commands from an air data computer to increase the wing's camber and lift. Manoeuvres at high angles of attack are facilitated by the fitting of forebody wing strakes – forward extensions of the wing-root leading edge which delay stalling. The unusual positioning of the engine intake beneath the forward fuselage was determined by the need to maintain an uninterrupted flow of air to the powerplant during violent manoeuvres, when conventional side-mounted intakes could become masked by the forward fuselage.

Finally the F-16's agility is improved by its fly-by-wire controls. A pilot operating conventional controls would find the F-16 difficult to fly, but the electronically-signalled fly-by-wire flight control system provides automatic stability and it also gives a near instantaneous control response to the pilot's signals. The F-16's high manoeuvrability is not its only novel

feature from the pilot's viewpoint. His cockpit is fitted with a sidestick control column, mounted on the starboard side of the cockpit together with an arm rest, which takes the place of the conventional centrally-mounted control column. Furthermore, instead of sitting on an ejection seat set back at a slight angle of 13 degrees, the F-16 pilot reclines on a seat positioned at 30 degrees and consequently increases his tolerance to G forces. His view through the single-piece frameless canopy is outstandingly good upwards, over the side and to the rear. And with essential flight information projected onto a head-up display within his field of view, plus radar and armament controls to hand on his sidestick and throttle, the F-16 pilot can give his undivided attention to searching for the enemy.

Although the F-16 was conceived as an air superiority fighter with the primary mission of clearing the skies of enemy fighters, it has in fact emerged as a multi-role aircraft able to take over most of the duties of the F-4 Phantom. This capability is due in no small measure to its Westinghouse APG-66 radar, which can not only search for and track airborne targets (including those flying at low level to escape ground-based radar detection), but can also switch to air-to-ground modes for mapping, target acquisition and target ranging. The F-16's armament options also reflect this versatility. A General Electric M61 Vulcan rotary cannon is built into the port wing-root, with 515 rounds of ammunition housed in a fuselage-mounted drum. Nine external ordnance pylons can carry up to six AIM-9 Sidewinder AAM (air-to-air missiles), or 7710kg (15,200lb) of bombs. Alternatively, a drop tank can be carried on the fuselage centreline, with two tanks underwing. In the air-to-air mission the F-16 will be armed with the AIM-120 AMRAAM (advanced medium-range air-to-air missile).

The F-16 entered USAF service in 1979, equipping the 388th Tactical Fighter Wing (TFW) at Hill air force base, Utah. In 1981 the first overseas USAF wing began to convert to the Fighting Falcon, when the South Korean based 8th TFW received its first F-16s at Kunsan air force base. Later that year a second overseas unit, the 50th TFW based at Hahn air force base in the Federal Republic of Germany,

The F-16 has not only proved itself a highly manoeuvrable air-superiority fighter (below left) but has been developed into a multi-role aircraft capable of delivering a bomb-load of up to 7710kg (15,200lb) (left). Right: An Israeli F-16 prepares for take-off, revealing the unusual positioning of the air-intake below the fuselage. Israel has bought both single (bottom) and twin-seat (below) versions of the F-16, and used them to good effect during the air war over Lebanon in 1982.

received its F-16s. Deliveries of the F-16 to European Nato air forces began early in 1979, with the first aircraft going to the Belgian Air Force. Although the F-16 has not enjoyed the remarkable sales success of the Starfighter in Nato, the air forces of Belgium, Denmark, the Netherlands and Norway have all ordered the Fighting Falcon. European licence production involves Fokker in the Netherlands, SABCA and Fairey in Belgium and Per Usden in Denmark. At present, planned totals stand at Belgium 160, Denmark 58, Netherlands 142 and Norway 72. Although basically similar to their American-built counterparts, Belgian F-16s have the Loral Rapport III internal ECM system instead of the USAF's external pods, while Norwegian F-16s are fitted with braking parachutes and can carry the Penguin anti-shipping missile.

In 1980 work began on the Multinational Staged Improvement Programme (MSIP), which is intended

to upgrade the capabilities of all F-16s. New equipment includes the AIM-120 AMRAAM, pods containing radar and infra-red systems for all-weather navigation and target acquisition, the General Electric 30mm GEPOD gun pod, Maverick air-to-surface missiles and Seek-Talk secure voice communications. Other modifications include the fitting of an enlarged tailplane to improve flying controls at higher all-up weights, the improvement of the radar and head-up display systems and a five-fold increase in the fighter's computer capacity. Aircraft modified for all-weather attack and to accept the AIM-120 will be designated F-16C, or F-16D in the case of two-seaters.

Supply of the F-16 has not been restricted to the United States' European Nato allies. Israel was one of the first export customers for the Fighting Falcon, with an initial order for 75 and a requirement to double this force. The first F-16s were delivered to Israel in July 1980 and in June the following year the aircraft took part in the raid on Iraq's nuclear reactor near Baghdad. This involved the eight participating F-16s in a 965km (600 mile) flight, each carrying a 1815kg (4000lb) bomb load. More recently Israeli F-16s were in action against Syrian forces during the invasion of the Lebanon in 1982, when the Israeli Air Force claimed 84 kills for the loss of only three aircraft. Israel's erstwhile enemy Egypt also flies the F-16, with 40 fighters in service and another 40 required. In Asia, Pakistan had taken delivery of the first F-16s of an order for 40, while South Korea's Air Force is scheduled to receive 36.

There have been several modified versions of the basic F-16A, including the F16B two-seater with the second pilot occupying space taken up with fuel on the single-seater. A low-powered variant of the F-16, fitted with the 8165kg (18,000lb) thrust General Electric J79-GE-119, which is on offer for export, while the F-16E fitted with a new double-delta wing is being considered by the USAF as a strike fighter. Other F-16s have been equipped with the 13,155kg (29,000lb) thrust F101 engine and radical new control systems as part of the USAF's advanced fighter technology programme. The F-16's future seems assured and it is likely to rival its predecessor, the F-4 Phantom, in both versatility and length of service.

F-16A Fighting Falcon

Type Multi-role lightweight fighter
Dimensions Span 9.45m (31ft); length 14.52m (47ft 8in); height 5.01m (16ft 5in)
Weight Empty 6613kg (14,567lb); maximum take-off (air superiority mission) 10,570kg (23,000lb)
Powerplant One 1140kg (25,000lb) thrust Pratt & Whitney F-100-200 turbofan with afterburner

Performance Maximum speed at sea level Mach 1.2, or 1472km/h (915mph); maximum speed at 12,190m (40,000ft) Mach 2.05, or 2170km/h (1350mph)
Range Tactical radius with 1360kg (3000lb) 550km (340 miles); ferry range 4020km (2500 miles)
Ceiling Over 15,000m (50,000ft)

Armament One 20mm General Electric M61 rotary cannon and up to 7710kg (15,200lb) of external ordnance, including AIM-9 Sidewinder and AIM-120 AMRAAM missiles, bombs, rockets, ECM pods and air-to-surface missiles

The air forces of the Netherlands (top) and Belgium (above) have ordered the F-16 as part of a programme to replace the ageing Starfighter. Below: The advanced F-16E's extended wing area can dramatically improve the aircraft's fuel capacity, thereby increasing its combat radius.

Attacking the Radfan

British operations in the mountains of South Arabia

The war in the Radfan was probably the last old-style 'colonial' campaign fought by the British Army. It began on 4 January 1964 and active fighting ended by 31 August; but the Radfan continued to be a problem until the British left Aden three years later.

The Radfan is a wild and mountainous region less than 65km (40 miles) from Aden by air but about 115km (70 miles) by road, less than half of which is metalled. By night the lights of Aden can be seen clearly from the summit of Radfan's highest peak, Jebel Huriyah, 1867m (6125 feet), yet the Radfan was unadministered territory visited by only a handful of Europeans. It is a confusion of cliffs, ridges, precipitous *wadis*, and ravines dropping away into bottomless pits, inhabited by several small tribes who scratch a subsistence living from the barren soil. They are fanatical Muslims, resentful of authority.

Under the constant threat of poverty and hunger, the tribes of the Radfan had to rely upon various 'illegal' methods for augmenting their meagre lifestyle. For the Quteibi, the largest tribe in the Radfan, a constant source of wealth was provided by travellers along the Dhala road, which is flanked by the Radfan. This ancient trade route was the main road from Aden into the Yemen and under the guise of collecting tolls from merchants and pilgrims alike, the Quteibi extorted protection payments – their only concession being that all government traffic was exempted. In this way their poverty was, to a degree, alleviated.

With the formation by the South Arabian Federation of a Customs Union in 1962, however, this source of finance was effectively removed as all revenues were now government controlled. The Quteibi strongly resented the loss of what they had always considered their rightful income. Further to this, the tribe's nominal ruler in the Federation, the Amir of Dhala, was apparently milking off a good proportion of the tolls for his own pocket.

When their sheikh, Seif Muqbil, returned from exile in the Egyptian-dominated Yemen, he provided a lead to the tribesmen and civil unrest followed shortly. At first this was merely the resumption of attacks on travellers but soon developed (with the aid of a constant flow of arms from the Yemen) into a nightly fusillade against the Federal Guard fort at Thumier which stood at the entrance to their tribal stronghold, the Wadi Misrah. The Amir demanded action against them and the Federal government asked for the RAF to be used to dissuade the Radfan tribes from their attacks. This was rejected by the British government for fear of international repercussions.

The Commander-in-Chief Middle East Command (Lieutenant-General Sir Charles Harington) then suggested a short, sharp punitive operation by the Federal Regular Army (FRA), an Arab force led by British officers. The High Commissioner in Aden (Sir Kennedy Trevaskis) concurred, but not without misgivings. Harington and Trevaskis were strongly opposed by the Federal ministers of de-

fence and internal security who said the situation would escalate beyond the FRA's ability to control it – the FRA was only 4000 strong – and that it was a mistake to start a war on Aden's doorstep. As Commander of the FRA at the time, I agreed with the Federal ministers, but these objections were overruled. Trevaskis was to admit later that 'in every respect they (the ministers) were proved right'.

As it happened the FRA's campaign, Operation Nutcracker, opened very successfully. Three battalions, supported by J Battery 3rd Royal Horse Artillery (3 RHA), RAF Hunters, Shackletons and Belvedere helicopters from Khormaksar and Wessex helicopters of 815 Naval Air Squadron disembarked from HMS *Centaur*, fought their way

Below: Two Quteibi tribesmen, proudly independent in the mountain fastness of the Radfan, guarding a wadi.

into the Radfan up the Wadi Rabwa and compelled the tribesmen to evict 12 named dissidents who had recently returned from the Yemen. This was the only political aim given to the force commander and it was hard to discern any other worthwhile result from the operation.

All but a few troops were withdrawn by early March 1964, whereupon the Quteibi went back to their old tricks, but this time with a difference. Arms, ammunition and mines had been smuggled down from the Yemen, then itself in the throes of civil war, and with them men trained in their use. Many wore a kind of khaki uniform and owed allegiance to the Egyptian-sponsored National Liberation Front (NLF) which was about to launch a terrorist campaign in Aden itself. With the whole of the Federation to look after, the FRA was overstretched and unable to cope with the rapidly deteriorating situation in the Radfan; but clearly the government's authority had to be restored. Early in April the British Army took over from the FRA and Major-General John Cubbon, General Officer Commanding Middle East Land Forces, was nominated overall commander. Cubbon then deputed Brigadier Louis Hargroves, newly arrived as Commander Aden Brigade, to be the field commander on 14 April. He was told to produce a plan within three days and to be ready to begin operations 11 days later.

Closing in

Initially Hargroves had to organise a field headquarters because Aden Brigade had basic internal security and administrative responsibilities in Aden itself. Through strenuous efforts he cobbled together an operational staff and set up his headquarters at Thumier on the edge of the Radfan. On 17 April he presented to the General Officer Commanding his plan 'to end the operations of the dissidents in the defined area' given to him as the military aim.

Radforce, as it became known, consisted of 45 Commando, Royal Marines, with B company, the 3rd Battalion the Parachute Regiment (3 Para) under command; 1st and 2nd Regiments of the Federal Regular Army (1 and 2 FRA); D squadron, 4th Royal Tank Regiment (4 RTR), equipped with armoured cars; J Battery, 3 RHA; and a Field Troop of the Royal Engineers. The 3rd Troop of the 22nd Special Air Service Regiment (22 SAS) joined just before D-day (30 April) and the 1st East Anglian Regiment (1 East Anglians) on 3 May. Air support was given by RAF Khormaksar. It was a much stronger force than that provided for Operation Nutcracker and the aims of the operation, both political and military, were more clearly defined.

The problems facing the force were formidable – extreme heat, the rugged terrain, shortage of water and lack of reliable information. On 25 April Hargroves set off from Thumier on a reconnaissance accompanied by Brigadier McWilliam, newly-appointed commander of the FRA, and Lieutenant-Colonel Roy Watson who, as officer commanding 2 FRA, had been in the area since January. They had not travelled far before Watson's Land Rover ran over a mine which exploded, killing two senior staff officers, Major Lintott and Major Monk, who were in Watson's vehicle. Watson and his radio operator were wounded, but less seriously. It was an unhappy start to the operations which were to follow.

The direct route into the Radfan was via the Wadi Rabwa. This had been used in Operation Nutcracker

Right above: While his colleague uses a telescope to spot sniper positions, a gunner of the 1st East Anglian Regiment prepares to engage Radfani rebels with a belt-fed 7.62mm GPMG (general-purpose machine gun). Right: A patrol of heavily laden paras pushes on determinedly in the fierce heat of the midday sun while scouring the area for rebels.

Above: A Belvedere helicopter lowers a 105mm medium artillery piece into position for troops urgently in need of artillery support against rebel strongholds.

The Radfan

Wadi Boran · *Danaba basin* · Cap Badge · *Wadi Teym* · *Rabwa Pass* · El Naqil (Pegasus) · *Wadi Rabwa* · *Bakri ridge* · Dhala road · Thumier · *Wadi Misrah* · *Wadi Bulbar* · Jebel Haqla · *Wadi Dhubsan* · to Aden · *Jebel Huriyah*

Sana · Harib · Shabwah · Hodeida · Beihan · WESTERN ADEN PROTECTORATE · YEMEN · Habban · Taiz · *Radfan* · Thumier · RED SEA · Lahej · Aden · GULF OF ADEN

Below: A patrol of the 3rd Battalion the Parachute Regiment, moves cautiously through the Radfan foothills. Note that ammunition for the 7.62mm GPMG is carried by all the troops.

Right: British paras use medium artillery pieces to bombard rebel positions. British ground patrols found it difficult to pursue tribesmen into the mountains, and without support they could easily be pinned down.

and therefore Hargroves discarded it; the tribesmen would be on the alert. Instead he chose the Wadi Boran a few miles to the north, passable only by men on foot but undefended. It led into the fertile Dabana basin, well populated by Radfan standards, which led in turn into the Wadi Teym. Hargroves' intention was to dominate the area which meant capturing the high feature overlooking the Dabana basin, code-named Cap Badge. The plan was for the Marines to move by night on 30 April up the Wadi Boran to secure the entrances to the Dabana basin by dawn on 1 May. Meanwhile B Company 3 Para would be dropped at midnight on 30 April close to Cap Badge to capture it by dawn. Their drop zone was to be marked by a patrol from 22 SAS who were landed just before nightfall on 29 April by helicopters some distance from the Dabana basin. Unfortunately the SAS, who had to lie up during daylight on 30 April, were spotted by a shepherd. There followed a fierce fight that lasted all day long. The enemy were well armed and very determined. Only the RAF could provide the SAS with support and this they did superbly; but Captain Edwards, the patrol commander, decided to withdraw after dark. He was killed, as was his radio operator, Sapper Warburton, whose radio was damaged. The rest of the patrol got back safely but the parachute drop was cancelled.

The fight for Cap Badge

B Company 3 Para, waiting in Aden to emplane, were rushed up to Thumier in trucks to reinforce the Marines who had caught the enemy off guard – a diversionary attack up the Wadi Rabwa on 30 April having misled them as intended. The Marines were then moved forward with the object of taking Cap Badge, with 1 East Anglians (brought up from Aden) relieving them on the high ground captured on 1 May. The Marines made good progress but the paras ran into trouble near a village on the lower slopes of Cap Badge. They were soon fighting for their lives and the battle continued all day. Out of range of their own guns B Company was dependent on the RAF Hunters who were magnificent, rocketing and machine-gunning within 140m (150 yards) of the forward troops.

It was 1500 hours, however, before the enemy withdrew, mainly because the Marines, by then securely established on Cap Badge, were able to outflank them. The paras had put up a splendid fight for 10 hours after a gruelling approach march lasting 11 hours, in burning heat with little water. Only the Company Sergeant Major had been in action before. They lost two killed and six wounded and the village (El Naqil) they had fought so hard to take was named Pegasus Village in their honour.

Hargroves was now established in the Radfan and by 5 May was patrolling down to the Wadi Teym. But it was clear that more troops would be needed to deal with the main massif, as well as a properly constituted headquarters to control the battle. Headquarters 39th Infantry Brigade were accordingly flown out from Northern Ireland and Brigadier 'Monkey' Blacker took over from Hargroves on 11 May. This meant there had been no less than three different field commanders since the campaign began.

Above: A typical supply dump in the Radfan countryside; the lack of suitable roadways and the consequent logistical problems were overcome by such supply centres. Above right: A lance-corporal and private of the FRA manning a forward observation post. Right: The commander of the FRA, Brigadier Lunt, talking to a Rabbizi tribesman. Below: One method of patrolling the terrain was by camel. Here, British soldiers move through the Wadi Teym in the Radfan mountains in December 1964. Although most units had already withdrawn some remained to keep the peace.

by 3 Para against the steep-edged Bakri Ridge on 18 May, portering ammunition and supplies because helicopters were not available. There was some stiff fighting along the way but eventually the paras achieved all their objectives. An advance up the Wadi Misrah on 19 April was less successful because the force had to be withdrawn after a cloud burst. By 27 May, largely due to the thrust of 3 Para and excellent air support, Blacker was firmly established in the heart of the Radfan. It now remained to deal with the Quteibi in their stronghold deep in the Wadi Misrah.

The task was given to 1 East Anglians, supported by the 2 FRA and D Squadron, 4 RTR. The objective was Jebel Huriyah, from the base of which the Wadi Misrah wound through beetling cliffs for nearly 16km (10 miles). The conditions were appalling. The East Anglians were to picquet the south side of the wadi and 2 FRA the north side. The advance was slow, due as much to the terrain as to the opposition, but there was a particularly stiff battle on 7 June when 2 FRA distinguished themselves. This proved to be the Quteibis' last fling – although this was not realised until the final assault on Jebel Huriyah took place during darkness on 10 June. By dawn the East Anglians were on the summit without opposition and at 0600 hours the regimental flags were flying proudly from the mountain peak. This, to all intents and purposes, marked the end of active operations in the Radfan and on 14 June Brigadier C. Blair arrived to take over from Brigadier Blacker.

It was Blair's task to consolidate the victory which he set about doing with vigour. But the situation in Aden and elsewhere in the Federation was fast deteriorating and this led to a rapid reduction in Blair's force. By 24 August most of the troops had been withdrawn and the Radfan continued to be a problem until the British withdrawal from Aden two and a half years later. Whether this withdrawal was hastened by the decision to intervene in the Radfan in the first place is hard to assess but it was certainly a campaign which might just as easily have not been fought. For the troops who participated it provided excellent training, particularly in mountain warfare and cooperation with the RAF. Very valuable lessons were also learned about the use of helicopters in support of ground troops, until that date rarely practised, and the tribes were certainly taught a lesson, mercifully with relatively few casualties on either side. **James Lunt**

Meanwhile General Cubbon had been involved in an unpleasant incident with newsmen and politicians. On 3 May he had stated that the heads of the two killed SAS men had been exhibited on stakes in the Yemen. This caused a furore in parliament and the press. Needless to say, it was denied by the Yemen and Cubbon was taken to task for talking out of turn. But on 13 May an FRA patrol discovered two headless bodies which were identified as Captain Edwards and Sapper Warburton. It was also established that it was Yemen Radio that had announced the decapitation in the first place. The General Officer Commanding and his staff were vindicated, the Secretary of State for Defence apologising publicly in the Commons, but it left a sour taste in the mouths of the troops taking part in the operations.

Penetrating the Radfan
Blacker's force was gradually built up until at its strongest it contained no less than seven infantry battalions, almost two armoured car squadrons (4 RTR and the Federal Regular Army), J Battery 3 RHA (who had been there since the beginning) and a section of medium artillery (5.5in) from 170 Battery, 7th Royal Horse Artillery. There was also a troop of Centurion tanks from the 16th/5th Queen's Royal Lancers. Helicopter support was also augmented by eight Wessex's from HMS *Centaur*. Blacker was now poised to penetrate deep into the Radfan where the enemy was still resisting strongly. The attack was led

The divided island

Greek against Turk in Cyprus of the 1960s

After four years of violent upheaval, Cyprus gained independence from Britain on 16 August 1960. The independence agreements, to which the British, Greek and Turkish governments were a party, displayed all the hallmarks of compromise. To allay Turkish Cypriot fears that the Greek Cypriot majority might try to achieve their ambition of Enosis (union of Cyprus with Greece), the constitution specifically stated that there should be no union of Cyprus with any other state. Partition was also explicitly ruled out in deference to Greek Cypriot fears that Turkish Cypriots might want to divide the island. Britain, Greece and Turkey retained the right to intervene in Cypriot affairs, jointly or singly, to guarantee the constitution and the independence of the new republic.

Britain kept its sovereignty over two Sovereign Base Areas – at Akrotiri and Dhekelia in the south of the island – where British forces remained in place. Greece also exercised her right to have 950 troops stationed on the island, and Turkey stationed 650 troops there too.

The most difficult problem encountered by the negotiators had been the detailed creation of a constitution which would overcome the deep-seated hatred and fear between the country's 78 per cent of Greek Cypriots and 18 per cent of Turkish Cypriots. Power was to be shared between the two communities to protect the Turkish minority against excessive Greek Cypriot domination. The president was to be a Greek Cypriot elected by Greek Cypriots and the vice-president a Turkish Cypriot elected by Turkish Cypriots. The council of ministers and the house of representatives were similarly divided. At each level of government the Turkish Cypriots had a right of veto on major issues, and thus the system could only work

if there was inter-communal trust and goodwill.

The civil service and the police force were also to be appointed on a quota system, with 70 per cent Greek Cypriot and 30 per cent Turkish Cypriot personnel, as was the army with 60 per cent Greek Cypriot and 40 per cent Turkish Cypriot recruitment. This over-representation of Turkish Cypriots was resented by Greek Cypriots. In the five main towns of Nicosia, Famagusta, Limassol, Larnaca and Paphos, the Turkish Cypriots were given control of local government in Turkish areas and the Greek Cypriots in Greek areas. This provision caused considerable difficulty since it enabled the two communities to continue to build up their own exclusive identities.

Murder and massacre

At first, most Cypriots were prepared to see whether the new arrangements could be made to work. Archbishop Makarios, the undisputed leader of Cypriot independence, was elected president by the Greek Cypriots, and Dr Fazil Kütchük became vice-president unopposed. But difficulties soon accumulated, as differences between Greeks and Turks reduced the administration to stalemate. Many provisions of the constitution were never fully implemented. Makarios was mistrusted by the Turks and, on the other side, was accused by some Greeks of betraying the cause of Enosis. Through 1962 and 1963, both communities began stockpiling weapons, ready for confrontation.

On 30 November 1963, Makarios proposed 13 constitutional amendments, particularly attacking the Turkish Cypriot right of veto. Many Turkish Cypriots believed that his intention was the establishment of Greek Cypriot domination, which might ultimately lead to Enosis. Makarios' proposals would

Above left: From well protected positions, Turkish rebels cover a possible Greek advance. The man in the foreground is armed with a double-barrelled shotgun while the man to his left holds a bolt-action Lee Enfield. Above right: The bloody result of a typical sectarian killing. Two Turkish Cypriots lie dead in the hallway of their home as relatives stand aghast.

Inset right: General George Grivas (right) observes Turkish positions from a bunker. Right: A Greek patrol boat comes under fire from four Turkish Super Sabre aircraft. After a 20-minute attack the Greek crew, all seriously wounded, managed to ground the burning vessel.

have left the Turks with little or no right of appeal against Greek Cypriot government. On 21 December, the murder of two Turkish Cypriots heralded an outbreak of violence in Nicosia which spread rapidly across the whole island.

The Greek Cypriots were superior in numbers and in preparation. Operating in groups of about 100 irregulars, mostly members of the old EOKA organisation which had fought the British, and often led by armed policemen, they attacked Turkish Cypriot districts with great ferocity. Turks were gunned down in their homes and hundreds of hostages taken. Towns and villages were quickly partitioned as Turkish Cypriots barricaded themselves into their own areas. Turkish Cypriot counter-attacks also inflicted heavy loss of life and property on their enemies. In a matter of days, several hundred people had been killed and the bi-partisan administration of the island had broken down.

As vandalism, murder and reprisal attacks took their toll, there were urgent moves to organise an intervention to restore order by the British, Turkish and Greek troops stationed on the island. On 26 December, a British battalion under the command of Major-General Peter Young moved out of the Sovereign Base Area and into the Republic. The British established a presence between the two communities to keep them apart. In Nicosia the division of the city, which was intended to be temporary, became a permanent ceasefire line known as the Green Line.

Although Greek and Turkish liaison officers were appointed to the British force, their troops did not join in the operation. Indeed, Turkish troops had already intervened in support of the Turkish Cypriots, occupying positions which controlled the southern end of the Nicosia-Kyrenia road. Possession of this road would ensure any Turkish invasion force landed on the north coast of Cyprus immediate access to Nicosia. It was fear of a possible invasion by the Turks – fighters from the Turkish mainland flew low over Nicosia on Christmas Day – which largely motivated Makarios' acceptance of the British intervention to stop the fighting.

In early 1964 Makarios agreed to a ceasefire under the supervision of the British peace force, and on 15 February 1964 a conference in London brought together representatives from Britain, Greece and Turkey, as well as President Makarios who by now represented an all-Greek Cypriot government, since the Turkish Cypriots had withdrawn their participation. The conference was a failure, but Britain took the opportunity to make it quite clear that she did not wish to continue her peacekeeping role in Cyprus. The possibility of a Nato peacekeeping force was

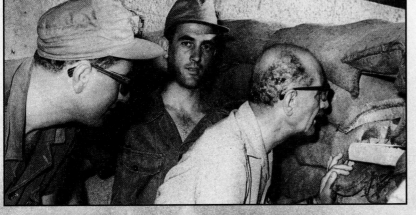

Problems of peacekeeping

'The story of how the Greeks launched their land attack last week and how the United Nations mission collapsed, at least for the time being, was told to me today by Colonel Jonas Waern, commanding the Swedish contingent, and Major Allan Olsson, one of his company commanders. Though they did not intend it, their vivid account was proof of the unwelcome fact that a United Nations peacekeeping force is in the last resort powerless unless it is willing to inflict and incur bloodshed.

'Both officers emphasised that the Greeks had made a planned attack.... The first signal of attack was firing at the shore by two patrol boats. "We did not get a warning," Colonel Waern said. "They promised they would warn us of any attack – they promised they would not attack at all.

"I went to try to get their plan and intentions and speak about agreements. At each place they said no one responsible was around. Not the commander, not an officer – no one.

"It was hide and seek – just hide and seek. We were blocked at Pomos by armoured cars. A police sergeant stopped me personally.

"Our men must have cooperation. I cannot work if they are blocked or shot at. I think we had a regiment of angels protecting us. We will always try to stop fighting, but in the situation of the last week you must try to concentrate your men and try to save their lives."'

Report in The Times, *11 August 1964*

Above: A Greek Orthodox priest stands on a Nicosia street corner, double-barrelled shotgun in hand. Religion and history – the long-term enmity between Christian Greeks and Muslim Turks – fuelled the bitterness of the civil war in Cyprus.

subsequently mooted, but Makarios would only consider a United Nations intervention, and so it was agreed that Britain should approach the UN Security Council.

In the meantime, the situation on the island had deteriorated. February saw renewed outbreaks of violence. Greek Cypriot attacks drove the Turkish Cypriots from key positions in Limassol after heavy fighting. As well as effective military operations of this kind, designed to improve their tactical situation, the Greek Cypriots carried out punitive raids on vulnerable Turkish communities. In some cases, Turkish Cypriots provoked attacks in the hope of forcing military intervention from the Turkish mainland and achieving partition of the island. The 5000 British troops repeatedly came under fire, chiefly from the Greek side. Supplies from mainland Turkey were smuggled into the country as Greek Cypriots imposed an economic blockade on Turkish Cypriot areas.

UN involvement

On 4 March 1964 the Security Council adopted a resolution which authorised the creation of UN-FICYP – the United Nations Peacekeeping Force in Cyprus. Strictly, the UN should not have got involved in what was a domestic conflict, but it did so at the request of the Cypriot government and under circumstances in which international peace and security might well have been threatened because of the close interest of Greece and Turkey in Cypriot affairs. UNFICYP was the first peacekeeping force to include a contingent from a member of the Security Council, since the British troops on the island took part in the UNFICYP force. As the British ran their numbers down to 2700 troops, and later 1000, reinforcements came in from Canada, and later from Australia, Austria, Denmark, Finland, Ireland and Sweden. At its peak UNFICYP reached a strength of 7000 men. The force first became operational on 27 March 1964. By June it was up to strength and had been sup-

plemented by 170 unarmed civilian police, known as UNCIVPOL, contributed by Australia, Austria, Denmark, New Zealand and Sweden.

The multi-national force was deployed as a series of national contingents, only truly integrated at headquarters level. Spread throughout Cyprus, UNFICYP was reasonably successful in reducing the level of inter-communal violence. It could effectively counter minor clashes and talk-down many local incidents, although it could not prevent more determined attacks. The UN also fulfilled a humanitarian role by helping the movement of supplies to the Turkish Cypriots who were cut off by the Greek Cypriot economic blockade, and by operating convoys to ensure the safe passage of Turkish or Greek Cypriots through hostile areas. UNFICYP was fortunate in having the British Sovereign Base Areas to provide logistic support. The mobility of the force enabled it to move in quickly when trouble threatened and prevent the escalation of incidents.

The UN also provided the mechanism through which the two sides could talk to one another. The UN Secretary-General, U Thant, first appointed Ambassador Tuomioja from Finland to act as mediator. After Tuomioja's death, Galo Plaza, a former president of Ecuador, took his place. But neither man had any success in producing a compromise between the two communities.

Despite the UN presence, both Greek and Turkish Cypriots continued to accumulate arms and expand their fighting forces. Both Turkish and Greek army officers from the mainland were involved on their respective sides. In June 1964 the Greek Cypriots introduced conscription to increase their numbers, and in August the former EOKA leader General George Grivas took over command of the Greek Cypriot National Guard. In that month the Greek Cypriots launched major attacks on Turkish villages

in the northern coastal area, advancing on Kokkina, which was reputedly the centre for arms smuggling from Turkey to the Turkish Cypriot irregulars. Mansoura fell to the Greek Cypriots and it seemed that Kokkina must be overrun. But on 9 August the Turkish Air Force launched extensive bombing raids on Greek Cypriot targets, reportedly using napalm. This intervention halted the Greek Cypriot advance and put an end to major fighting for three years.

From 1964 onwards both Greek Cypriots and Turkish Cypriots in effect controlled their own areas and the two communities defended these areas with their own armed forces, the Turkish Cypriot Freedom Fighters and the Greek Cypriot National Guard. The division of towns and villages produced 'ghettos' defended by the community forces with UNFICYP interposing itself whenever violence threatened. As a police force UNFICYP functioned well, but it could not effectively contribute to a long-term political solution.

In 1967 the tense stalemate once more rose to a crisis. On 15 November, the Greek Cypriots launched an assault on the Turkish Freedom Fighters' strategic stronghold of Kophinou which resulted in the gutting of numerous homes. In response to the new flare-up, the Turkish government began preparations for war. Only intense diplomatic activity and concessions by Makarios's government – including the removal of Grivas from the island – averted an invasion.

From 1967 it was clear to everyone that a new situation had emerged. The Turks had demonstrated that they were ready and able to invade Cyprus if Greek Cypriot extremists got the upper hand. Therefore the outcome hinged on Makarios's ability to keep control over his own side. When he finally lost the struggle against Greek Cypriot extremists in 1974, the Turkish invasion and the partition of the island which the Greeks had always feared swiftly came to pass. **David Johnson**

Above: While his friend covers him from a doorway, a Turkish irregular dashes forward along a street to take up a new position. He carries a sub-machine gun and two spare magazines in his left hand.

Below: A Ferret scout car moves through the streets of Kophinou, by-passing a civilian casualty, in pursuit of Greek Cypriot terrorists who have just launched an attack.

Soldiers of peace

UN peacekeeping and observer missions

The Charter of the United Nations, signed in San Francisco in June 1945, was dedicated primarily to preserving peace in the world. By 1983 this was still the most important function of the UN despite the fact that by then it had diverse interests in a whole range of international issues and problems. The record of the UN as a force for peace is mixed: UN forces have contributed widely to the preservation of peace, but the UN itself has failed to take action in many situations where such forces might have been deployed. Sadly, the ideological and political considerations of member states have often conspired to make the UN powerless.

Under Chapter Seven of the Charter the UN can initiate collective enforcement action to deal with threats to international peace and security. Such action was taken in 1950 when military enforcement measures were introduced during the Korean War. Sixteen nations sent troops to Korea when the South Korean government claimed that it was the victim of North Korean aggression. South Korea survived as a result, but the UN was unable to find a solution to the problem that had caused the conflict. After hostilities ended in 1953, the UN retained a presence in South Korea and has done so ever since. This was the only occasion when the UN implemented collective military enforcement measures, but collective economic measures were taken under Chapter Seven of the Charter to instigate international economic sanctions against Rhodesia in 1966 and to impose an arms ban on South Africa in 1977. Theoretically compulsory, these measures secured only minimal success since some nations ignored them, and there was little that the UN could do to force member states to comply with UN resolutions.

The UN can also authorise peacekeeping measures under Chapter Six of the Charter but only with the consent of the governments involved. They also officially have control of the stationing of the force and its composition. International agreement in the

UN has been more forthcoming in this area than in that of enforcement action, and numerous peacekeeping forces and military observer missions have been created since 1945. The aim of UN peacekeeping is to help bring about a cessation of hostilities and to prevent their recurrence, thus contributing to a normalisation of relations between the states in dispute. Peacekeeping forces are composed of contingents of armed troops made available by member states to serve under the light-blue beret that the UN has adopted. In theory, the value of the UN presence in this respect lies in the impartiality of the force, which enables the UN to gain the confidence of both sides in a dispute. Peacekeeping forces are normally tasked to use force only in self-defence and as a last resort, and only exceptionally, as in the Congo operation in the early 1960s, has a peacekeeping force moved on to the offensive. By far the most common activities for peacekeeping forces are persuasion, observation, fact-finding, patrolling, and the prevention of the escalation of violence by controlling incidents that occur. Their role is often, therefore, that of an international fire brigade and police force at the same time.

Peacekeeping worldwide

Since 1945, peacekeeping forces have served in the Middle East (United Nations Emergency Force, UNEF I, 1956-67; UNEF II, 1973-79; United Nations Interim Force in Lebanon, UNIFIL, 1978 – present day); the Congo (Force de l'Organisation des Nations Unies au Congo, ONUC, 1960-64); and Cyprus (United Nations Peacekeeping Force in Cyprus, UNFICYP, 1964 – present day).

There have been many problems for UN

Left: Norwegian troops of the UN contingent in Lebanon wearing flak jackets and armed with standard 7.62mm Nato G3 semi-automatic rifles, hold a forward observation post. Below: UN troops move up a road in Lebanon in 1978 adopting the classic staggered file formation.

Left: Two soldiers of the United Nations Emergency Force during a motor patrol in the Gaza Strip in 1957.

peacekeeping forces. On many occasions they have suffered from a lack of clear operational guidelines from UN Headquarters, although this has sometimes been turned to the advantage of commanders in the field, giving them greater flexibility and the opportunity to judge situations on the spot – as in the Congo. The mandates of the forces have often been vague and contradictory. Problems have also arisen from the complexities of the command, control and organisation of a multi-national force – including difficulties over language, diet, training, operational concept, equipment, acclimatisation and impartiality. Logistic back-up has sometimes been difficult; it was good in Cyprus, largely due to the presence of British bases on the island and to the relatively small geographical area of operations; in the Congo it was correspondingly poor.

Most of the problems encountered are in fact the result of the UN having no standing forces of its own and the consequent requirement for the Secretary-General to raise *ad hoc* multi-national forces at short notice, and with little or no prior planning or organisation. The cost of peacekeeping operations has inevitably been high, especially since they have often continued for longer periods of time than originally anticipated. The cost falls on the UN itself, although this burden is reduced by those states contributing forces paying their own personnel and by the big powers contributing finance and sometimes logistic support too, although many states in the UN are in arrears in their payments for peacekeeping operations. In general, however, the peacekeeping forces have operated remarkably smoothly and have overcome these difficulties through experience, adaptability and patience.

Unarmed observers

In addition to peacekeeping forces, the UN has also created military observer missions. These forces are usually unarmed and are interposed between disputants when a ceasefire has already been established. Their purpose, therefore, is to watch, patrol and report violations in the hope that the presence of UN officers will be a deterrent to the resumption of hostilities. Observer missions have operated in the Middle East (United Nations Truce Supervision Organisation, UNTSO, 1949 – present day; United Nations Disengagement Observer Force, UNDOF, 1974 – present day) and in Kashmir (United Nations Military Observer Group in India and Pakistan, UNMOGIP, 1948 – present day). Provisional arrangements have also been made for a new UN force to go to Namibia in the event of a South African withdrawal from that country. The United Nations Transitional Assistance Group for Namibia: (UNTAG) was only in the planning stage in 1983 and the operational use of UNTAG will depend upon future developments in Southern Africa.

Enforcement and peacekeeping together represent the UN in action, with the use of armed forces in the service of international peace and security, and as such they attract the attention of world opinion. The UN operations to date have been a success given their fairly narrow aims and operational limits. It should not be forgotten, however, that many of the successes of the UN have been achieved in the fields of diplomacy and economics, and that these have also contributed significantly to peace, stability and prosperity.

David Johnson

Tools of the trade

Infantry company weapons

In any modern army, the infantry remains the basic fighting arm, and since World War II the proliferation of small wars and guerrilla struggles has proved the need for a versatile, flexible, well armed infantryman. Those armies which have placed most emphasis upon armour – such as the Israeli Defence Force during the 1960s – later found to their cost that armour without infantry support can be terribly vulnerable to modern anti-tank weapons. A major role of today's infantry unit is to support armoured advance and exploit any field successes in their offensive role, while in a defensive role they may be required to delay or destroy any enemy armoured advance allowing their own armour to exploit a possible enemy retreat. Both roles are based upon the ability of a single well-armed soldier to pack plenty of firepower while still remaining a diminutive target. But in addition to this role on the full-scale battlefield, the infantryman can fight in jungle against guerrillas, or in city streets against urban terrorists. And to fulfil these different roles, the infantry units need adaptable weapons.

The basic tactical infantry unit in most armies is the company, of about 120 men. In the British Army, companies are organised into battalions. Generally speaking a battalion is formed of four to five infantry companies (depending upon whether the battalion is mechanised or wheeled); a company of from three to four platoons; and a platoon of from three to four sections (usually a section will comprise eight men).

In order fully to grasp the levels to which the modern British infantry company is armed it is best to begin with the infantry section. This eight-man unit, usually commanded by either a corporal or a sergeant, comprises a driver, five riflemen armed with the standard British Army 7.62mm self-loading rifle (SLR) – one of whom will also man the radio and another of whom acts as the number two on the General Purpose Machine Gun (GPMG). Further to these, the second-in-command of the section (usually a lance-corporal), operates the GPMG, and another soldier carries the 84mm L14A1 Carl Gustav anti-tank gun. Ammunition for the GPMG is carried by the number two gunner.

At company level there is an extra headquarters section with more radios, a fire support section with an extra GPMG and a company mortar section which may in the future carry the 51mm Light Mortar. At battalion level, the mechanised battalion (mechanised battalions are based on the FV432 armoured personnel carrier (APC) whereas wheeled battalions move by Land Rover) will include two extra support weapons platoons. These two platoons are usually four-section platoons, one of which will carry two 81mm mortars per section while the other will carry either two Wombat 120mm guns per section or more usually four Milan firing units per section. Thus from battalion level down, the infantry unit of today's army is extremely well-equipped.

Despite the increasing tendency towards mechanised army units, the value of the infantryman and the assorted weapons he can carry is priceless. The basic weapons of the infantryman remain the rifle and the machine gun. To date, the 7.62mm SLR remains the standard British Army weapon, although the conflicting requirements for range, accuracy, lethality, volume of fire, maintenance, weight, and interchangeability between ammunition and parts, have led to moves to replace it.

The SLR 7.62mm L1A1 is the British version of the Belgian FN FAL and has included such variations as the removal of the automatic fire operation. This weapon is well thought of among infantry since replacing the Rifle No.4 Mk1 as the army's standard service rifle. Using a gas-operated return system for the breech-block, the weapon is easily maintained in the field and is a highly-dependable rifle not noted for a liability to jam under combat conditions. When fully loaded with a magazine of 20 rounds, the rifle weighs approximately 5kg (11lbs). Although the maximum effective range of the SLR is noted as being 600m, this is a capability of the weapon that remains largely unused as a rifleman will rarely be able to pick out a target with any considerable accuracy beyond a range of 300m. The rate of fire at 40rpm is generally considered inadequate. Apart from this, Nato has recognised that 7.62mm is an unnecessarily large calibre for a standard smallarm (the standard US smallarm, the M16, is a 5.56mm calibre weapon) and the move for a smaller calibre weapon led to the development of the 5.56mm Individual Weapon (IW) XL70E3. Although not yet in service, this new IW will have considerable advantages over its predecessor. Much shorter than an SLR and calibred to a Nato standard 5.56mm, the weapon will be compact enough to be easily carried in the confined spaces of an APC or helicopter.

Close-quarter fighting

Although generally not recognised as an infantryman's weapon, the 9mm L2A3 Sterling sub-machine gun deserves mention in that it is particularly robust and has proved its effectiveness in close-quarter fighting. This is a straightforward blowback-operated weapon with a single-shot or automatic capability, usually carrying a 30-round magazine (the actual capacity of the magazine is 34 rounds but 30 rounds is a standard fill). It has a cyclic rate of fire of 550rpm, although in real terms this will probably approach not more than 120rpm. The main limitation of the weapon is found in its range: its maximum effective range is only 200m and its combat range is standardised at only 100m. This weapon is generally used by tank crews, artillerymen and second-line support services. The US Army does not carry any equivalent weapon, as the M16 rifle has an automatic facility discharging some 150-200rpm (practically not cyclically).

In support of any infantry assault, the General Purpose Machine Gun (7.62mm) L7A2 provides effective and sustained fire. In the infantry unit the GPMG is used in two roles, either 'light' or SF (sustained fire). In its light role the GPMG is mounted with a spring-released bipod – thus allowing the infantryman to provide accurate supporting fire, but also allowing him to move position quickly, preventing enemy units from locating and eliminating him. At least, this is the theory; however, the weapon is in fact far too awkward and heavy to allow the comfort and mobility which have been a feature of more recent weapons designs. The GPMG is converted from its light role (where the bipod is used) to its SF role by the addition of a dial sight, a tripod mount and a heavy-duty barrel. Generally three such kits are held by each rifle company. The main drawback of the GPMG in its SF role is that it lacks high fire volume and the barrels are prone to overheat very quickly (the US equivalent, the M60, is built to withstand a firing rate of 250rpm but for not more than three minutes at a time). This of course not only makes the weapon

Far left: British troops, carrying their 7.62mm SLRs and full '58 pattern webbing, march through soaking conditions during an exercise on Salisbury Plain. Left: A mortar team prepares to fire an 81mm mortar. This weapon has a maximum range of 5800m, and is a weapon that an infantry unit could expect in immediate support.

Left: Night firing exercises in Cyprus in 1963. Note the converted Nato 7.62mm Bren gun (furthest from camera) which has since been replaced by the 7.62mm GPMG, able to operate in both light and heavy machine gun roles. Although the Bren gun has been in service for many years with the British Army and was a popular weapon, its slow cyclic rate of fire and the inconvenience of a box magazine eventually led to its replacement.

dangerous to fire but also severely inhibits its accuracy. It has a maximum effective range of 800m in its light role and 1800m in its SF role. Ammunition is found in 100-round belts; there is no facility for magazine loading. Despite these drawbacks, the GPMG has remained the standard army weapon. Research and development are in progress on the 5.56mm Light Support Weapon XL73E2, but if this weapon enters service it will only act as an addition to overall firepower, not as a replacement for the GPMG.

The claim has been made, and not without evidence, that during World War II mortar fire accounted for more than 50 per cent of all land force casualties. Indeed, although the evolution of the mortar appears to be thoroughly pedestrian (the basic design has varied little), it still remains extremely effective against troops in the open. One of the two mortars usually carried by British infantry units is the 51mm Mortar L9A1 (the actual calibre is 51.25mm) which is replacing the 2-in mortar. This weapon has been designed to be carried and operated by one man, with a complete weight, less ammunition, of only 6.3kg (14 lbs). The 51mm mortar not only has a good battlefield range of some 750m but can also be adapted for close-combat situations by restricting the range to only 50m – this is achieved by the insertion of a sleeve into the main barrel which allows the gases to expand more than usual when a round is fired. As well as using smoke and illumination rounds, the weapon can fire a High Explosive (HE) round with serrated case interior which, upon detonation, produces a large number of steel segments that are murderously effective against troops. The other mortar common to the British infantry unit is the Ordnance Muzzle-Loading 81mm L16A1. This weapon is relatively heavy at 36.7kg (80lbs) but has the advantage of a maximum range of 5650m which can be extended to 5800m using HE L31E3 rounds. This weapon is normally carried mounted on an adapted FV432 but may be mounted on a Land Rover or even, at its most basic, may be broken down into three man-pack loads. The HE rounds used are still under development, but the L15A3 HE round has a ductile cast-iron shell ensuring that over 40 per cent of the casing shatters to provide lethal fragments upon detonation.

Rockets and missiles

The development of anti-tank weapons has taken an increasingly important role in modern warfare. Infantry-manned anti-tank rockets and missiles, where deployed intelligently as part of a combined-arms operation, are easily capable of blunting the heaviest of armoured attacks. The two most common to the British infantry are the 84mm L14A1 Gun or Carl Gustav and the Milan. The Carl Gustav is basically a shoulder-fixed semi-automatically guided (i.e. the gunner merely maintains sight contact with the target up to impact) recoilless gun. Although it can be fired by a single man, two men usually make up the gun team with one loading and the other aiming and firing. Using a HEAT round, this weapon can penetrate up to 228mm (9ins) of armour and has an anti-tank range of 400m mobile and 500m static. It weighs only 16kg (35lbs) complete. As well as being man-portable, this weapon can be fired from a vehicle though the back-blast, which is substantial, suggests that an open-top vehicle would be necessary.

The Milan, a second-generation infantry anti-tank

system, is easy to transport, has a rapid launch preparation time, a semi-automatic infra-red guidance system and a high-probability hit rate at up to 2000m. At a tube-loaded-and-ready-to-fire weight of only 11.5kg (25lbs) the weapon is truly a one-man system, yet as with all such weapons, one or two others will complete the weapon team by carrying extra ammunition. Milan also has a good armour-penetration capability up to 352mm (13.9ins) although the Soviet equivalent, the Sagger, weighs 11.3kg (25lbs) and has a maximum range of 3000m and an armour-penetration cability of 400mm (15.8ins).

This combination of weapons gives the infantry company the ability to take on the variety of tasks it may face: from confronting tanks to flushing out guerrillas. And it means that even in the nuclear age the individual soldier is still of great importance.

Alexander McNair-Wilson

Above: A gun team of the Royal Irish Rangers prepare to fire their 7.62mm GPMG while a spotter is ready to call out range and hits. Note the optic sight on this weapon, an unusual feature for a weapon that normally mounts fixed sights.

Below: Two infantrymen in NBC protective clothing using a Carl Gustav anti-tank weapon during an exercise on Salisbury Plain. The Carl Gustav has a maximum range of 500m.

Key Weapons

SOVIET SPGs

The idea of mounting a field artillery piece onto a caterpillar-tracked chassis saw fruition during World War II. The great advantages of the SPG (self-propelled gun) over conventionally-towed artillery were, firstly, its far greater mobility which allowed it to accompany the forward deployment of armour and be at hand to bombard centres of enemy resistance with minimal delay, and secondly, the degree of protection offered to the SPG crew, enabling the artillerymen to operate in hostile environments, immune from smallarms fire and deadly shell splinters.

Since World War II the primacy of the tank as the single most important tactical element on the battlefield has not altered – despite the emergence of sophisticated anti-tank weapons – but it has been realised that to be successful the tank has to operate as part of an all-arms team including artillery. The advent of NBC (nuclear, biological and chemical) warfare and the ever-increasing mobility of modern armies has ensured that the SPG's importance has increased progressively since 1945, a fact acknowledged by the number of SPG types in service with the armies of both Nato and the Warsaw Pact.

Although an SPG looks similar to a tank it has never been expected to fulfil that role; far cheaper to produce than the heavy, well-armoured tank, the SPG is essentially a forward-operating artillery piece, although the lightweight assault gun is designed to operate as a cost-efficient tank-killer.

While the Soviet Union has not developed the range of SPGs available to Nato – and until recently relied extensively on conventional artillery – the first

Russian SPGs emerged during World War II as a means of disrupting the German Panzer formations and supporting the Soviet T-34 offensives. The SU-122/152 series, which first saw combat in 1943, was an effective amalgam of the KV heavy tank chassis and a 122mm or 152mm gun. Towards the end of the war the KV chassis was discarded in favour of IS (Josef Stalin) chassis, and redesignated ISU-122/152. This SPG remained in Soviet Army service until the early 1970s.

The Soviet ability to utilise a tank chassis for SPG mounts ensured that the highly successful T-34 would be likewise employed. Armed first with a 76mm gun

Previous page: The business end of an ASU-85 assault gun. Top: ASU-85s parade through Moscow as part of a public demonstration of the Soviet Union's military strength. Above: An ISU-122 crosses the River Spree by pontoon bridge during the closing stages of World War II.

The SAU-152 on parade (below) and in the field (left). Despite its formidable appearance the SAU-152 – like other SPGs – lacks any real armour protection and would be no match for a tank in close combat.

but soon uprated with an 85mm main armament, the SU-85 medium SPG was deployed as a direct support weapon for T-34 tank formations. Towards the end of the war the SU-85 was further uprated to take the 100mm M-1944 gun and redesignated the SU-100; its high-velocity gun proved capable of dealing with the German Panther and Tiger tanks, being able to fire armour-piercing rounds, and an HE round up to 19,200m (21,000yds). In its capacity as the standard armoured support gun in the Soviet Army it was only replaced in front-line usage in 1957, and as an export success to the Warsaw Pact and pro-Soviet Arab nations it remains in service to the present day. Even as late as 1973 both Egypt and Syria were deploying SU-100 battalions with their armoured and infantry divisions, although obsolescent in face of the latest Israeli armour and anti-tank weapons.

Despite the Soviet Army's interest in SPGs, little development work in this field was carried out in the postwar years, the army apparently being content with their existing models. It was only in the 1970s that a new generation of SPGs came into service, which today form the basis of Soviet self-propelled artillery.

The 20-tonne SAU-122 or M-1974 was first observed at a military parade in Warsaw in July 1974, and consists of a modified 122mm D-30 howitzer mounted in a rotating turret upon an MT-LB chassis.

Above left: The heavy weight of the SAU-152's main gun necessitates an asymmetrical arrangement of road wheels to provide extra support for the turret. Right: A unit of SAU-152s maintains strict formation during a Soviet parade. Below: The high-velocity gun of the ASU-85.

Left: One of the most effective elements within the Soviet Union's artillery forces are the SAU-122 SPGs, shown here taking a salute.

Embodying a number of features to be found on the PT-76 amphibious tank, it is fitted with seven rubber-clad road wheels with Christie-type torsion-bar suspension and two hydraulic dampers to provide a suspension system capable of traversing rough terrain. Two track widths are available, the broader of the two for movement across soft ground. The 240bhp diesel engine provides a maximum road speed of 60km/h (37mph) and affords some degree of frontal protection to the four-man crew. The driver sits forward at the front left-hand side of the SPG while the commander, gunner and loader are situated within the turret. In keeping with its PT-76 ancestry the SAU-122 has an amphibious capability and its boat-shaped hull facilitates the crossing of water obstacles, which by means of track propulsion can be traversed at a rate

of 4.5km/h (3mph).

The main armament has a fume extractor and is fitted with a double-baffle muzzle brake. Some 40 rounds of ammunition are carried and by employing a semi-automatic breech a rate-of-fire of five rounds per minute can be achieved. Ammunition types include HE and HEAT and it is reported that the SAU-122 can also fire an RAP (rocket assisted projectile) to a range of 22km (14 miles).

The SAU-152 or M-1973 SP howitzer entered service in 1973-74 and like its smaller counterpart has a turret-mounted main gun. The chassis, however, is based on that which carries the SA-4 Ganef SAM

Above right: A side-view of an SAU-122 reveals the clean lines of this SPG. Right: An ASU-57 is loaded onto a pallet ready for air transportation within the An-22 in the background. The ASU-57 can be para-dropped by utilising cluster parachutes. Below: ASU-85s drive off to an assembly point after having been landed by An-22 transport plane.

(surface-to-air missile) and as a consequence lacks the amphibious capability of the SAU-122. Due to the considerable weight of the modified 152mm D-20 gun/howitzer the six road wheels are asymmetrically positioned in order to provide greater support for the turret. The 500bhp diesel engine enables the 24-tonne vehicle to travel at 50km/h (31mph). The crew configuration is similar to the SAU-122 although an extra member can be carried. Ammunition capacity is 40 rounds and in addition to HE and APHE rounds it is thought that an HE/RAP round can be fired, capable of a highly impressive range of 37km (23 miles). In addition the SAU-152 has a nuclear capability and can fire a 0.2 kiloton-yield nuclear round.

Both SAU guns have standard NBC systems and although they possess only limited armour protection, their mobility and speed of deployment and redeployment (about one-fifth of the time of conventional guns) will considerably increase their chances of battlefield survival.

The SAU-122 SPG is designed to replace the D-30 towed howitzer, and the SAU-152 to replace the D-1 towed howitzer, as well as forming an SPG battalion within the Soviet tank division. Organised into six-gun batteries the Soviet SPGs operate either at battery or regimental level (three batteries) with front-line manoeuvre units. The high degree of low-level SPG/armoured unit integration contrasts strongly with Nato practice, in that each battalion commander has his own individual artillery support, although because of the overall rigidity of the Soviet artillery system other adjoining units within range cannot call upon another unit's artillery support. While the SAU-122 SPGs are deployed at manoeuvre level, often in a direct-fire role, the SAU-152s tend to be held back at

SOVIET SPGs

SAU-122
Crew 4
Weight 20,000kg (44,100lb)
Performance Maximum road speed 60km/h (37mph); range (road) 500km (310 miles)
Armament One 122mm D-30 howitzer, HE range 15,000m (16,700yds)

SAU-152
Crew 3-5
Weight 24,000kg (52,900lb)
Performance Maximum road speed 50km/h (31mph); range (road) 300km (186 miles)
Armament One 152mm D-20 howitzer, HE range 24,000m (26,250yds)

ASU-57
Crew 3
Weight 3450kg (7600lb)
Performance Maximum road speed 45km/h (28mph); range (road) 250km (155 miles)
Armament One 57mm Ch-51 anti-tank gun, HE range 6000m (6560yds)

ASU-85
Crew 4
Weight 14,000kg (30,900lb)
Performance Maximum road speed 44km/h (27mph); range (road) 260km (162 miles)
Armament One 85mm M-44 gun, HE range 15,300m (16,700yds)

Above: An ASU-57 depicted in winter conditions.

Below: These Western photographs of an ASU-57 reveal the rather primitive nature of its construction; and its small 57mm gun can have only limited use on today's battlefield.

regimental or divisional level in an indirect over-fire role.

In 1980 a new self-propelled heavy artillery piece was reported to be in service with front-line units; possessing a long-barrelled 203mm gun, it is thought to have a nuclear capability. Like the SAU SPGs it has been employed in Afghanistan, although details of the weapon are as yet unavailable.

The Soviet airborne forces have their own self-propelled guns, specifically designed for air-portability. The ASU-57 was introduced in 1957. Mounting a 57mm Ch-51 anti-tank gun, it was designed to be as weight effective as possible. The ASU-57 weighs under four tonnes and can be air-dropped from the Antonov An-12 transport aircraft, pallet-mounted with cluster parachutes and retro-rockets which are fired when the pallet hits the ground to provide an acceptably soft landing. The major weaknesses of the ASU-57 are that its 57mm gun is ineffective against modern armour and its own minimal armour makes it vulnerable even to infantry support weapons.

Altogether more effective is the ASU-85 which, while employing the PT-76 chassis, dispenses with its amphibious capability. The 85mm gun is effective against light armour and its own thicker armour provides more effective protection for paratroop units, which because of their airborne weight restrictions are woefully short of effective artillery support weapons. The increased weight of 14 tonnes means that the ASU-85 cannot be para-dropped but nevertheless is air-transportable. Each Soviet airborne division fields 18 ASU-85s and since their introduction in 1961 they have seen service in Prague in 1968 and more recently in Afghanistan.

Since the introduction of the SAU series in the early 1970s the Soviet Army's commitment to replacing its conventional towed artillery with SPGs has begun to gather momentum. Before the 1970s only a small proportion of the Soviet Union's vast artillery forces was mounted on tracked vehicles. In 1978, 17 per cent of Soviet artillery in front-line positions in Europe was self-propelled and by the early 1980s it was estimated that the proportion could be as high as 40 per cent. Clearly, in the light of these dramatic advances, the importance of Soviet self-propelled guns will steadily increase especially as they meet the modern requirement of mobility and firepower.

Winds of change

Independence for black Africa

In 1945 the map of Africa was a colonial patchwork in which the pink of the British Empire and the blue of the French predominated. There were only four independent countries in the continent. Three of these – Egypt, Liberia and Ethiopia – were still subject to considerable colonial influence. The fourth country was South Africa, ruled by a white minority which allowed the black majority even less political rights than did some of the colonial regimes further north.

The lines of the colonial map had been drawn up in the 19th century as a consequence of the scattered initiatives of adventurers or missionaries and piecemeal bargaining around international conference tables. Where Africans resisted the imperial advance, repression was brutal. Most of the continent proved unsuitable for white settlement; the European presence comprised a motley of soldiers, administrators, missionaries and businessmen. Where European settlers established themselves – notably South Africa, Kenya, Rhodesia, Algeria, and later Angola and Mozambique – a more complex relation grew up between the colonial power, local whites, and the original natives.

With few exceptions, resistance to colonial rule died out quickly. Africans submitted to second-class status in their own lands; even when subjected to forced labour or obliged to watch while their best land was given to white settlers or used for large-scale plantations, they suffered with resignation. The more obvious benefits of Western civilisation, such as medicine, improved communications and a modest level of education spread slowly through the continent. The white administrators were buoyed up by the notion of a civilising mission – which assumed, naturally, the fundamental inferiority of black Africans, often spoken of as if they were children to be encouraged, protected from themselves, and if necessary disciplined. Even in 1945, at the end of a war fought for freedom and democracy, there were few who thought that black Africans might achieve, or even desire, self-government for many years to come.

Yet a new generation of African nationalists, dedicated precisely to the principle of 'Africa for the Africans', was already active in the 1940s. The leaders of this African nationalism were beneficiaries of the colonial powers' limited extension of Western education to blacks. Such figures as Kwame Nkrumah from the Gold Coast, Jomo Kenyatta from Kenya, Léopold Senghor and Félix Houphouët-Boigny from French West Africa, were inspired by

Below: The end of an era as, on 17 April 1980, in the presence of Prince Charles, Zimbabwe became independent and the Union Jack was lowered for the last time in Africa. Zimbabwe's independence came only after bitter armed struggle – unlike the peaceful handover in Britain's other African colonies two decades earlier.

the Western concepts of self-determination and equality of opportunity. They were men of great personal ambition, but also pursued high ideals of liberation for all of Africa. A highly sophisticated, elitist poet and philosopher like Senghor – who discoursed on the inherent values of *négritude* (blackness) as opposed to white culture, but did so in brilliant French – could claim little contact with the mass of Africans, rural or urban, but the ability to meet the colonial powers on their own intellectual and political ground proved a valuable weapon.

The existence of the black elite in which nationalism grew was not an accident. It was a product of the colonial 'civilising mission'. The French, the Belgians and the Portuguese all shared the notion of

creating black 'imitations' of themselves, people who would be certified – more or less formally – to have passed from the status of uncivilised native to that of black European. The British never operated quite such a system, but the effect of their education policies was much the same. The prospect was one of long-term change in which, eventually, the Africans would be fit to replace colonial administrators, colonial army officers, colonial doctors and missionaries. The formation of this elite proceeded at a different pace in different parts of the continent – relatively quickly in West Africa, disastrously slowly in the Belgian Congo – but everywhere it brought the same problem: the newly privileged guests at the feast of Western civilisation wanted more than they were offered, and they wanted it more quickly.

The more sophisticated colonial authorities saw that the leaders who had emerged must be turned into allies, even groomed for the eventual replacement of their masters. In 1951, Nkrumah was elected to form a government in the Gold Coast with limited powers: the colonial authorities released him from prison to take up office. In the neighbouring French Ivory Coast, Houphouët-Boigny was elected as a deputy to the French parliament in Paris (all French colonies were represented in Paris) and by the early 1950s had actually become a minister in the French government, the first black to feature in a European cabinet. Léopold Senghor achieved the same status later.

Times were changing, not only in Africa but in the

The powerful tide of African nationalism brought to prominence a generation of forceful leaders, such as Joshua Nkomo (far left) in Rhodesia, Jomo Kenyatta (left) in Kenya and Julius Nyerere (right) in Tanzania. Some of these nationalists, like Kenyatta and Nyerere, established durable regimes but more typical was the fate of Ghana's Kwame Nkrumah, overthrown by a military coup in 1966, his grandiose statue (below) defaced and forgotten.

wider world. The growing preponderance of the US in the Western alliance favoured African nationalism, because the Americans were opposed to the continuance of the old empires. After the Suez debacle, in which US opposition to British and French intervention in Africa was crucial, both the major colonial powers were weakened. France had met with military defeat in Indochina in 1954 and the outbreak of a guerrilla war in Algeria, her most important colony. Britain had withdrawn from Libya in 1951. In 1956 she withdrew from Anglo-Egyptian Sudan, and in the same year France left Tunisia and Morocco. Colonialism was losing its credibility. The advantages of granting independence were becoming obvious: it would save vast sums of money spent on administering the colonies; it would avoid possibly embarrassing and costly colonial wars; and it would ward off international criticism from the United Nations, the Third World and the Americans, calling for national liberation. The problem posed was how to maintain control of the situation after independence.

Although left-wing politicians had been prominent in anti-colonial agitation in Britain and France, it fell to right-of-centre governments in both countries to set off the wave of decolonisation in black Africa. Prime Minister Harold Macmillan and President Charles de Gaulle determined separately on a policy of swift withdrawal. In March 1957 the Gold Coast became independent as Ghana, with Nkrumah as head of the new state. Coming to power in France in 1958, de Gaulle pushed forward a referendum in French West Africa and French Equatorial Africa: the population was asked to choose between full independence at once or independence 'in association with France' in the near future. Only one country, Guinea, under the influence of a former trade union leader and radical nationalist Sékou Touré, chose full independence. In October 1958 the French withdrew from Guinea totally, cutting off all economic aid, destroying military equipment and not leaving behind even essential technical staff. Guinea's economy was severely disrupted, but under Sékou Touré the country survived.

An end to colonialism

For most of France's other African colonies, independence came in 1960 – no less than 14 French-ruled countries received their independence in that year, from Mauritania on the Atlantic coast to the island of Madagascar in the Indian Ocean. The process was smoothly accomplished. The new states were tied closely to France by a series of financial and military agreements. After Harold Macmillan's famous 'wind of change' speech in February 1960 heralded withdrawal, the British proceeded at a slightly less precipitous rate but none the less surely. Independence came to Nigeria and Somalia (the latter combining the former Italian and British colonies) in 1960, Sierra Leone and Tanganyika in 1961, Uganda in 1962, Kenya and the island of Zanzibar (the latter soon to join with Tanganyika as Tanzania) in 1963, and Malawi (formerly Nyasaland) and Zambia (formerly Northern Rhodesia) in 1964. The other smaller fry followed in the subsequent years, but there was one major failure: the decolonisation of Southern Rhodesia did not follow in sequence. The white settler population, backed by neighbouring South

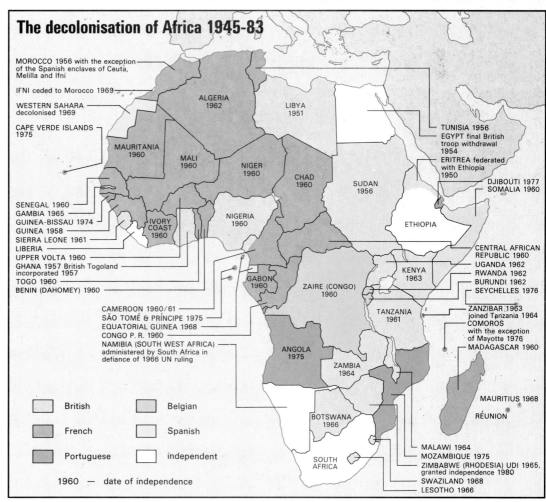

The decolonisation of Africa 1945-83

MOROCCO 1956 with the exception of the Spanish enclaves of Ceuta, Melilla and Ifni
IFNI ceded to Morocco 1969
WESTERN SAHARA decolonised 1969
CAPE VERDE ISLANDS 1975
MAURITANIA 1960
ALGERIA 1962
LIBYA 1951
MALI 1960
NIGER 1960
CHAD 1960
SUDAN 1956
TUNISIA 1956
EGYPT final British troop withdrawal 1954
ERITREA federated with Ethiopia 1950
DJIBOUTI 1977
SOMALIA 1960
SENEGAL 1960
GAMBIA 1965
GUINEA-BISSAU 1974
GUINEA 1958
SIERRA LEONE 1961
LIBERIA
UPPER VOLTA 1960
GHANA 1957 British Togoland incorporated 1957
TOGO 1960
BENIN (DAHOMEY) 1960
IVORY COAST 1960
NIGERIA 1960
ETHIOPIA
CENTRAL AFRICAN REPUBLIC 1960
UGANDA 1962
RWANDA 1962
BURUNDI 1962
SEYCHELLES 1976
KENYA 1963
GABON 1960
ZAIRE (CONGO) 1960
CAMEROON 1960/61
SÃO TOMÉ & PRÍNCIPE 1975
EQUATORIAL GUINEA 1968
CONGO P. R. 1960
NAMIBIA (SOUTH WEST AFRICA) administered by South Africa in defiance of 1966 UN ruling
TANZANIA 1961
ZANZIBAR 1963 joined Tanzania 1964
COMOROS with the exception of Mayotte 1976
MADAGASCAR 1960
ANGOLA 1975
ZAMBIA 1964
MAURITIUS 1968
RÉUNION
BOTSWANA 1966
SOUTH AFRICA
MALAWI 1964
MOZAMBIQUE 1975
ZIMBABWE (RHODESIA) UDI 1965, granted independence 1980
SWAZILAND 1968
LESOTHO 1966

British
French
Portuguese
Belgian
Spanish
independent

1960 — date of independence

YOU BLIND AMERICAN, PORTUGAL, SOUTH AFRICA, RHODESIA WITH YOUR GOVERMENTS THE SIN YOU HAVE COMMITTED IS VERY GREAT WE SHALL NEVER FORGET

In newly-independent Tanzania demonstrators show their hostility to white domination (left), but before independence cheerful crowds greeted a royal tour (below) and black police units under British officers (bottom) put down nationalist demonstrations by their fellow Africans.

Africa, would not allow the British to install a black majority regime. By a Unilateral Declaration of Independence (UDI) in 1965 the white government of Ian Smith pre-empted British efforts and effectively ended the colonial regime; Britain protested but did nothing. Britain's links with its other ex-colonies were less explicit and formal than France's, but in most ways equally close.

Under the influence of British and French withdrawal, the Belgians made the disastrous decision to pull out of the ill-prepared Congo (now Zaire) in June 1960. The result was all that the most pessimistic commentators on African independence had foreseen: the breakdown of central administration, secession of provinces, tribal warfare and foreign intervention. Yet this was not the experience of the British and French colonies; whatever problems might lie ahead, the transfer of power was carried out in remarkable calm and good order. The contrast with the Belgian Congo shows what had been achieved by planning, cooperation, and the proper grooming of a local elite to take up the reins of authority.

The new leaders of independent Africa were in many cases men of real political and moral stature – as well as those already mentioned, there was Kenneth Kaunda in Zambia, Julius Nyerere in Tanzania, Modibo Keita in Mali, Sylvanus Olympio in Togo. For all their faults, these and other figures who had emerged

as the leaders of nationalism during the period of legitimate political activity allowed by the colonialists in the build-up to independence, were reasonably honest and intelligent. But their regimes quickly ran into insuperable difficulties. Without exception they were drawn from the elite, and although their leadership often evoked popular enthusiasm, they were cut off from the mass of Africans. The rule of the elite was insecure and soon became corrupt. The economic problems of the poorest continent in the world were beyond their power to tackle – indeed, direct influence from European interests and indirect influence from the world economy left them powerless.

To the more radical leaders, such as Nkrumah, Sékou Touré, or Modibo Keita, it appeared that only if Africans acted together could they have any power to solve their economic problems and influence inter-

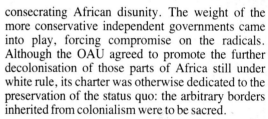

Above: Independent in name, African governments have repeatedly called on the former colonial powers to shore up their authority. Here a French para captures insurgents in Kolwezi in 1978 during a combined French and Belgian intervention in Zaire.

national events. The independent states were mostly too small and weak to defend themselves or avoid economic dependence on the West. In the early years of independence there were abortive attempts at mergers: between Mali and Senegal, between Ghana and Guinea, and between Guinea, Ghana and Mali. Nkrumah even proposed the creation of an international military force by African states to give them the power to defend themselves. In 1963 the Organization of African Unity (OAU) was formed, but it soon became clear that it was to be more of an organisation for consecrating African disunity. The weight of the more conservative independent governments came into play, forcing compromise on the radicals. Although the OAU agreed to promote the further decolonisation of those parts of Africa still under white rule, its charter was otherwise dedicated to the preservation of the status quo: the arbitrary borders inherited from colonialism were to be sacred.

Tribal rivalry

These colonial boundaries which defined the new states enclosed varied tribes speaking different languages, whose traditional rivalries had often been exacerbated by colonial policy. A leader like Kenyatta might aspire to national leadership, but his regime easily slipped into patronage of the leader's own tribe, the Kikuyu. As the difficulties of creating a sense of nationhood mounted, the new governments found themselves in peril. Where political parties were identified with tribal interests, the ideal of democracy foundered.

Many people came to doubt the wisdom of the rapid decolonisation which had taken place. Certainly, no high ideals were realised. The poorest continent in the world, Africa did not get richer. Most of its governments swiftly deteriorated: there were one-party states, military regimes, a few grotesque tyrannies. Some of the national leaders, such as Kenyatta and Nyerere, were forced to call on the armies of the ex-colonial powers to defend them; others, like Nkrumah, were overthrown to the joyous applause of the people they had claimed to liberate. But the fate of the Portuguese colonies and of Rhodesia, where the logic of decolonisation had not been accepted, shows what might well have happened elsewhere: prolonged guerrilla war and the eventual emergence of black governments less amenable to Western influence. Sooner or later the colonialists would have had to heed Nkrumah's plea, to leave the Africans to make their own mistakes. **R. G. Grant**

The Shifta War

Somali nationalism and nomad resentment

The nomadic Somali tribes have roamed the Horn of Africa since ancient times, leading a frugal existence in those barren lands. During the colonial period, the Somalis came under the rule of the British, French, Italians and Ethiopians. Their territory had no clear boundaries, and when the prospect of decolonisation arose, the borders of an independent Somalia were hard to establish. The republic that emerged in 1960 did not include the largely Somali-populated areas of the Ogaden (controlled by Ethiopia) and northeastern Kenya.

In 1962, when Kenya was still under British rule, a fact-finding commission was sent to northern Kenya and duly reported that the majority of the population wished to join Somalia; Britain ignored these findings. As Kenya approached independence, fixed for December 1963, Somalia stepped up its claims to the three northeastern provinces of Mandera, Wajir and Garissa. From an economic point of view the 170,000 square km (65,000 square miles) in dispute were of little value. Mandera is a region of barren, rocky mountains; Wajir and Garissa are expanses of desert where camel thorn is the only vegetation. But the nomadic tribes that roamed the area were mostly of Muslim Somali extraction.

In November 1963 the first raids by armed Somali nomads, labelled Shiftas (bandits), were reported. Their activities increased in December and by January 1964 five Kenyans, three of them policemen, had been killed and 32 wounded. In response to these acts of violence, Kenya's President Jomo Kenyatta declared a state of emergency, but effective counter-measures were slow to get under way.

Kenya's army consisted of units of the old King's African Rifles. It later grew to divisional strength with an armoured regiment and small all-purpose air force, but in 1964 it was reckoned that a bare brigade group, three infantry battalions each of three companies, was ready to take the field. There was another problem. Although 'Africanisation' was under way, Major-General Freeland was still the commanding officer and most of the senior posts were still occupied by whites. For many blacks this remaining trace of colonialism was intolerable and there were mutinies in January 1964.

Promising that African control would be complete by the end of the year – and with the help of men of the 3rd Royal Horse Artillery – Kenyatta was able to crush the mutineers, but such teething troubles could well have had a disastrous effect on the campaign in the northeast. However, the Somalis were unwilling to commit their national army, leaving the fighting entirely to the Shiftas who showed themselves incapable of organising on even a semi-regular basis.

Operations were inevitably on a small scale and, because of the vastness of the country, fluid in the extreme. Keys to success were the ability to control the wells, at the same time outpacing and outmanoeuvring the enemy. As both sides were utterly dependent on water, there was no recourse to that ultimate horror of desert warfare, the poisoning of the wells. The Kenyans were fortunate in being able to count on support from a small air force of transport and spotter planes. This meant that although the Shiftas did not have to contend with the threat of the helicopter gunship or the fighter bomber, they could

Top: Somali chiefs, one armed with a sword, meet at Wajir in Kenya's Northern Frontier district to discuss the impending Kenyan independence and Britain's refusal to recognise their demands to join Somalia. Above: While the problems were merely discussed at higher levels, the feelings of the people were expressed in vociferous and violent protest. Here a unit of Kenya 'riot squad' police control Somali demonstrators.

be tracked down with comparative ease since the camel thorn which restricted ground observation provided little cover from the air.

By mid-March 1964 the Kenya command had worked out a specific plan of campaign. To preserve maximum mobility, the company was the largest single tactical unit employed – a wise move considering the enormous distances to be covered chasing an enemy preferring to stick to proverbial 'tip and run' methods. According to one white officer retained after 'Africanisation' on President Kenyatta's orders, no encounter featured more than 100 men on either side. At the end of the day some 10 dead might be counted, and perhaps 20 to 30 wounded. The clashes were nonetheless ferocious. It was very much a question of 'woe to the vanquished', no prisoners being taken.

An elusive enemy

As the war progressed, the Shiftas learnt not to stand their ground for long when cornered. Their objective was not so much to destroy their better-equipped enemy – though they themselves were well armed with light automatic weapons of Eastern bloc origin – but rather to harry and wear down, hoping probably that in the end the Kenyan government would come to the conclusion that so much effort and money, and so many lives, being spent to retain stretches of basically hostile, unproductive, barren territory was not worthwhile. Confirming this unwillingness to 'stand up and fight', an officer reported that on more than one occasion he had seen Shiftas throwing grenades when a good two hundred yards still separated them from their attackers, prior to taking to their heels. In fact, from the Kenyan point of view, the greatest danger arose from the Shiftas' use of Czech land mines on the few inferior roads and tracks crossing the deserts, which inflicted heavy material damage and surprisingly high casualties.

The Kenyans retaliated against the Somali nomads by confiscating their herds of cattle and camels and marching the livestock off to be sold at some distant market. On one such punitive raid, herds totalling some 10,000 head were seized. The first night the Kenyans were camped by a well having penned the animals in a thorn zariba, when the camp was attacked by Shiftas who broke down the zariba and stampeded the herds. Many of the sleeping Kenyans could well have been trampled to death, had not one individual had the presence of mind to let off a number of flares. This provoked an even greater panic among the terrified animals, which turned about in a counter-stampede, scattering the attackers.

On much the same pattern the desultory campaign dragged on until late 1968 when the dispute was brought before the Organization of African Unity (OAU) with President Nyerere acting as mediator. Perhaps a little surprisingly the outcome was a triumph for Kenya; all frontiers, whatever the origin of their imposition, were to remain unchanged.

To discourage further secessionism, the Kenyan government launched an all-out attack on the nomads' way of life. They decreed that all nomads should regroup within a 50-mile (80km) radius of designated 'centres' in the three provinces, where they would be forced to adopt a semi-sedentary pattern of existence. Draconian penalties were applied to any nomads who failed to comply. Kenya had won its Shifta war. **Patrick Turnbull**

Above: Shiftas, the Somali nomad fighters of northern Kenya, surrender their arms (including a Thompson sub-machine gun, right) to Kenyan Security Forces in 1967 after President Kenyatta had offered amnesties to the rebels. As well as this inducement to surrender, the Kenyan government launched a programme of nomad re-settlement.

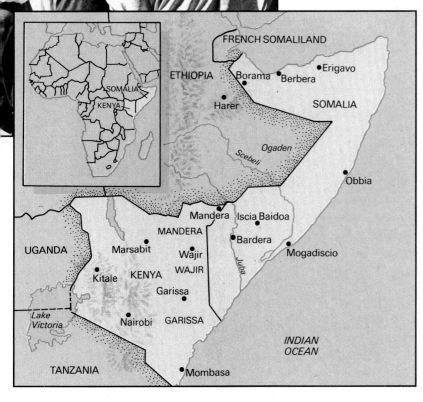

African involvement

British operations in the early 1960s

Above: British troops, armed with 7.62mm SLRs, man a barbed wire roadblock in Zanzibar. The British had withdrawn from Zanzibar by 10 December 1963 when the island achieved independence – though they almost returned in early 1964 after a violent coup seemingly threatened the remaining British community.

Between September 1960 and January 1964 Britain mounted military operations in five African territories – the Cameroons, Swaziland, Tanganyika, Uganda and Kenya. The nature of these operations varied from peacekeeping to intervention, but in each case the British units involved were able to fulfil their mission efficiently, successfully and with minimum loss of life. Indeed, on the British side no fatalities were incurred.

The operations were carried out against a political backdrop of rapid African decolonisation, heralded by Harold Macmillan's celebrated Cape Town speech of 3 February 1960. Referring to the rise of African nationalism, Macmillan declared that a 'wind of change' was blowing through the African continent and warned his hosts, the members of the South African parliament, that Britain would be revising its policies accordingly.

It soon became evident that Macmillan was not merely indulging in rhetoric. Within the year the British government had granted independence to Britain's most populous African colony, Nigeria. By 1965 Britain had withdrawn from most of Africa. This rapid withdrawal had a profound effect on the British Army. It was spared the unenviable task of suppressing African nationalism by force – having been promised independence, African nationalist leaders had no incentive to promote conflict against the colonial authorities. But this did not mean that the

British armed forces had no role to perform. They found it necessary to mount a series of operations during the early and mid-1960s in order to cover the withdrawal.

The first of these operations took place in the British-administered United Nations trust territory of the Cameroons and began in September 1960. The purpose of the operation was to keep the peace until the constitutional status of the territory had been settled by plebiscite. The plebiscite was duly held in February 1961. The results indicated that the people of the North Cameroons wished to join the neighbouring state of Nigeria, while the people of the South Cameroons wished to join the adjacent Republic of Cameroon (formerly a French trust territory). These wishes were granted on 1 June 1961 and 1 October 1961 respectively. In the meanwhile, order had been maintained in the plebiscite areas by the 1st Battalion the King's Own Royal Border Regiment, between September 1960 and May 1961, and by the 1st Battalion the Grenadier Guards between May and October 1961.

A second operation, carried out in 1963, involved the despatch of British troops to the High Commission territory of Swaziland, the so-called 'jewel of Africa'. The purpose of this operation was to deal with internal unrest. The trouble had started on 20 May 1963 when some 1400 African workers at the Havelock asbestos mine near the capital, Mbabane, went on strike for better pay and conditions. By early June, the situation had deteriorated. Nationalist elements, hoping to capitalise upon the unrest, called for a general strike on 10 June to back up their demand for immediate independence. As a result some 3000 men demonstrated in the capital and clashed with police. Two days later, over 1000 workers at an important sugar plantation went on strike. At this juncture, the British government placed their troops based in Kenya on alert. On the following day, 13 June 1963, the 1st Battalion the Gordon Highlanders was airlifted into Swaziland by RAF Beverley and Argosy transport aircraft. With the help of the troops, the police were able to restore order swiftly and effectively. By 20 June 1963 the country had returned to normal and the Gordons were able to depart.

Putting down the mutinies

Seven months later, British forces were back on active service in another part of the continent – east Africa – carrying out more or less simultaneous operations in Tanganyika (now Tanzania), Uganda and Kenya. On this occasion, the circumstances were rather different. Whereas the Cameroons and Swaziland operations had been executed in territories still administered by Britain, the east African operations took place in independent states recently freed from British rule. Moreover, the east African operations had a different purpose. Whereas British troops had been called on to keep the peace in the Cameroons and restore order in Swaziland, their task in east Africa was to put down mutinies by the armies of the fledgling states. These interventions were potentially hazardous, because in each case the mutinous forces were several hundred strong and well armed.

The mutinies were preceded by a revolution in the island of Zanzibar, which had become independent from Britain on 10 December 1963. Violence erupted, and amidst scenes of considerable carnage,

Above: A wounded Tanganyikan Army sergeant is carried from a helicopter aboard HMS *Centaur* after the mutiny. Below: Gordon Highlanders question Swazi warriors. Below right: Sheikh Mohammed Shamte Hamadi signs the agreement for Zanzibar's independence, watched by British Colonial Secretary Duncan Sandys.

the Sultan of Zanzibar, Seyyid Jamshid bin-Abdullah and his prime minister, Sheikh Mohammed Shamte Hamadi, were overthrown on 12 January 1964; power was seized by radical republicans. The Hamadi government, with no army and only a small police force at its disposal, had asked Britain to come to its aid but the British government, fearing that the Sultan had already lost control of the situation, refused to help directly. It did, however, take military action of a sort. Because the safety of the British community on Zanzibar looked to be in jeopardy, the frigate HMS *Rhyl*, with a company of men from the 1st Battalion the Staffordshire Regiment on board, was ordered to sail from Mombasa (Kenya) and wait off the coast of Zanzibar for a possible evacuation of British subjects. Also standing by was the survey ship HMS *Owen* and the fleet auxiliary *Hebe*. In the event, the precautions proved unnecessary. The danger to British lives subsided, a fragile calm returned to the island and the Sultan and his prime minister escaped by sea to Tanganyika and thence by air to England.

Within days of this revolution, mutinies broke out

in the armies of Tanganyika, Uganda and Kenya. The basic causes of the mutinies appear to have been professional: the African soldiers involved in the revolts wanted an improvement in their pay and conditions of service and resented the fact that senior positions were still held by British officers. Whether the mutinies were connected or not is unclear, but the pattern of events was the same. Army units went out of control and the governments of Tanganyika, Uganda and Kenya had to call upon the former colonial power, Britain, to quell the rebellions.

The first of the three east African states to be affected was Tanganyika. On 20 January 1964 soldiers of the 1st Tanganyika Rifles based at Colito near the capital, Dar-es-Salaam, revolted against their officers and detained some 30 British officers and NCOs. The mutineers, joined the following day by men of the 2nd Battalion at Tabora, went on to seize the airport and enter the capital, where they arrested among others the acting British High Commissioner. A new commander of the Tanganyikan Army, Elijah Kavana, was appointed by the rebels in place of Brigadier Sholto Douglas.

British lives in danger

These developments naturally caused alarm in Britain, particularly when the safety of several thousand British subjects in Dar-es-Salaam seemed to be threatened. On 20 January, therefore, the British government ordered HMS *Rhyl* to move from Zanzibar to the waters off Dar-es-Salaam. At the same time the aircraft carrier HMS *Centaur* with men of 45 Royal Marine Commando aboard, and with a complement of 21 aircraft, left Aden and made for the same destination. As it happened, these forces were not immediately needed. British lives were not endangered, the acting High Commissioner was released and the officers and NCOs of the 1st and 2nd Battalions of the Tanganyika Rifles, together with their families, were allowed to leave for Nairobi (Kenya). Nevertheless, by 24 January the Marines were in action. For on that day, Tanganyika's president, Julius Nyerere, formally appealed to Britain to intervene.

The action taken was short and sharp. *Centaur* had arrived off Dar-es-Salaam on 24 January and that evening Brigadier Douglas, who had been in hiding, was taken back to the carrier to discuss plans. In the early hours of the next morning, Douglas, together with a company of Marines, was put down by helicopter near to the mutineers' barracks. The Marines seized the entrance to the barracks and Douglas called on the rebels to surrender. When they refused, the Marines fired off an anti-tank rocket and destroyed the front of the guard room. This demonstration of firepower had the desired effect and the mutineers decided to give up the fight. Three of their colleagues had been killed, six or so wounded and the rest surrendered. Thus the barracks were captured without a single casualty being incurred on the British side. It fell to the other companies of 45 Commando to round up those mutineers still roaming the streets of Dar-es-Salaam.

In the meantime, Uganda and Kenya had also been affected. In Uganda, which had become independent on 9 October 1962, the troublespot was Jinja, where the 1st Uganda Rifles, plus elements of a newly created 2nd Battalion, were based. On 23 January 1964 several hundred Ugandan soldiers mutinied.

Above: Soldiers of the 2nd Battalion, the Scots Guards man a machine gun post overlooking Entebbe airport during the Ugandan military revolt of 23 January 1964 when Britain came to the aid of the Ugandan government after Premier Milton Obote had appealed for help. While the Scots Guards held Entebbe, the 1st Battalion, the Staffordshire Regiment was making rapid progress to Jinja where a daring initiative brought the revolt to a close.

They took control of the armoury and British officers and NCOs were forced to take refuge in the orderly room of the barracks. Milton Obote, the Ugandan prime minister, asked the British government for assistance. Britain immediately acceded to this request and that same day some 450 men of the 1st Battalion the Staffordshire Regiment and the 2nd Battalion the Scots Guards were flown by Beverley transport aircraft from Nairobi to Entebbe, where they were placed under the command of Colonel Tillett, the commander of both battalions of the Ugandan Army. The Scots Guards were left to hold the aerodrome at Entebbe, while the Staffords, who had managed to acquire a number of vehicles, drove the 110km (70 miles) to Jinja. Having been met *en route* and advised by two British officers who had broken out of the camp, the Staffords decided to drive straight into the camp and take the mutineers by surprise. This they did in the early hours of 25 January. As dawn broke, the rebels found themselves

Above: Well-armed Royal Marines march a group of captured rebels along a roadway in Tanganyika in January 1964. The prompt British intervention was a very small-scale exercise in military terms, but it probably prevented the fall of the government of Julius Nyerere.

Top right: Gunners of the 3rd Regiment, Royal Horse Artillery prepare to move against mutineers of the 11th Kenya Rifles at the base camp at Lanet in Kenya during late January 1964. The mutineers put up little resistance to the well-armed and organised British force.

surrounded by the bayonets of the travel-weary Staffordshire Regiment and had no other recourse but to surrender without a fight.

While all this was happening, Kenya was also in the throes of a crisis. Here the troubles began at Lanet, where some 250 men of the 11th Kenya Rifles were based. Disturbances at the base on 23 January led to a request for assistance from the Kenyan government. On the evening of 23 January, a battery of men from the 3rd Royal Horse Artillery (RHA), based some 35km (20 miles) away at Gilgil, were ordered to the area of Lanet. The following day, the gunners reconnoitred the camp and established radio contact with British personnel inside. That evening, some 75 men of the RHA drove into the camp, captured the guardroom, the armoury (though many of the weapons had already been removed), the ammunition magazine, the officers' mess and the telephone exchange, but were unable to overcome the rebels completely. Just over an hour later reinforcements – more gunners, as

well as some sappers and Gordon Highlanders – arrived.

After holding his position overnight, the British commanding officer attempted to get the mutineers to surrender. Lengthy negotiations took place on 25 January and the rebels eventually decided to give in, but only on condition that they be disarmed by African officers. As the British troops pulled back, however, some of the mutineers tried to regain possession of their weapons while others who had not yet been disarmed attempted to break out of the camp. This attempt failed, but some of the mutineers did manage to regain control of the armoury. Their success was short-lived. The gunners attacked the armoury, entering the building at great speed. The defenders, taken by surprise, surrendered. For the third time within the space of 48 hours, British troops had quelled a mutiny and saved a Commonwealth government from possible collapse, without losing a single man.

Francis Toase

939

MUTINY!

Collective indiscipline or combat refusal?

Mutiny is an emotive word and there is frequently a reluctance either to use the term at all or to admit that mutiny has occurred. In World War I the French High Command referred to the open mutiny affecting 40,000 men in 68 divisions as 'collective indiscipline'. When a mutiny occurred in the 5th (Indian) Native Infantry at Singapore in February 1915 one British politician described it as more 'of the nature of a regimental riot than of anything which could possibly be described as a mutiny'. Even more obscurely the Singapore authorities spoke of an *emeute*, which somehow did not convey the essence of a mutiny that left 39 Europeans dead and resulted in the public execution of 37 mutineers. The mutiny of over 1500 troops of the Canadian 15th Infantry Brigade at the Terrace camp in British Columbia in November 1944 (over government repudiation of earlier promises on conscription) was similarly called an 'incident'.

In Vietnam, mutinies were generally described by the euphemism 'combat refusals'. Figures given by Senator Stinnis in 1971 revealed 68 such combat refusals in seven US combat divisions in Vietnam during 1968 and 35 cases alone in the US 1st Air Cavalry Division in 1970; it has been estimated that there might have been at least 245 combat refusals in Vietnam in the latter year. Some cases became known through the press – such as the refusal of men of B Company, 1st Squadron, 12th Cavalry to patrol from Firebase PACE in October 1971 – but official American statistics for 'insubordination, mutiny and other acts' total only 131 convictions in 1970. In a sense, too, the murder of American officers and NCOs by their own men – 'fragging' – was a kind of perishable mutiny which amounted to at least 730 known cases in Vietnam between 1969 and 1971. Similarly, the Soviet Union has never admitted that mutiny occurred on its destroyer *Storozhevoi* in November 1975, for which 82 Soviet seamen were reportedly shot.

Strikes or mutinies?

While mutiny may thus be sometimes concealed or obscured, it can equally be argued that many cases of indiscipline treated as mutiny appear somewhat less serious in hindsight, although military authorities can hardly ignore such threats to cohesion. Many of the mutinies associated with British troops at the end of World War I, such as those at Folkestone, Dover, Southampton and Calais in January 1919, are better characterised as strikes than as mutinies. The growing body of conscripts in the British Army introduced into a military context the forms of collective bargaining with which they were familiar in civilian industry. Much the same could be said of the mutinies in the Imperial German Navy in August 1917 and October-November 1918. The true nature of the opposition to slow demobilisation in the US Army at the end of World War II, which led 4000 troops to demonstrate in Manila in December 1945 and over 20,000 in January 1946, as well as to mass petitions to the White House and similar disturbances in Europe, was recognised by the general leniency afforded the demonstrators by the authorities. In October 1968, however, a sit-down protest following the death of an inmate at the Presidio military prison outside San Francisco resulted in 27 men being charged with mutiny. The severe 16-year sentences given the first defendants caused such widespread public opposition that subsequent sentences were as light as three months imprisonment. Similarly, the conviction of 255 men of the

British 13th Parachute Battalion for mutiny for refusing to obey orders in protest at conditions at Muar camp in Malaya in May 1946 also aroused a public outcry and the sentences were quashed altogether.

Many causes are often advanced by contemporaries for the outbreak of mutiny. An apparent explanation in wartime, for example, for any refusal to fight can be simple cowardice. This was the charge made against the 191 British soldiers of the 50th and 51st Divisions who refused to be employed as a reinforcing draft for the 46th Division at Salerno in September 1943. In fact, detailed psychological investigations of the men highlighted group loyalty towards previous formations, as well as the interplay of rumour and sheer mismanagement by the military authorities. Quite frequently external influence is held to be chiefly responsible for mutiny. In 1917 the French suspected pacifists and communists of being behind the widespread mutinies when it was more a case of a refusal to fight the war in a certain manner than of refusing to fight at all. The worst cases occurred in those units which had suffered heaviest officer casualties in the ill-fated Nivelle offensive which preceded the mutinies and they were also underlain by a series of grievances on pay, rations and leave. The mutiny of the Royal Indian Navy in February 1946 involving 45 warships and 11 shore establishments was not due, as the British believed, to communist or nationalist agitation, but derived from the discrimination displayed against Indian personnel by a European officer corps too rapidly expanded during the war.

The mutiny of the British Atlantic Fleet at Invergordon in September 1931 cannot be adequately explained without reference to long-term grievances on the lower deck denied an adequate airing for too long. At Muar in May 1946 it was the condition of the tented camp, subsequently accentuated by heavy rainfall, and continuing administrative failures, which precipitated mutiny. Similarly, the 'Presidio 27' in the USA, most of whom had been persistently

Above: A Zambian mortar crew train with live shells on an 81mm mortar under the instruction of a white officer. The continuing presence of white officers in the armed forces of independent black African states was a prime cause of the mutinies in the Congo (Zaire) in 1960 and in east Africa in 1964.

Far left: After the mutiny by soldiers of the Tanganyika Rifles on 20 January 1964, men of 45 Royal Marine Commando launched a lightning operation against the rebels who were holding the barracks at Colito near Dar-es-Salaam. The operation was completely successful and not a single British casualty was incurred. Here a Royal Marine calmly disarms one of the rebels. Left inset: Behind a screen of banana leaves, troops of the mutinous 1st Battalion Uganda Rifles hand in their weapons as they are herded into a barbed wire enclosure at the sprawling Jinja camp. British troops had stormed the rebel-held camp and restored order almost immediately without opposition.

'We didn't have to salute nobody'.

The fragile nature of military discipline in the US Army in Vietnam is well illustrated by this excerpt from an interview with a US infantryman:
'We had a sense that we was no longer that GI who had to march, who had to salute. That was shit. We didn't have to salute nobody. We dressed the way we wanted to dress. If I wanted to wear the boony hat, I wore the boony hat. If I wanted one sleeve up and one sleeve down, I did it. If I didn't want to shave, I didn't. Nobody fucked with nobody in the field. An officer knows if he messed with you in the field, in a fire fight you could shoot him in the head. This was standard procedure in any infantry unit. Anybody tells you differently, he's shitting you.'

absent without leave during their military careers, had faced a regime of brutality and appalling conditions which had resulted in 33 suicide attempts (or 'gestures' in official parlance) in the 21 months prior to the mutiny.

A common basis of mutinies has been a strained relationship between an officer corps and a rank and file recruited from different races or nationalities. Some of the incidents in Vietnam, as well as the near mutinies on the American aircraft carriers *Kitty Hawk* and *Constellation* in November 1972, certainly appear to have had a racial implication in the same way as did the mutiny of black American truck companies at the USAAF station at Bamber Bridge in Lancashire in June 1943. The mutiny of the *Force Publique* in the (former Belgian) Congo in July 1960 against its European officers appears another clear case of this, as does the mutiny of naval and police units in East Pakistan in March 1971 when Bengalis generally revolted against their West Pakistan Punjabi rulers.

But just as in other mutinies, more mundane issues may be involved. This is well illustrated in the case of the east African mutinies of January 1964. The mutinies of the 1st Tanganyika Rifles at Colito on 20 January and of the 2nd Battalion at Tabora on the following day, as well as the subsequent upheavals in the 1st Uganda Rifles at Jinja and of the 11th Kenya Rifles at Lanet on 23 January 1964, demonstrated a frustration with the slow progress towards 'Africanisation' of the officer corps. However, it also involved a root dissatisfaction with rates of pay. Once the Tanganyikan authorities had caved in to demands for pay rises of up to 300 per cent there was a 'knock-on' effect throughout east Africa. The Kenyan mutiny resulted from the silence of the Kenyan government following the events elsewhere, as well as from the 11th Kenya Rifles being placed on stand-by for possible use against mutineers with whom they sympathised in Dar-es-Salaam. In the event the intervention of British troops led to a rapid disarming of the mutineers, but the mutinies did succeed in securing the withdrawal of expatriate officers.

Invariably, then, mutinies are concerned with defending or acquiring privileges and are caused by lack of leadership, poor administration and a failure in the channel of communication between officers and men or between armed forces and governments. Their prevention lies in giving adequate attention to those specific areas. **Ian Beckett**

Top: Members of the mutinous 'Presidio 27' continue singing 'We shall overcome' while the Mutiny Act is being read to them. Immediately after the act had been read, all of them were charged. This photo was used in evidence at the subsequent trial. Above: Armed guards stand by as Kenyan soldiers, arrested after the Lanet mutiny, leave a police van on arrival for their courts martial in Nairobi.

Key Weapons

MORTARS

The infantry mortar is the personal support artillery of the battalion commander, directly under his control and possessing the ability to respond very quickly to calls for fire. The near-universal pattern for mortar construction is of a weapon divided into three elements: a smoothbore barrel, resting on a baseplate which transmits the recoil thrust directly to the ground, and supported at the desired angle of elevation by a bipod. The bomb is a streamlined teardrop with fins at the tail end to give stability. The tail unit carries a shotgun-type cartridge of powder in its centre, and auxiliary charges of smokeless powder are clipped around the fins. When the bomb is loaded, by dropping it into the muzzle tail-first, it slides down the barrel until a fixed firing pin at the bottom strikes the central ignition cartridge, whereupon the auxiliary charges are fired and the resulting explosion lifts the bomb out and discharges it towards its target.

The mortar, by definition, fires only above 45 degree elevation, so that the bomb describes a high, arching trajectory which carries it over obstacles and delivers the bomb very steeply on to the target. This angle of approach means that the bomb is almost vertical when it detonates, and thus can distribute lethal blast and fragments in all directions; in this, it differs from an artillery shell which strikes the ground at a much shallower angle and is more directional in its effects.

Given these basic features, it is not surprising that most mortars have a resemblance to each other, even in calibre. Almost every Western army uses an 81mm infantry mortar, while the armies of the Warsaw Pact use an 82mm model; the difference between the two is negligible, though in general the mortars in use in the West are of more modern and efficient design, are more accurate and have something like 40 per cent more range than do the Soviet designs.

An example of technological superiority is seen in the British 81mm L16 mortar, which replaced the wartime 3-inch model. One of the problems with mortars is that the bomb must be smaller than the interior of the barrel, so that it can slide down, displacing air as it does so. But when the cartridge explodes, the gas which should be lifting the bomb is able to leak away through the 'windage' between

Previous page: British paras prepare to fire an 81mm light mortar. Above: The FV432 APC mortar variant mounting an L16A1 mortar. The mortar has a full 360 degree traverse and is provided with 160 rounds of HE ammunition. Right: Light mortars can be broken down into three main elements and carried by infantry over difficult terrain.

bomb and barrel, so reducing the theoretical performance. Wartime bombs were made of cast iron and had a smoothly machined belt around the point of largest diameter; some had grooves machined in the belt so as to cause turbulence when the gases tried to pass and thus make some sort of a seal. The 81mm design, however, has the bomb made of special graphite iron and carefully machined all over. Around the waist is a groove into which a plastic sealing ring is snapped. This remains in the groove during loading, and allows the bomb to be dropped into the barrel. But when the explosion gases rise alongside the bomb, the shaped

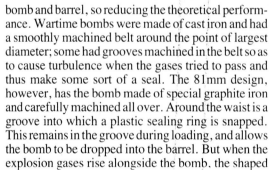

Below left: A French Hotchkiss-Brandt MO-120-RT-61 120mm mortar in the firing position. The barrel is rifled and fires a range of ammunition including the 18.7kg (41.2lb) PRPA rocket-assisted bomb which has a range of 13,050m (14,750 yds). Below right: Troops training with an Austrian 120mm M-60 mortar.

Right: An Israeli 160mm self-propelled mortar carrier. Israel has modified a number of AFVs to meet its own requirements and the 160mm Soltam mortar has been mounted on both the M7 and M4 Sherman chassis.

Below: A rear view of the 160mm SP mortar carrier with kit laid out. The mortar is breech loaded by a crew of between four and seven men and achieves a high rate of fire with a maximum range of 9600m (10,500 yds).

plastic ring is forced outwards and up against the groove, so that it makes a gas-tight seal. This device improves the efficiency and accuracy of the 81mm by a considerable amount, so that a maximum range of 5800m (6350yds) is quite possible.

Moving up from the 81mm level, several armies employ 120mm mortars, though in many cases they are considered as light artillery and are not manned by infantry. The average 120mm mortar can deliver a bomb weighing about 14kg (31lb) to ranges in excess of 6000m (6560yds) but the penalty for this is weight: many 120mm weapons have wheeled carriages incorporated in their baseplates and can weigh up to 600kg (1320 lb) or more.

One advantage of the 120mm calibre is that it allows the designer some space in which to make improvements to the basic bomb. While the standard 120mm bomb is much the same sort of projectile as the 81mm, the French Hotchkiss-Brandt company.

long leaders in mortar development, have developed a rocket-boosted bomb. The bomb has a central rocket motor and a tail unit which is detachable. It is loaded and fired in the normal way, the explosion of the cartridge throwing the bomb high into the air. But the explosion also ignites a pyrotechnic delay element which, after some seconds of flight, blows off the tail unit and ignites the rocket motor. As the tail unit falls away it also unlocks a set of fins on the bomb which has, until then, been folded away. The bomb now accelerates under the impulse from the rocket motor, stabilised by the unfolded fins. With this PRPA RAP their standard 120mm mortar has its maximum range

Above centre: An Israeli 160mm Soltam M-66 mortar. In the firing position the wheels are angled inwards and the mortar can be turned through 360 degrees.
Above: An Israeli 120mm Soltam M-65 mortar in the travelling position. Although usually towed behind a truck, the M-65 can be broken down into four elements and loaded onto pack mules.

Left: A FRELIMO unit in Mozambique. Light mortars are particularly effective weapons for guerrilla operations and ambushes since they can be broken down quickly and carried out of the combat area before enemy reinforcements can be called up.

Below left: The massive Soviet 240mm M-240 heavy mortar. The M-240 is breech loaded and fires 100kg (220lb) HE bombs to a range of 9700m (10,600 yds). Below right: A Soviet M-1943 120mm mortar. Six M-1943s equip the mortar battery of each motorised rifle battalion. Bottom: The seven-man crew of a Dutch YP-408 APC PW-MT variant deploys a French 120mm Brandt mortar.

increased from 4250m (4600yds) to 6550m (7100yds).

Another Hotchkiss-Brandt 120mm mortar design uses a rifled barrel, an idea which may seem to run counter to the basic idea of a simple weapon. The idea is not new; it was first put forward during World War I by an Australian officer, and a mortar to his design was developed by the US Army in 4.2-inch calibre and is still in use. In this type of mortar there is no need for fins on the bomb, since stability in flight is obtained by spinning the projectile just like a gun shell. The bomb looks rather like a shell, but with a short tubular extension at the base in which the ignition cartridge is carried and around which are the auxiliary cartridges. At the bottom of the bomb is a dished copper plate, smaller in diameter than the interior of the mortar barrel; below this is a flat steel plate. When the bomb is drop-loaded it slides down the barrel, leaving sufficient windage for the air to escape. When the cartridge explodes, the steel plate is driven forward against the dished copper plate and straightens it out so that it is now of slightly greater diameter than the bomb and digs into the barrel rifling. This causes the bomb to be spun as it passes up the bore, as well as making an efficient gas-tight seal, and as a result the 4.2-inch mortar was extremely accurate and had a range of just over 3660m (4000yds). Its present-day equivalent, the 107mm M30, uses the same system with an improved mounting and fires its bomb to 6800m (7400yds) range.

The Hotchkiss-Brandt rifled 120mm mortar is used by the French and several other armies. They approach the problem slightly differently, using a conventional copper driving band on the bomb which is pre-engraved to fit the rifling; this means that the loader has to fit the bomb into the rifling before he can drop it, which makes for a slight delay. In addition, there is also a rocket-boosted bomb for this mortar. With the standard spinning bomb the maximum range is 8135m (8850yds), while the rocket boost improves this to 13,000m (14,200yds).

Even larger mortars are employed by some countries. The Tampella company of Finland makes a 160mm weapon which fires a 40kg (88lb) bomb to a range of 10,000m (10,900yds), and a similar weapon, made by Soltam of Israel, who are linked with Tampella, is employed by the Israeli Army. The Soviet Army also uses 160mm mortars, though these are large and complex breech-loading weapons analogous to light field-artillery guns.

At the other end of the scale there is ample scope for

Above: The British 51mm is designed to be carried and used by one man and was introduced to replace the old 2in mortar. Early versions provided a monopod for support but this was deleted and a webbing gaiter fitted around the barrel for the firer to hold the barrel steady.

Modern Mortars: Weights and Ranges

Country of origin	Type	Total weight	Maximum range
Great Britain	51mm mortar	4.6kg (10.15lb)	800m (875yds)
Israel	60mm Tampella mortar	14.5kg (32lb)	2555m (2800yds)
Canada/ Great Britain	81mm light mortar	36.7kg (80lb)	5800m (6350yds)
Soviet Union	82mm M1937 mortar	56kg (125lb)	3040m (3325yds)
France	120mm RT-61 mortar	580kg (1280lb)	8135m (8900yds) PRPA RAP: 13,050m (14,750yds)
Israel	160mm Soltam M-66 mortar	1700kg (3750lb)	9600m (10,500yds)
Soviet Union	240mm M-240 mortar	3610kg (7940lb)	9700m (10,600yds)

Left: Two views of the French EMC 81mm mortar gun carrier. The EMC is a variant of the Panhard ERC armoured car fitted with an open-topped turret and armed with a Hotchkiss-Brandt 81mm breech-loaded mortar. The EMC is extremely mobile with a road speed of 110km/h (68mph) and a range of 950km (595 miles) and carries 72 HE bombs. The EMC's mortar can also be used in an anti-tank role, with APFSDS bombs.

Below: The French Panhard M3 APC can mount a wide variety of armament including the Hotchkiss-Brandt 60mm mortar. Like the EMC mortar gun carrier, the M3 provides a highly mobile platform and is fully amphibious.

very small mortars. The favoured calibre for this mortar type has been 60mm (51mm in the British Army) which is, today, almost the standard for what are usually called 'patrol' or 'commando' mortars. These can be carried by one man and put into action very quickly. The bomb they throw is only about 2kg (4.4lb) in weight and the maximum range is about 2000m (2190yds), but these weapons form a very useful support for the infantry platoon.

Another aspect of mortars which is currently wit-

nessing much exploration is their mounting on armoured personnel carriers. The general policy is to strengthen the vehicle and mount the standard 81mm or 120mm weapon inside, firing through an open hatch. By using the standard weapon, and carrying the normal baseplate, it is possible to dismount it and use the mortar on the ground in the conventional manner should this be desirable. But some authorities are against this method, since they feel that the open roof of the vehicle makes the crew too vulnerable. They suggest that a better answer is the French 'gun-mortar', another Hotchkiss-Brandt invention. This is a 60mm or 81mm mortar barrel mounted in a recoil system and carried in the turret of an armoured car. It can be breech-loaded from inside the armour, so allowing maximum protection for the crew, and duplicates the performance of the standard 60mm or 81mm mortar. In addition, special ammunition can be provided to permit firing the weapon like a gun, so that anti-tank projectiles or mortar bombs can be fired on a flat trajectory. This gun-mortar has been adopted by several armies and it will probably find more adherents in the future.

The unwinnable war

US strategy in Vietnam

In his 1974 examination of the failure of American policy in Vietnam, Brigadier-General Douglas Kinnard described a 'deep-seated strategic failure: the inability of the policymakers to frame tangible, obtainable goals.' Yet one of those same policymakers – Secretary of Defense Clark Clifford who took over shortly after the Tet offensive – confessed himself horrified at the failure of the military experts, the generals, to give him any concrete advice: 'It was startling to me to find out that we had no military plan to win the war.' So the generals blame the politicians for not giving them a goal, while the politicians claim that the army had no strategy worthy of the name.

The US did have a goal in South Vietnam, of course: the establishment of a stable regime, able to defend itself against internal insurgency, rather along the lines of South Korea. But by the time the decision was taken to commit 125,000 combat ground troops in July 1965, they faced overwhelming obstacles that practically doomed the US forces to defeat. Perhaps the problem was one of over-confidence. The US had never lost any war in its history; and it was the most powerful nation the world had ever seen. It was US confidence that somehow, sometime, they were bound to overcome these problems that led the generals and the policymakers to subscribe to a military strategy that failed, in effect, to address itself directly to the major obstacles to victory.

The first obstacle was that South Vietnam itself was a collapsing, corrupt state. The overthrow of Diem in 1963 had initiated two years of political instability in Saigon, while the situation in the countryside steadily deteriorated, with 75 per cent of the country under communist control by early 1965, according to President Thieu. The South Vietnamese Army, the ARVN, was of poor quality: the desertion rate in 1966 was 21 per cent, or 124,000 men. Yet the US could find no answer to this problem beyond pouring in massive quantities of money and aid, which added to the corruption rather than alleviating the problems. There was just a vain hope that the South Vietnamese generals and politicians could put their own house in order and that somehow, under the umbrella of US military victory over North Vietnamese and Viet Cong mainforce units, the weak, corrupt and unpopular Saigon regime could bind the people to it. The Americans' efforts were constantly hampered by the independence of the South Vietnamese regime which, although denounced by its enemies as a 'puppet' government, always in fact pursued its own line. Initiatives designed to win popular support, such as land reform, could be urged on the government in the South by its American allies, but Saigon could not be forced to carry them out.

The failure to attend to very basic levels of counter-insurgency amazed many observers – particularly those British who had experience in Malaya. But the Americans felt the Malayan experience was not fully

Above: A US Marine aiding a wounded comrade shouts against the powerful downblast of a helicopter as he gives the order for battle casualties to move out. The category 'died of wounds' virtually ceased to exist for the Americans in Vietnam, such was the speed of evacuation to military hospitals, yet the carnage was still appalling – the US forces suffered some 45,000 battle deaths during the conflict.

Monty speaks out

Some prominent military men voiced serious doubts about United States policy in Vietnam. For example, in an interview on BBC television in September 1968 Field-Marshal Lord Montgomery, Britain's best-known wartime general, had this to say:

'I have never been able to determine what is the strategy of the United States in the Far East. I asked Richard Nixon once.... He made a very good speech for a quarter of an hour. At the end I had to repeat the question, because he couldn't answer it. That's why I asked it.

'The general on the ground has got to pursue the policy which is laid down by his political masters in Washington, and my view is that they can't win that war, ever.

'I consider that the first thing the United States should do is to stop the bombing of Vietnam. Then they must organise a conference of North Vietnam, South Vietnam and the Viet Cong, all together round a table, and draw up a government which would have to be communist controlled. There's no harm in that.

'If they want to be communists, I say well let them be communists. That's their business. But don't let it come our way. That's the point.'

relevant, since in Vietnam the insurgents were not a clearly defined minority and the level of external intervention – from the North – was far higher. Yet the experience of the Korean War did not fit Vietnam either. Korea had given rise to Limited War theory, under which fighting was to be strictly circumscribed both in geographical scope and in terms of the weapons used, avoiding escalation to a superpower conflict. Total victory – the conquest of the enemy – was not sought; controlled destruction was to be used to teach the enemy he could not win and must desist from his actions. At first the Americans tried to separate the Vietnam War in two – they would carry out a limited war against the North while the ARVN dealt with local insurgency. But since the ARVN failed in its task, the Americans turned the limited war techniques of controlled destruction against insurgents in the South, making effective counter-insurgency – with the ultimate goal of political and social stability – impossible.

The second major problem was that South Vietnam was extremely vulnerable to infiltration from outside, along its long western border with Laos and Cambodia, and that North Vietnam was prepared to keep the communist forces in the South supplied with a constant stream of reinforcements and war material. The obvious answers to this external threat were to invade North Vietnam, or to place a block along the most convenient line across Laos. Neither of these two alternatives was really considered, however. The option of invading the North was always ruled out of court. As Assistant Secretary of State William Bundy put it: 'the arguments against doing so – to all of us in

Top left: South Vietnamese troops and US advisers go scrambling for cover as they come under enemy fire while unloading supplies from a helicopter about to take off. Top right: A US sergeant rides shotgun at the door of a UH-1B helicopter. Note the use of knotted flexicord to support his M60 machine gun. Above: A peaceful dawn over the Mekong as a river patrol boat docks. Right: The sudden glare of a Viet Cong phosphorous grenade, tripped by US Marines, penetrates the gloom of the jungle.

the Johnson administration – seemed overwhelming. It would change the whole nature of the war. It might not work militarily.... we would very likely see a massive Chinese counter-intervention.'

Nor was permission given for a massive intervention into Laos to cut the Ho Chi Minh Trail there. The US ambassador in Laos, William Sullivan, strongly opposed such a move, and in 1966 he successfully resisted General Westmoreland's plea for three divisions to go into the country. In 1967, there were renewed calls for an invasion, but President Johnson rejected them, ordering discussion to cease, while the so-called 'McNamara Line' was set up. This was to be an electronic barrier of minefields and sensors, backed up by firebases, that would, it was hoped, prevent infiltration. Meanwhile, the bombing attacks on the Trail were growing in intensity; more weight of bombs was dropped on the Trail between 1965 and 1971 than in the whole of World War II.

In 1967, however, Westmoreland estimated that 90,000 troops a year were entering South Vietnam along the Trail; and a report commissioned by McNamara concluded that only 60 tonnes, or 20 truck loads, of supplies per day were needed to keep the communist war effort going at its then level. Trying to fight a war within South Vietnam while the enemy had complete strategic initiative along the borders seems clearly, with hindsight, an insuperable problem.

The third, and most intangible, of the obstacles that the Americans somehow believed they would overcome was the will to fight of the North Vietnamese. In 1964, the US estimated that North Vietnamese industry could be destroyed within 12 days of starting a bombing programme; in November 1964, Johnson

was told that two to six months of 'surgical bombing' would force Hanoi to abandon its campaign. Both of these were absurdly optimistic forecasts, based on a misappreciation of the nature of the enemy.

The politbureau in Hanoi were ruthless nationalists who had fought the French to a standstill, and were happy to do the same to the Americans. In the end, they were prepared to sacrifice one million dead in the communist forces as a reasonable price for victory, while much opinion in the US felt that the total of 47,000 American dead was unacceptable. Graduated air strikes were no answer to the North's will to win; nor were bizarre CIA schemes to capture the politbureau in a lightning raid, or send the Hanoi chief of secret police poisoned apricot brandy.

General Westmoreland's strategy in Vietnam during the period 1965 to 1968 must be seen in the light of these three basic obstacles, which both the generals and the politicians either vaguely hoped would be overcome, or failed to identify as existing. For Westmoreland did have a coherent strategy, which he pursued with a great deal of success in tactical terms. It was just that these three surrounding factors doomed this strategy to defeat.

Put most simply, Westmoreland's strategy was to use the US forces, with their enormous firepower and mobility, to pin down and destroy large communist units, while the ARVN was to control the population, by establishing itself in the villages and preventing small-scale insurgency. And this policy seemed at first to be successful. In August 1965, at Chu Lai, Marines and the 1st Cavalry Division won an impressive victory against communist forces in their first major engagement, and during the next six months the

VIETNAM 1965-68

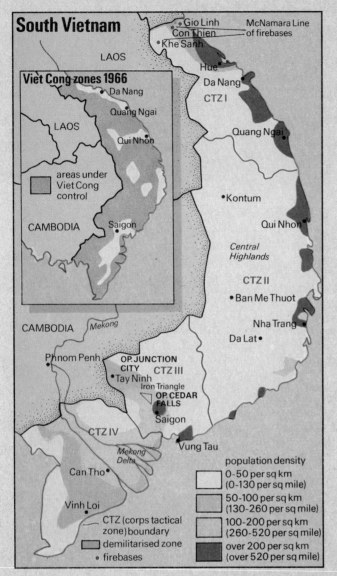

South Vietnam

LAOS
Gio Linh
Con Thien
Khe Sanh
McNamara Line of firebases
Hue
Da Nang
CTZ I

Viet Cong zones 1966
Da Nang
Quang Ngai
LAOS
Qui Nhon
areas under Viet Cong control
CAMBODIA
Saigon

Quang Ngai
Kontum
Qui Nhon
Central Highlands
CTZ II
Ban Me Thuot
Nha Trang
Da Lat

CAMBODIA Mekong
Phnom Penh
OP. JUNCTION CITY CTZ III
Tay Ninh
Iron Triangle
OP. CEDAR FALLS
Saigon
CTZ IV
Mekong Delta
Vung Tau
Can Tho

Vinh Loi

CTZ (corps tactical zone) boundary
demilitarised zone
firebases

population density
0-50 per sq km (0-130 per sq mile)
50-100 per sq km (130-260 per sq mile)
100-200 per sq km (260-520 per sq mile)
over 200 per sq km (over 520 per sq mile)

US military commitment
South Vietnam 1965-68 (as of 31 Dec)

	1965	1966	1967	1968
Military personnel	184,300	385,300	485,600	536,100
Deaths in action	1369	5008	9378	14,592
Wounded in action	6114	30,093	62,025	92,820

areas, but such a passive role soon proved untenable. Increasingly, the US armed forces moved on to the offensive. A rough-and-ready division of labour was worked out with the ARVN: the American troops took on North Vietnamese and Viet Cong main forces and attacked communist-controlled areas, while the South Vietnamese patrolled and pacified areas held by the government.

American forces were augmented by troops from South Korea, Australia, New Zealand, Thailand and the Philippines. At the peak of their contribution, these allies were providing more than 65,000 men, but their main usefulness was a bolster to the US diplomatic position, confirming that the Americans were acting as part of an alliance of regional powers rather than as a superpower pursuing its own interests.

Deploying their extraordinary firepower, the US troops and their allies had considerable success in the field. They advanced into the Central Highlands to pre-empt a possible conventional offensive by the Viet Cong and North Vietnamese Army which might have split South Vietnam in two (as was indeed to happen in 1975). In the north of South Vietnam, and in the Iron Triangle near Saigon, US forces took the war into areas that had been dominated by the Viet Cong for a decade or more. To prevent communist infiltration from North Vietnam, the Americans built a series of firebases, known as the McNamara Line, just south of the Demilitarized Zone. It was possible, however, for the North Vietnamese to circumvent the US line by passing through Laos and Cambodia; US troops did not have political authorisation to operate outside Vietnam's borders.

The combat successes of US troops did not have the expected effect on the North Vietnamese leadership; instead of drawing back or seeking negotiation, they committed ever larger forces to the South. Despite the loss of perhaps 330,000 troops in the three years 1965-67, the number of Viet Cong and North Vietnamese operating in the South probably increased over the same period from about 180,000 to 260,000.

But the North Vietnamese leadership was undoubtedly worried by the military situation. After an especially grave series of set-backs in the first half of 1967 – defeats in the Saigon area in Operations Cedar Falls and Junction City, and the failure of attacks on the McNamara Line firebases at Khe Sanh, Gio Linh and Con Thien – the North Vietnamese decided on a new strategy to reverse the situation by an all-out offensive at the Lunar New Year (Tet) in 1968, combining a major siege of Khe Sanh and small-scale attacks on cities throughout South Vietnam.

The period 1965-68 had been the time of the US build-up, reasonable morale and military success. There is no doubt that by 1968 the military situation in South Vietnam was tenable whereas in early 1965 it had been almost hopeless. But from the time of the Tet offensive in 1968 onwards, the US Army was to face an agonising period of withdrawal, disillusionment and disintegration.

By the end of 1964 US policy-makers confronted what they saw as a 'lost strategic situation' in South Vietnam. Since the fall of President Ngo Dinh Diem in November 1963, South Vietnamese military governments had succeeded one another with dizzy rapidity. Despite the help of some 20,000 US advisers, the ARVN was usually worsted in its encounters with Viet Cong insurgents. Large areas of South Vietnam were under communist control. As North Vietnam began to commit battalions of its regular army in support of the insurgents, Saigon seemed doomed.

Under the blanket powers voted to the president by Congress after the Gulf of Tonkin incident in August 1964, Lyndon B. Johnson was able to step up US military action at will. On 7 February 1965, after a Viet Cong raid on a US barracks had left eight Americans dead, regular bombing raids on North Vietnam were initiated. They had no effect on the desperate military situation in the South. Johnson was faced with a stark choice: accept defeat, or commit a major US military force to Vietnam.

From spring 1965 ever-increasing numbers of American troops moved in, the force deployed rising from 45,000 in May to 125,000 in July 1965, reaching 265,000 by June the following year and almost 500,000 in 1967. When the first detachment of Marines was deployed in March 1965, its instructions were to defend US base use of helicopters and mass bombing and shelling in the Central Highlands appeared to give the Americans the initiative against the communist forces there. It seemed that the Americans could smash down on the enemy whenever he dared show himself, and that the communists must realise that they could not win, that they would be worn down in a war of attrition.

The three obstacles began to make themselves felt in 1966, however, and doomed Westmoreland's tidy division of the war into various phases and compartments. First of all, the idea that the ARVN could cope with the populated areas was proved false. The real Viet Cong strength was in the villages, and so the American forces' 'search and destroy' operations soon had to be directed against the villages of South Vietnam – as in Operation Cedar Falls. But trying to apply maximum pressure and enormous firepower in short sharp sweeps was no real answer to the problems of insurgency. By 1968, over one third of South Vietnam's population had become refugees. Unable to destroy the Viet Cong in the villages, the US strategy had become one of destroying the villages themselves.

The failure to stem the flow of men and supplies into the South meant that although the Americans could win any single engagement, they had lost the strategic initiative. The communists fought when and where they wanted. There was no territorial indicator as to success or failure, and so the only statistics that had any meaning were the 'body count', a macabre and, from 1966, absurdly over-inflated set of figures. Westmoreland believed that even though the North Vietnamese held the initiative, they were so stretched that it would only be a short time before they had to wind down their force levels in South Vietnam. But this ignored two vital factors: firstly, that the strategic initiative held by the communists meant that they could

Below: Members of an immediate-response combat unit of the US Army leap from a Bell Huey helicopter hovering a few feet from the ground to reinforce a hilltop position recently taken from the Viet Cong. A radio operator and his colleague remain in position, ready to give covering fire if necessary.

choose a level of casualties they were able to sustain; and secondly that the communists were prepared to take far higher casualty rates than the Americans had ever imagined. Soon, American dead began to mount up. Casualties tripled in 1968 as compared to 1966. If this carried on, then the balance of attrition might well work the other way.

Not that the communists were necessarily winning the war at this stage; they were incurring heavy losses, and found the tactical superiority of American forces difficult to cope with. But the American Army was not winning the war either, and, as all the government enquiries emphasised after Tet, had no plan that could realistically alter the situation. The failure of American strategy in Vietnam was that the three critical elements of the war – the unpopularity and incompetence of the Saigon government; the vulnerability of the country to infiltration from the Ho Chi Minh Trail; and the ruthless determination of the North Vietnamese leadership were never adequately faced. Only if these issues had been directly and effectively addressed could the US have formulated a winning strategy.   **Ashley Brown**

The Gulf of Tonkin

Pretext or provocation?

By the spring of 1964 it was clear that communist insurgency in South Vietnam was beginning to attain its ends, partly because of its own efforts and partly because inherent political instability within the country inhibited an adequate response.

In January of that year a junta headed by Major-General Nguyen Khanh had seized power in Saigon, without much popular support. Khanh believed that the communists could only be defeated if US ground troops became actively involved in the war. This was a course of action which the administration of President Lyndon B. Johnson was extremely reluctant to take, although it was already supporting the South Vietnamese government with economic aid, military equipment and teams of tactical advisers.

Khanh argued that the source of communist aggression lay in North Vietnam, although at that period no units of the North Vietnamese Army had been identified south of the Demilitarized Zone. He hinted that South Vietnam might well invade the North in retaliation and arranged carefully orchestrated demonstrations in the capital which gave the impression that the United States was failing to honour its commitments. Johnson, facing an election year, was in a difficult situation and Khanh maintained the pressure, suggesting that if matters continued as they were, South Vietnam might be forced to reach an accommodation with the communists, the results of which could hardly be favourable to American interests in Southeast Asia. At this point General Nguyen Cao Ky, commander of the South Vietnamese Air Force, entered the debate, declaring that his pilots were already training for missions against the North. Wishing to retain some control over events, Johnson agreed to joint planning which, in certain contingencies, could result in joint United States/South Vietnamese air activity over North Vietnam. This seemed to satisfy Khanh, but Ky had already further embarrassed the Americans by announcing publicly that the US was already involved in the insertion of sabotage teams into North Vietnam.

There was sufficient truth in this for Hanoi to be forced into some kind of reaction. The US Navy was providing cover for South Vietnamese commando raids along the enemy's coastline, and its destroyers patrolled the Gulf of Tonkin on intelligence gathering missions. By now, prestige and propaganda were taking over from purely military considerations. If an apparently defensive strike could be made against an intrusive US naval unit, the communists could turn the situation to their advantage by mobilising world opinion against American aggression within North Vietnamese territorial waters. At the same time, both the South Vietnamese government and those parts of the US establishment that wanted more US involvement in Vietnam would be only too happy to use an attack on US vessels as proof of North Vietnamese aggression and as a good opportunity to bring America more directly into the conflict.

On 31 July 1964 South Vietnamese assault boats carried out a hit-and-run raid against North Vietnamese offshore islands under cover of darkness. Some 100km (60 miles) to the southeast, an American destroyer, the USS *Maddox*, was bearing towards the Gulf of Tonkin. It has always been unclear whether the *Maddox* was backing the South Vietnamese raid or merely on routine patrol.

Cruising off the coast

During the afternoon of 2 August, some 36 hours later, the *Maddox* was cruising in the Gulf some 16km (10 miles) off the coast of North Vietnam, within the 20km (12 mile) limit of territorial waters claimed by North Vietnam, although outside the 5km (3 mile) limit recognised by the Americans. Three contacts were observed on the destroyer's radar and these were quickly identified as North Vietnamese torpedo boats. When these had closed to a range of 9000m (10,000 yards) *Maddox* fired a warning salvo, but they continued to close and at 8000m (9000 yards) the destroyer commenced the engagement in earnest.

The torpedo boats, which were photographed during their attacking run from the deck of the American ship, launched two torpedoes; *Maddox* turned towards them and they missed by 185m (200 yards). The carrier USS *Ticonderoga* had already been alerted and four of her F-8E Crusaders streaked in to attack the enemy craft with missiles and cannon fire. As a

A North Vietnamese torpedo boat (top), the only survivor of three, retreats after the unsuccessful torpedo attack against the American destroyer USS *Maddox* (shown above), with shells from the *Maddox* bursting close to its stern.

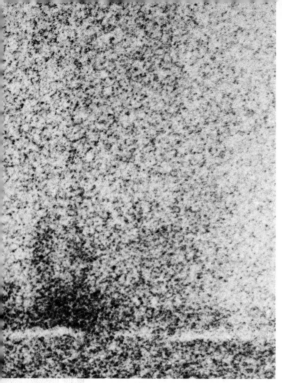

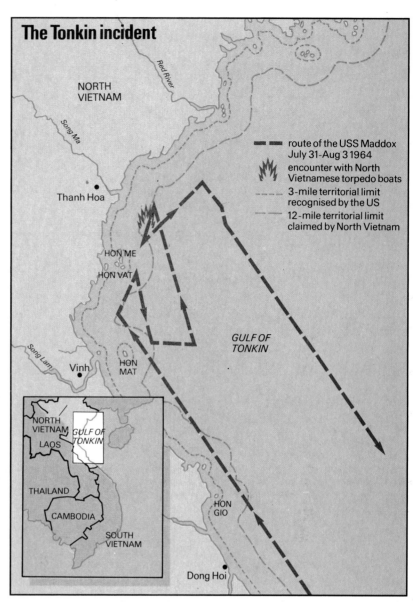

The Tonkin incident

NORTH VIETNAM

Red River

Song Ma

Thanh Hoa

- - - route of the USS Maddox July 31-Aug 3 1964
- encounter with North Vietnamese torpedo boats
- - - 3-mile territorial limit recognised by the US
- - - 12-mile territorial limit claimed by North Vietnam

HON ME

HON VAT

Song Lam

Vinh

HON MAT

GULF OF TONKIN

NORTH VIETNAM

LAOS

GULF OF TONKIN

THAILAND

CAMBODIA

SOUTH VIETNAM

HON GIO

Dong Hoi

Below: Pilots pose for a photograph on board the carrier USS *Ticonderoga* with an F-8E Crusader in the background. Four Crusaders were quickly scrambled during the incident of 2 August 1964, and helped eliminate the enemy threat.

result of this and the *Maddox*'s gunfire one torpedo boat was left dead and blazing fiercely, a second limped off seriously damaged, and the survivor sped away. Next day, Johnson issued a stern warning: 'North Vietnam will be under no misapprehension as to the grave consequences which will inevitably result from further unprovoked military action against United States forces.'

Contact and retaliation

Maddox resumed her patrol on 3 August, accompanied by a second destroyer, the USS *C. Turner Joy*; that night, there were further South Vietnamese raids on the Northern coast. During the following night of 4/5 August the US destroyers' radar picked up five suspicious surface contacts moving into attack positions. At 5500m (6000 yards) these were engaged with gunfire and towards midnight they disappeared. Immediately news of this second incident reached Washington, Johnson ordered a start to preparations for retaliatory air attacks on North Vietnam. By the morning of 5 August, the Pentagon was in receipt of further cables from the Fleet casting doubt on the original report – the weather had been very stormy, and it was suspected that the contacts might have been imaginary, based on inaccurate interpretations made

by inexperienced radar operators. But the air strikes went ahead. The carriers *Ticonderoga* and *Constellation* flew off 64 aircraft which struck at North Vietnamese naval bases. The oil storage depot at Vinh was set ablaze and hits were recorded on 29 ships.

The most important consequence of these events, however, was undoubtedly the Gulf of Tonkin Resolution rushed through Congress on 7 August and signed by Johnson four days later. This stated that America would 'take any necessary measures to repel any armed attack against the forces of the United States... including the use of armed force to assist any member or protocol state' of Seato (including South Vietnam). It was under the umbrella of this resolution that the president was able to start a major bombing campaign against North Vietnam (Rolling Thunder) and the engagement of US ground forces in the South in March 1965.

Some congressmen, such as Senator William Fulbright, were later to feel that the president had railroaded them into support for this far-reaching resolution through an adept exploitation of the Gulf of Tonkin incident. Many anti-war campaigners were convinced that the second attack was a pure invention. The exact truth of these events may never be known.

Bryan Perrett

Years of uncertainty

The communists adapt to US intervention

The crucial years of the Vietnam War for Hanoi were those spanning the period just before, during, and following the advent of full US military might in Vietnam. For Hanoi's Vo Nguyen Giap and his High Command, they were years of battlefield improvisation and tactical experimentation, a time of extended search for ways to meet and overcome a new and awesome challenge.

The period 1964 to 1967 forms the first part of the central phase of the Vietnam War. That phase, commonly called the Big Unit War period (General Giap called it the 'regular force strategy' period), ran from the moment the US fully committed itself to large-scale intervention in Vietnam (in February 1965) to the signing of the Paris Agreements in January 1973. This central period had been preceded by a revolutionary guerrilla war phase (1959-65) and was followed by the post-American phase which North Vietnamese historians refer to as the 'talk-fight' period (1973-75). During these changing phases, the North Vietnamese High Command's estimate of its situation and its tactical response to various exigencies of war changed markedly and in complex fashion. Throughout the central period particularly, Giap and his associates showed a marked lack of certitude and a great deal of doctrinal casting about in their hunt for a formula that would achieve victory.

To understand Hanoi's tactical response and to appreciate the nature of the unfolding military events, it is necessary to take note of three aspects of the war: firstly the structure of the insurgent forces in the field; secondly the unique nature of the struggle; and thirdly the basic strategic concepts of the communists.

The forces in the field on the communist side consisted of the People's Army of Vietnam (PAVN) – the North Vietnamese armed forces – and the People's Liberation Armed Forces (PLAF), formerly the Liberation Army, which was the military wing of the National Liberation Front (NLF) in South Vietnam

and technically under the control of the Provisional Revolutionary Government (PRG) of South Vietnam. The PLAF consisted of two elements: the full military force, or main force; and the paramilitary force or guerrilla force. The guerrilla force was in turn divided into the combat guerrillas and the village guerrillas. Both the PLAF and the PAVN were under the operational command of the Vietnamese Communist Party's Central Office in South Vietnam (COSVN) throughout the war. The term Viet Cong was sometimes used indiscriminately to describe any South Vietnamese communists, or even to cover North Vietnamese communists as well. But in any discussion of communist methods it is necessary to distinguish clearly between these elements – and especially between the PLAF and the PAVN.

Ambushes and assassinations

Basic Vietnamese communist strategy, which predated US military involvement, was built around a peculiar but effective concept called *dau tranh* which can be roughly translated as 'struggle'. This formed a whole, but broadly speaking was divisible into two types: armed dau tranh and political dau tranh. The first, armed dau tranh, consisted of military actions such as attacks and ambushes by regular forces and guerrillas; also assassinations and kidnappings of village officials. Political dau tranh was not politics in the usual sense but rather what might be called politics with guns, that is techniques of persuasion and intimidation designed to mobilise Vietnamese villagers. But the core of this doctrine was that both forms of dau tranh must be used simultaneously and consistently (although there was room for differing opinion on allocation of greater or lesser resources to one or the other). Only in combination, like hammer and anvil, could the doctrine work. And together they created the communist trinity; organisation, mobilisation and motivation.

Left: While his comrade gives him covering fire with a type 56 Chinese-made assault rifle, a Viet Cong guerrilla primes and prepares to throw a grenade at advancing enemy units before melting back into the jungle. Below: A small unit of guerrillas move across a rice paddy. Bottom: Well-armed Viet Cong troops in action during fighting in Quang Tri province in 1969.

Within the Viet Cong there were two distinct groups; the paramilitary and the full military unit – though both divisions rigorously maintained the concept of the self-contained combat unit.

Paramilitary units were exclusively guerrilla warfare units and were made up of ordinary villagers who did much of their sabotage at night. They were regarded as local and civilian as opposed to outside soldiers. They received only basic military training and were usually armed with only the most primitive weapons. Within the paramilitary itself, two further divisions existed; combat and village guerrillas.

Village guerrillas were older, poorly armed and trained and basically intended to provide static defence for a village. The presence of village guerrillas was a psychological boost to the prestige of the Viet Cong. Combat guerrillas were a younger better-trained force who provided a pool of manpower for the full military units to draw upon. They were often used as peripheral troops for such things as porterage to mobile columns. From this pool were also drawn fanatical young men to form suicide and assassination squads – known as special activity cells.

The full military units were also divisible into two main groups; the regionals and the main force. The regionals were not specifically a combat force and though well armed and trained concentrated on propaganda and political indoctrination. The main force was the fighting core of the Viet Cong. It was made up of both independent battalions and larger, combined formations and was able to carry out large-scale actions against US and government forces.

The last months of 1964 were a period of almost unrelieved deterioration for the South Vietnamese, and consequently of general satisfaction for the communist High Command. By the end of 1964 PLAF forces controlled perhaps two-thirds of the 2500 villages in South Vietnam. The Army of the Republic of (South) Vietnam (ARVN) strategic reserve battalions were being reduced one by one and few remained. Once an army's strategic reserve forces are gone, of course, fixed installations can be picked off one by one.

It was a moment of agonising choice for the US. Either it could cut its losses in Vietnam and allow the collapse of the South and subsequent communist victory, or it could commit itself to the use of direct military force. The fateful latter decision came on 7 February 1965 with the White House announcement that air strikes and bombing had been authorised in North Vietnam and that ground troops were to be despatched to South Vietnam.

The announcement did not immediately alter the communist High Command's conclusion, reached a month earlier, that 1965 would prove to be the year of final victory. It considered the rot too far gone in South Vietnam and thought the US had acted too late – not an unrealistic estimate. In fact, it still is something of a puzzle as to why the communists did not win the war in early 1965. The only important US strategic contribution at the time was the air strikes into the North, which had little meaning in the South. Some vital US military hardware – most importantly helicopters in numbers – began arriving in early summer, but not until the end of the year was the logistic pipeline in full flow. Much of 1965 was devoted simply to getting US military forces into position and had General Giap pressed on with his campaign to decimate ARVN reserves he might well have ended the war before the Americans got into place. But ever the cautious commander, Giap ordered his forces to scale down their activities; he felt he needed a re-evaluation, calculating that he faced a new war against a new enemy requiring new tactics and a re-adapted grand strategy.

During this period a great doctrinal debate raged at Politburo level over proper strategy for war – between those such as party theoretician Truong Chinh, who advocated primary emphasis on political dau tranh, and General Giap and others who sought to place chief emphasis on armed dau tranh on the grounds that victory could be achieved only militarily, on the ground, in the South.

The importance of air power

Having failed to win the war in 1964, the communists then had a whole new set of military problems to face – a major one of which was US air power. In the pre-1964 period air power had played only a minor role in the Vietnam War. Tactical air power, what there was of it, made a small useful contribution, while strategic air power was virtually uninvolved. In the 1964 to 1967 period close air support wrought enormous changes; it saved the day in several key ground battles, beginning with the battle of Binh Gia in early 1964; and certainly at Khe Sanh beginning in December 1967. The PAVN response to air strikes in the North was to augment its air defences. With Soviet assistance it developed the most powerful air defences the world had ever seen in action, far beyond the primitive defences of either side in World War II. This response, more and more SAM sites, was of course about the only response possible for the PAVN High Command.

The ground war in 1966 and 1967 tended to be amorphous and indeterminate, the ARVN fought the PLAF guerrillas while US and allied forces took on the regular PAVN troops and the PLAF main force. The communists mounted as many small-sized operations as possible, while their opponents built their military operations around artillery and air strikes, attempting to reduce communist offensive capability. It was tactics which bled against tactics which spoiled.

Giap meanwhile worked to perfect a new set of tactics which he hoped would nullify enemy advan-

While some of the Viet Cong weapons were of dubious effectiveness, such as bamboo crossbow anti-aircraft harpoons (right), the adaptation of grenades as landmines often inflicted heavy casualties against foot patrols (far right, a Chinese-made grenade buried at the side of a road linked to a fishing line tripwire). Indeed, Viet Cong ingenuity in the use of natural resources as weapons was staggering. The Punji stick traps, often smeared with faeces, were sharpened bamboo sticks buried upright in the ground. Such was the success of these primitive weapons that all US units in Vietnam were given entirely new combat boots whose soles could not be pierced. This caused the Viet Cong to redesign their lethal weapon (right) so that pressure on a wire caused two spiked panels to pierce the leg above the boot. A further refinement of the concept was the placing of large amounts of bamboo spikes in clearings thus preventing the landing of troops (far right, Viet Cong women plant a clearing).

Sabotage and subversion

In 1967 the US Mission in Vietnam produced this account of Viet Cong terror tactics:

'Psychological objectives dominate Viet Cong sabotage and subversion efforts. In the early years the guerrillas were under strict orders not to destroy or interfere with permanent fixed economic installations such as power stations and port facilities. But beginning in 1965 these became targets of sabotage efforts.

'In the cities there has been no end to the ingenuity employed in terroristic sabotage. The grenade is the most common instrument, often rolled into a cafe by a young boy who escapes on a bicycle. Sometimes the bicycle itself is the instrument of death. Its hollow tubular frame is packed with plastic explosive and a time device is located under the saddle. Terrorists ride the bicycle into the area, lean it against the building to be destroyed, set the fuse, and walk off. Two such explosive devices were employed in Saigon in May 1963 using a motor bicycle and a motorcycle to blow huge holes in the side of a US military warehouse. The Brink officer's billet in Saigon was dynamited by an explosive-packed vehicle which had been driven into the parking lot on Christmas Eve, 1964. The Pershing Sports Field explosion in Saigon was caused by explosives packed into a length of soil pipe under the grandstand with a calendar watch detonator....

'Grenades lobbed into vehicles stopped for traffic lights; poison injected into bottles of wine with hypodermic needles; poisoned darts; doors, drawers or automobile engines booby-trapped – all are used. Often merely the threat of violence is enough. In November 1964, a young Vietnamese girl typist in a US aid program office was caught with program plans in her purse. She told security officials a man came to her apartment and told her that unless she stole the documents her family, living in the rural Quang Tri Province, would be harmed.'

tage in mass (men and firepower) and movement (particularly the ubiquitous helicopter). He engaged in a great deal of what might be called experimental combat. This began with the important Battle of Ia Drang Valley (November 1965) and continued for the next two years. It included Operation Junction City (February-May 1967) and three important but relatively small set-piece battles at Loc Ninh (Binh Long province, September 1967); Con Thien (near the DMZ, November 1967) and Dac To (Kontum Province, November 1967). All of these proved to be defeats for the communist forces, but Giap learned much from them.

By the end of the summer of 1967, after two years of trial and error, General Giap had arrived at what he felt was a new, workable military formula. He outlined it in his book *Big Victory, Great Task* (1967), the most innovative and creative of his writings; it was virtually a blueprint (although not recognised as such until later) for the 1967-68 winter-spring campaign in which the 1968 Tet offensive played such a prominent role.

Giap's 'fighting methods'

The way to shunt aside the enemy's advantage in mass and movement, wrote Giap, was through use of two distinct kinds of tactics or what he called 'fighting methods'. The first was the 'coordinated fighting method' by which he meant attacks by fairly large PAVN units against relatively important targets, but

The Viet Cong deployed women in the field after a period of military training. Left: A Viet Cong woman trainee negotiates a barbed wire entanglement. Right: a group of women maintain a forward observation post using a shell-case as a warning gong.

Below left: One of the great strengths of the Viet Cong campaign was its logistical back-up system. Women often performed tasks such as arms, ammunition and rations resupply. Here, bicycles provide a convenient means for carrying heavy loads over a distance.

only given favourable terrain and never if the outcome of the battle was strategically decisive. Ideally the target would be in some wild inaccessible region which would reduce the manoeuvrability of enemy troops brought in as reinforcements. The initial assault should bring the attackers close under the umbrella of the target's no-strike zone, eliminating the threat of air attack. Then the target would be overrun and the attackers would vanish. The 'independent fighting method' involved a large number of small-scale attacks mounted simultaneously and over a wide area, no single one of which was militarily important but which had great cumulative effect. The two methods were to be employed first alternately, then combined into a 'comprehensive offensive'.

Finally there would come some psychologically oriented *coup de grâce*, a Dien Bien Phu to break the enemy's spirit, cause his armed forces to unravel and thus end the war. Such was the new Giap concept.

All in all this period, from late 1964 to the end of 1967, was well used by Hanoi. The communist cause managed to weather the advent of US forces without losing self-confidence and its leadership remained as determined as ever, surviving all pressures, internally in the North and from its allies, to consider a political settlement. General Giap and his High Command had adapted to the kind of warfare the PAVN was now obliged to fight. And they had devised a new grand strategy that they hoped, and expected, would deliver victory before the end of 1968. **Douglas Pike**

Above: The waterlogged terrain of the Mekong Delta region forced both sides to resort to river craft. Here Viet Cong women carry out a river patrol to monitor enemy movements.

Search and destroy

US ground operations in Vietnam 1965-67

Left: A radio operator guides in heliborne supplies as troops establish a forward operations base during the US logistic build-up.

Around 1600 hours was reckoned to be the worst time for mines and booby traps in South Vietnam. Earlier in the day an American patrol would normally be fresh and alert, while nearer the evening it would be suffering less from the oppressively sticky heat. In mid-afternoon, however, the defences would be down. The patrol would grow careless and forget to stay on the lookout. If it was unlucky, it might blunder into one of an awesome variety of death traps. 'Bouncing Betties', 'Toepoppers', Claymores and giant shrapnel mines were all to be found by troops on foot, and there was a further range of specialised types to be encountered by men in armoured vehicles or helicopters.

Sometimes the mines might be covered by fire from local guerrillas or Viet Cong snipers; but normally they would be left unattended as a random weapon of attrition. Their role in the war was simply to keep reminding the Americans that they were not wanted in rural Vietnam – and to maintain a steady drain of

casualties. About 11 per cent of US deaths in the field were caused by such methods; the men died without being in combat with the enemy and were kept constantly on edge.

Something similar could be said of random sniping, mortar or rocket attacks. These were all techniques for long-range harassment which, although they might often be deadly, could not hope to be decisive. Their effect was to show the Americans that nowhere was truly safe, not even the centre of the biggest base areas. There was not usually a great deal that could be done to eliminate these stand-off attacks, even with 'harassment and interdiction' counter-fire or standing ambushes outside the US perimeters. No fully effective countermeasure was ever found against mines, and such technical aids as the AN/MPQ 4A radar for locating mortars proved disappointing in action. The AN/MPQ 4A achieved less than 20 per cent success in spotting incoming rounds, and hence could do little to identify their source. All too fre-

Above: A US patrol moving through soaking jungle conditions with extreme caution. The band-aid strips around the point-man's M16 are to aid his grip.

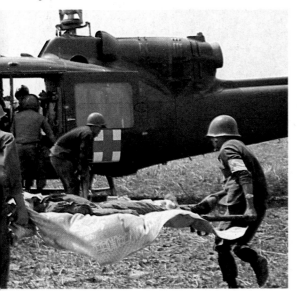

Left: Troops and medics hurrying to load a casualty for 'medevac' by a helicopter ambulance after contact with Viet Cong units.

quently, in fact, the American ground troops could do nothing but grin and bear it.

An amazing fact about the US serviceman in Vietnam between 1965 and 1968, however, was precisely that he *could* keep grinning. Disenchantment and bitterness may have set in after the Tet offensive and the decision to withdraw; but until that point was reached the morale and combat efficiency of the 'grunts' seems to have held up remarkably well. There was apparently no reason to doubt that Uncle Sam would win this war just as he had won all his others, and even if the soldiers did not relish their task they did nevertheless perform it, by and large, with dedication, courage and skill.

An education in war

Perhaps this was because most front-line infantrymen were little more than schoolkids, and members of the least-educated and least-privileged strata of American society. They did not enjoy the wider perceptions which came with a college education, since college also brought draft-deferment or at least a relatively sheltered military technical speciality. Instead, the men who actually walked point into the boondocks were educated only in the hard school of the boot-camp and the war itself. They were sufficiently uncomplicated to make excellent fighting soldiers – although by the same token they were quite unqualified to act as sensitive or diplomatic ambassadors for the American way of life.

It was with some reason that an early decision was taken to keep US personnel as far apart from the local population as possible. Their base areas were deliberately designed to be self-contained slices of America, segregated from the alien and often hostile Vietnamese. When it came to military operations, also, the US troops were tasked with large-scale conventional jungle warfare against the North Vietnamese and Viet Cong main force, leaving the delicate business of the so-called 'village war' in the hands of the ARVN.

It is misleading to suppose that major American formations in Vietnam were much concerned with counter-insurgency, as that expression is widely understood, for they were not. Instead, they were usually sent out to remote and uninhabited places to 'find, fix and destroy' the formed enemy regiments and divisions which lurked there. Only at a few points

did these operations overlap with the 'village war' – most notably in the Mekong Delta and along the coastal strip of the northernmost corps area. It was perhaps no accident that this latter area saw the massacre at My Lai, near Quang Ngai, in March 1968.

The aim of the US 'search and destroy' operations was to seize back the initiative from the enemy, disrupt his base areas and gain revenge for his harassment or attritional attacks. By the time American deployment was complete, towards the end of 1967, the techniques needed for 'search and destroy' were well understood, and the system was running in top gear.

It is true that in the first couple of years the Americans had suffered some unexpected slippages in their timetable for victory. The logistic build-up took much longer than anticipated, and the North Vietnamese caused considerable surprise by 'reinforcing failure' and matching the US escalation by one of their own. Several leading American commanders were badly embarrassed to find that their confident predictions of an early triumph proved premature. It is nevertheless the case that at the start of 1968 these predictions were at last starting to be fulfilled. The communist decision to launch the Tet offensive itself owed a very great deal to this fact.

On the other hand there were few 'search and destroy' missions which could truthfully be described as anything but very blunt instruments. They seldom attained anything like the degree of precision and effectiveness which was intended by their designers, and had to be repeated incessantly before they started to achieve their effect. They did have an important effect, and they did succeed in eroding the North Vietnamese freedom of manoeuvre; but it was a wearing and exhausting process.

Working on water

A major problem lay in the nature of the terrain which, although it varied greatly from one part of the country to another, was almost universally difficult. In the Mekong Delta it was waterlogged and often impassable to ground vehicles. A special riverine task force had to be created there, equipped with a weird and wonderful assortment of specialised armoured boats. There were barges converted into floating artillery platforms; gunboats and monitors for direct fire support; and landing craft to carry infantry, helicopters, medical posts or headquarters. There was even a floating barracks to act as a base for this miniature armada, and a floating workshop for running repairs.

Inland from Saigon lay the heavily-forested 'war zones' of the piedmont region. These provided bases for communist activities in the capital, and staging points along the line of supply from Cambodia. Throughout the war this area attracted a particularly heavy share of the fighting and, indeed, of the US defoliation efforts. Gradually the jungle was mastered and the enemy base camps uprooted; but it was a laborious business which took several years, and thousands of lives, to complete.

Further north, the jagged line of the Central Highlands wound its way up the borderlands between Vietnam and Cambodia or Laos. Some of these mountains rose to 2100m (7000 feet) above sea level and attracted cloud cover which restricted flying at many times of the year. The population, however, was sparse in these areas. It consisted of a few planters, the occasional tribe of Montagnards and a rich variety of jungle fauna. On 23 December 1968 a US Marine fell victim to attack by a tiger.

It was difficult enough merely to enter these inhospitable arenas of conflict, and the helicopter rapidly became indispensable to the US campaign. Hopping from one landing zone (LZ) to another at speeds of around 100 knots, the helicopter could mock the jungle, the hills, and even the debilitating heat. It could cruise at 600m (2000 feet) where it was beyond the reach of effective smallarms fire, and it could whisk a casualty from battlefield to hospital in a matter of minutes. The category 'died of wounds' almost ceased to exist for the Americans in Vietnam, since those who were hit would either be killed outright or they would be evacuated and survive. The medical helicopter (or 'Dustoff') became an essential and unavoidable component in any operation.

The main difficulty with helicopters, however, was the fact that sooner or later they had to come down to earth. Their approach to an LZ was notoriously dangerous if the area was covered by the enemy's fire, so whenever possible any LZ had to be 'prepped' by a bombardment, or secured by ground troops, before it could be used. The LZ itself also had to have enough room for helicopters to land, which in triple-canopy jungle could often be a tall order. Innumerable operations were distorted by the sites of available LZs, or delayed while fresh ones were cleared. Each one might have to be strenuously hacked out by machetes or chain saws, although the Americans did eventually make experiments with giant blast bombs – 6800kg (15,000lb) 'Daisy Cutters' – in their search for more rapid methods. Techniques of this kind were developed only later in the war, however, and like so many of the Americans' tactical refinements they could not affect the action during the decisive first three years.

Danger on the ground

Finally, no helicopter could enhance the mobility of troops on foot once they had stepped off their LZ. From that point onwards they were on their own, and were no better off than the enemy. They had to manpack all their weapons, and could move no faster than their legs could carry them. In jungle a speed of half a kilometre (600 yards) per hour might be considered good going, and in Vietnamese conditions one could not expect to march for very many hours at a time. Only tracked vehicles could have improved the situation in these respects, but the Americans mistakenly believed that such vehicles would be too vulnerable to guerrilla harassment and would lack manoeuvrability in difficult terrain; they were not widely used until later in the war.

The cumbersome nature of US manoeuvres gave the enemy many opportunities to monitor their progress. Communist intelligence was generally very good, and where possible they would try to sidestep the blow and present the Americans with a frustratingly 'dry hole'. Alternatively, the communists might manoeuvre around a network of prepared positions and ambush a detached sub-unit of the American force. On many occasions this type of action led to combats in which the odds were surprisingly unfavourable to the theoretically stronger side. With their agility, their skills in dispersion, in digging and in concealment, and their stubborn persistence in the face of danger, the Viet Cong and North Vietnamese

infantry often succeeded in pinning the Americans down. Firefights could then become very lengthy, and might be terminated only when the communists chose a propitious moment to slip away. The Viet Cong proved so skilful at evading contact with American forces whenever they chose that they earned the nickname 'ghosts'.

The Americans had little difficulty in killing large numbers of the enemy when he chose to make massed rushes against a defended perimeter. The firepower of almost any US base was truly prodigious. Even in mobile encounter battles the Viet Cong and North Vietnamese casualties would be high. But what the Americans found they could not do was to destroy entire enemy formations. It was rare for whole communist battalions or regiments to be surrounded or captured, since they were normally capable of escaping from the scene of a battle to fight another day. With their clumsy mixture of helicopters which needed LZs, and infantry which needed heavy supporting fire, the Americans rarely enjoyed much of an advantage when it came to mobility for the pursuit. They could often 'find' the enemy and could sometimes 'fix' him. They could almost always 'destroy' some of his soldiers – but they could not effectively destroy his order of battle, and therefore they were unable to bring the war to the speedy conclusion which they so desperately needed. **R.E.M. Foster**

Above: US infantry on patrol during Operation Oregon in May 1967 question a crippled villager. Collecting intelligence from the local population was not, however, generally considered one of the main tasks of the US ground forces. Most 'grunts' were drawn from the rougher, less educated sectors of US society, and although their unquestioning patriotism encouraged high morale in the early part of the war, they were singularly ineffective ambassadors for the US way of life.

Key Weapons

MINES AND MINESWEEPING

Although the first underwater mine was successfully exploded during the American War of Independence (1775-83) it was not until the 20th century that the mine developed into one of the most flexible weapons available to the maritime powers. But as the importance of the mine grew then so did measures to counteract its influence; each development in naval mine technology has been swiftly paralleled by appropriate countermeasures. And while mines can be laid by almost any ship, submarine or aircraft, their neutralisation has necessitated the construction of purpose-built vessels, the minesweeper and minehunter.

Compared with the greater majority of marine weapons, the mine is a simple, cheap and yet highly flexible weapon: it can be constructed to be activated by virtually anything afloat or it can discriminate between surface ships and submarines or even particular classes of each; it can be used offensively or defensively, and, not least, it can be laid by a wide range of vehicles. Once laid it can prove difficult to sweep and even the suspicion of its presence can exert a powerful psychological effect, disrupting sailing schedules and demanding a large commitment in time, effort and expense to prove a sea-lane clear. Two world wars have demonstrated conclusively that a well-organised mining policy will yield a handsome return on a small outlay. The mine is highly cost-effective and techniques in deployment and countermeasures are ignored by a maritime power only at its peril.

Many similarities exist between the use of mines ashore and at sea. Fields may be laid overtly or covertly, they may be self-contained or 'controlled' and those announced may not actually exist. They should create doubt in the mind of the enemy tactician, restricting his freedom of movement while improving one's own.

Orthodox mines can be divided into contact or influence types. The contact mine is the simpler of the two and for its detonation relies on the surface vessel crushing one of several lead horns that protrude from the mine. The influence mine responds to one or more types of 'signature', which can be magnetic, acoustic or pressure in origin. These methods of triggering a mine have been used for some considerable time but refinements in micro-electronics have given the mine an increasing degree of intelligence, for instance in its powers of target discrimination and in its ability to identify a false target, thereby increasing its resistance to countermeasures and sweeping.

All types can be made buoyant for moored laying in deep water, or negatively buoyant for bottom laying in shallow water. Pure contact-type mines are now rare, their lethal radius being too restricted.

Magnetic mines, once laid, are situated in a known condition of the earth's magnetic field. A metal ship, passing within a practical range, will distort this field, altering the electrical coupling between a pair of coils in the mine. The minute signal thus derived is amplified to detonate the mine. On the other hand, if a ship's magnetic signature can be diminished, so also will be its likelihood of triggering such a mine. Cruder mines of World War II vintage responded to the magnetism which is an inherent part of a ship's steel hull. This could be nullified or reversed by ringing the hull with a heavy 'degaussing' girdle, a charged electric cable fed from an on-board generator which encircled the vessel's hull. Indeed, it was often sufficient to 'wipe' the ship periodically on a specialist de-magnetising range, to ensure a reasonable level of immunity.

Present-day mines, however, are sensitive enough to respond even to electrical machinery within a hull. To counter these, high-risk ships such as a mine countermeasure vessel (MCMV) incorporate several large coils built into the hull in different planes. A range-calibration of the ship will quantify her magnetic field for any combination of active machinery and determine the levels of energisation needed to counter

Previous page: HMS *Ledbury*, a Brecon-class minehunter of the Royal Navy, undergoes sea trials in 1981. Above: A Soviet Whisky-class submarine, a vessel widely used by the Soviet Navy to carry out unobserved mine-laying duties.

Right: Hydrofoils – such as the US Navy's *Pegasus* – are useful vessels when employed in a minesweeping capacity.

the machinery's magnetic effect.

Acoustic mines can be designed to respond to a wide variety of noise input. Signal processing can enable them to be highly selective in their choice of target or, alternatively, to be triggered by any noise source that exceeds a normal ambient level. Noise transmitted underwater by ships derives from three main sources: the vibration caused by propeller cavitation (an imbalance in water pressure due to the action of the propeller), flow turbulence around the hull, and the action of machinery, particularly the propellers themselves. The first two sources radiate broad-band, high-frequency noise, hardly characteristic of a particular ship but which may be reduced by careful attention to design. Propeller-induced noise, however, is of low-frequency and highly individual, caused largely by the blades of the propeller working in an asymmetric wake pattern. Noise produced by machinery within the hull can be isolated to some degree through the use of resilient mountings.

Pressure mines work because a moving ship is surrounded by a three-dimensional pressure field. Where the sea is shallow, water is constricted between the sea bed and the ship's bottom, but then is forced outwards, its increase in velocity being accompanied by a corresponding decrease in local pressure which can be made to deflect a pressure-sensitive diaphragm in the mine. This type of mine is particularly difficult to sweep as only a ship-sized body can produce a large enough change in pressure. As this effect is also a function of ship speed, however, the safest course is to navigate slowly in suspect and shallow waters.

Minelaying can be conducted by surface ships of almost any type, by submerged submarines or by aircraft. Navies whose tasks include the control of maritime choke points, such as the Baltic or Black Sea exits, commonly include mine rails on the afterdecks of a wide variety of warships, even down to fast attack craft. As minelaying by surface ships tends to attract attention it is usually reserved for a defensive field. Submarines can penetrate enemy waters submerged, laying mines either through the torpedo tubes or from especially configured external stowages. Aircraft

Above: A US Navy Mk 25 mine is loaded aboard a P-3 Orion aircraft in preparation for an aerial drop. Right: A Mk 6 mine is positioned on launching rails prior to testing on an exercise in Subic Bay in the Philippines.

carry fewer mines but can lay them both rapidly and at short notice. It is in the interests of the layer to site a minefield with as much precision as possible, both to avoid it himself and to ensure that the enemy will be forced to travel through it. In this respect surface laying is the best method, as submarines and aircraft lack accuracy.

Classic minesweeping operations are arduous – and potentially hazardous – whilst being comparatively simple in concept. The minesweeper tows an underwater cable or sweep fitted with cutters which will sever the mooring wire holding the underwater mine to the sea bed. Once floating on the surface the mine can be located and dealt with.

Above: The Royal Navy minesweeper HMS *Cuxton* (displacement 400 tonnes, crew 27), on a mine-clearing mission.

Although not true sea-going vessels hovercraft are suitable for in-shore minesweeping work (above) and are largely immune from the effects of exploding mines (right).

Right: The Soviet Union places considerable importance on mine warfare and has a large fleet of minesweeping vessels, including this T58-class ocean-going minesweeper photographed in the Atlantic in 1966.

Below right: The *Eridan*, the first of the French Navy's tripartite minehunters. These ships represent the latest in MCMV technology and are equipped with devices such as the PAP 104.

Influence-type mines, laid on the sea bed in shallower waters, require different techniques. Magnetic mines can be detonated by a buoyant cable sweep, towed in a large loop through which are passed heavy bursts of electric current. Acoustic mines can be swept with a towed body housing a noise generator which emits a sound within the wavelength band normally radiated from a ship. But as the modern mine is capable of discriminating it may well ignore the sweep; it is a simple modification to incorporate a counter into the mine trigger circuit enabling it to ignore a set number of stimuli. A mine so fitted may well be 'swept' a dozen times only to explode on the thirteenth.

The growing sophistication of the influence mine has led to the development of minehunting as a replacement to sweeping. The idea behind minehunting is to pinpoint each suspicious object with a high-definition sonar, examine each and dispose of it, where necessary, with a countermining charge. During peacetime vital sea areas can be scanned by sonar in order to build up an accurate map of the sea bed, a process that needs to be updated regularly. Using this survey as a reference, an MCMV can then rapidly detect any new object by automated comparison techniques. The object is marked for investigation, either by a diving team working from the ship's inflatable boat or by a remotely-controlled vehicle. This latter device, such as the French-built PAP 104, is really a miniature submarine, and controlled from the ship is able to pinpoint the mine. If visibility permits, it is able to transmit television pictures back to the parent MCMV. Once alongside the mine it can then lay a small charge to ensure its destruction.

Current multi-role MCMVs, built of glass-reinforced plastic, packed with non-ferrous machinery and high precision electronics and built to stringent noise-emission standards, are very expensive. In the quest for cheaper alternatives, large hovercraft have been evaluated. They have the advantage of being very hard for the mine to detect, due to the air cushion, and if the mine should detonate they suffer little damage from an explosion. Though able to deploy most of the usual countermeasures equipment, they lack the seaworthiness of a ship and are

Left: A PAP 104 mine-hunting submersible is lowered into the water during trials in 1980.

Below left: The US Navy's Aggressive class is one of the more important minesweeping types and has been exported world-wide, here as the *Vinh Long* in the French Navy. Below: A type-498 minehunter of the Royal Belgian Navy.

really suitable only for fast-response day-running.

Mines so far mentioned have been termed conventional, their common feature being a passivity that requires the target to come to them. The American Captor (captive torpedo) mine, however, has proved a starting point for a new generation of active weapons. The mine consists of an encapsulated homing torpedo, and discharge system and advanced electronic devices for acoustic processing. Acoustic inputs from any passing vessels are received by associated hydrophones and then analysed; if they agree with a 'wanted' signature, the torpedo is automatically launched. The Captor mine is specifically designed to counter Soviet submarines in the North Atlantic; lines of these mines will be sown across strategic choke points to act as a barrier to submarines attempting to break-out into the Atlantic sea lanes.

If the Captor mine represents the way forward for future mine development then it seems likely that this trend will be paralleled by progress in the nuclear mine. Some defence commentators suggest that the submarines that breached Swedish territorial waters in the early 1980s were in fact Soviet submarines armed with nuclear mines. The advantages of such a weapon are considerable: it could be laid covertly and left dormant to be activated at a time of international crisis and its presence announced to strengthen the mine-layer's bargaining position. Attempts at clearance would risk detonation and possibly the loss of a coastal town or region. Certainly it seems likely that the nuclear mine will become yet another weapon in the superpowers' nuclear arsenal.

The agony of Aden

From nationalist revolt to civil war

The Aden Emergency began around 9 am on 10 December 1963 when a grenade was thrown at the High Commissioner, Sir Kennedy Trevaskis, as he waited to board a plane to attend a constitutional conference in London. An Indian lady was killed, the Deputy High Commissioner, George Henderson (who probably saved the High Commissioner's life by pulling him to one side) was mortally wounded, and several others, including Trevaskis, were injured. It was the curtain-raiser to a terrorist campaign that was to continue with ever-increasing viciousness and violence until the British left Aden four years later.

The British presence in Aden dated back to the 19th century. The Aden peninsula, including its fine deep-water harbour, had been offered to the British Government by the Sultan of Lahej as early as 1799. The offer was declined but in 1839, following ill-treatment of seamen shipwrecked on the South Arabian coast, the Governor of Bombay despatched a punitive force which took physical possession of the town after a short bombardment, and the reigning Sultan formally recognised British sovereignty. Lying close to the junction of the Red Sea with the Indian Ocean, Aden was now regarded as an important strategic acquisition and for the next century served as a coaling and bunkering station on the Imperial route to the Far East. It was governed from India until 1937, when it became a Crown Colony. British Petroleum built an oil-refinery in the Colony in 1954, after which Aden developed as one of the world's busiest oil-bunkering ports.

The actual land area of Aden Colony was comparatively small, but lying beyond its immediate boundary was a collection of autonomous sultanates, sheikhdoms and emirates whose rulers concluded a series of mutually beneficial protection treaties with

The terrorist campaign against the British which began in late 1963 with a grenade attack against the British High Commissioner, Sir Kennedy Trevaskis (left) was carried out by the NLF and FLOSY (above, Abdulla Al Asnag, head of FLOSY, on left of photograph) and was to herald a series of attacks against British military personnel (top, a Northumberland Fusilier collapses against a wall after being hit by grenade fragments).

the British. Britain intervened to protect them from the Turks in 1870 and 1915, and against the encroachments of the Imam of the Yemen in subsequent years. But on the whole the British government tried its utmost to avoid becoming involved in this mountainous interior region – 'up-country' as expressed in Aden – where tribe fought tribe and every man went armed. Eventually the area was organised into the Eastern and Western Aden Protectorates, but these remained separate from Aden Colony, with Britain only operating in an advisory capacity.

Building 'Murder Mile'

After World War II Britain attempted to persuade the Protectorate states to form themselves into a more coherent body. These efforts bore fruit in 1958 with the establishment of the Federation of South Arabia. The principal architect of the Federation was Sir Kennedy Trevaskis, then the British Agent for the Western Aden Protectorate and High Commissioner from 1962. The new Federation had a British-officered Federal Regular Army (FRA) and a local gendarmerie force, the Federal National Guard (FNG).

Below: Police wearing gas masks and carrying batons and shields prepare to meet angry demonstrators in the streets of Crater in September 1962. The decision to create a Federation of South Arabia linking the sheikhs 'up-country' with the more prosperous urbanised Adenis was the root cause of much nationalist resentment in the port.

In 1961 Aden became Britain's main overseas military base west of Singapore and Headquarters Middle East Command was established there. Both the military garrison and the RAF station at Khormaksar were greatly expanded. Large fortunes were made by contractors who built blocks of flats for service families on reclaimed land at Maalla, later to be called 'Murder Mile'. Britain's plan for the region, made explicit in the Defence White Paper of July 1964, was to grant independence to South Arabia while retaining the base in Aden. It was hoped that yoking Aden, with its busy port and its oil refinery, to the improverished up-country states would create a viable economic unit.

But most Adenis feared and distrusted the up-country tribesmen and their discontent grew after January 1963 when Aden Colony joined the Federation as Aden State. Many claimed that Aden had been hijacked into doing so only to forward Britain's plans. The native Adenis were for the most part shopkeepers, artisans, clerks, teachers and civil policemen. Much of the trade was in the hands of Indians or other foreigners who had little interest in the hinterland. Labour in the port was provided by migrant workers from the Yemen, up-country and Somaliland.

When the nationalist movement first began to manifest itself in the early 1960s it drew its main strength from young educated Adenis who were determined to achieve independence on their terms, and not on terms agreed between the British government and the feudal rulers of the petty states up-country. Although they were recruited into the Civil Police, Adenis were few and far between in the FRA and the FNG which recruited from the tribes up-country, as did the Aden Armed Police. There was therefore a deep antipathy between the Adenis and those supposed to protect them, to such an extent that the FRA and FNG were not involved in Aden's internal security until the last few years of British rule. That was the job of the Civil and Armed Police, and in the last resort British troops.

The wider context for the outbreak of terrorism was the tide of Arab nationalism sweeping the Middle East. After the Suez fiasco in 1956 the prestige of Great Britain throughout the Arab world had sunk to its lowest ebb, while the Egyptian leader Gamal Abdel Nasser was at the height of his prestige as the messiah of Arab nationalism. A revolution in the Yemen in 1962 brought Nasser's troops to the borders of the Federation.

Problems with the Yemen

The traditional ruler of the Yemen, the Imam, had an ancient claim to the Protectorates and to Aden itself which Britain had long resisted. This claim was renewed by the republican regime which ousted the Imam in 1962. During the subsequent civil war in the Yemen the royalist faction was supported by Saudi Arabia and the republicans by Egypt, the latter committing some 35,000 troops. Britain for its part rebutted Yemeni territorial claims and also refused to recognise the new republican government. The Egyptian Air Force made a number of strikes into South Arabian territory, notably against Beihan, and an RAF reprisal raid destroyed a fort on the other side of the frontier. Radio Cairo, together with Radio Taiz and Radio Sana in the Yemen, poured out a stream of anti-British and pro-nationalist propaganda beamed specifically at the Federation, which was vilified as

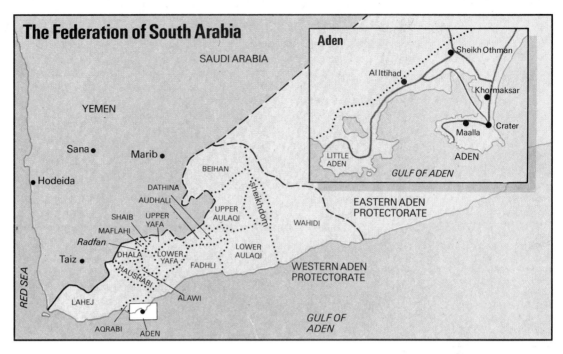

The Federation of South Arabia

Below: Sitting next to an anti-British poster, two soldiers of the Northumberland Fusiliers take time out from duty to relax and have a smoke.

the puppet creation of an imperial power. Such propaganda was well received throughout the Federation, where the Yemeni revolution had been widely acclaimed, inspiring nationalist demonstrations in the Crater district of Aden.

In 1963 the volatile tribes of the Radfan massif, north of Aden, began to receive arms, money and training from the Yemen. These tribes lived in a state of permanent armed feuding with each other, enjoyed fighting for its own sake, and were ripe for mischief, partly because the Federation no longer permitted them to levy their time-honoured but totally illegal tolls on the Aden-Dhala-Yemen road. By the end of the year the Federation's writ had ceased to be honoured in the Radfan and a joint British/FRA task force was sent in to restore order in January 1964. Following the success of this operation, the force was withdrawn. (Described on pages 909-913.) The withdrawal in itself was hailed as a tremendous victory by

the dissidents and trouble broke out afresh with renewed vigour. Ultimately it took the remainder of the year and a strong brigade battlegroup based in the Thumier basin inside the Radfan before the revolt was suppressed. The nature of operations varied between high-intensity and outright war, involving artillery, airstrikes, Saladin armoured cars and occasionally Centurion tanks employing direct gunfire against the rebels' sangars. Placed firmly on the defensive, the dissidents finally gave up. Not that the Radfan could ever be regarded as safe or secure; the only Britons whose safety could be guaranteed were the government's civilian water engineers, whose value to the tribes in this inferno of red, heat-shattered rocks was beyond price.

Although the revolt in the Radfan and the threat posed by the Yemen had been successfully contained, the influence of the local nationalist organisations was beginning to rise. Of these the oldest was the

South Arabian League, formed in 1951 at Lahej, but it played only a minor role in events. The much larger Front for the Liberation of Occupied South Yemen (FLOSY) drew most of its support from Aden and its environs. Most important of all was the National Liberation Front (NLF), formed in 1963 with assistance from Egypt, with a broadly marxist philosophy.

These groups cordially detested each other and the only point upon which they agreed was that whoever controlled South Arabia after independence, it would not be the hereditary state rulers who had formed the Federation. It was equally clear to all that to achieve this aim the British must be compelled to evacuate Aden altogether. Terrorism would be the major tool to drive them out.

Murder and manipulation

After the grenade thrown at the High Commissioner, the next act of terrorism occurred on Christmas Eve 1964 when a grenade was thrown into a British teenagers' party; one girl was killed and four others were wounded. There was very much worse to come. In 1965 there were 286 incidents; in 1966 there were 510; and in 1967 there were no fewer than 2900. These attacks resulted in 2096 casualties among troops and local inhabitants. The first attacks were amateur affairs which often resulted in the terrorists blowing themselves up with their own explosives. Gradually, however, their techniques became more efficient. The terrorist tactics were similar to those employed in Cyprus, using bazookas, grenades, smallarms, mortars and mines. The rabbit warren of huts that lay behind Maalla, in Crater (the business quarter) and in Sheikh Othman, 16km (10 miles) from Aden Town, provided safe refuges for terrorists among a population too scared to give them away.

Steady infiltration of the police and of the tiny state forces, accompanied by murder and threats against the families of loyal men, reduced to a trickle the flow of intelligence reaching the British. Mining of roads and grenade attacks were complemented by carefully staged riots, often designed to draw British troops within range of snipers.

At first the British authorities seemed at a loss as to how to tackle the problem. Although there had been plenty of previous British experience in Cyprus and Kenya, there were too many government agencies functioning independently, and a further complication was the reluctance of Adeni ministers in the Federal government to take strong action. However on 5 June 1965 the General Officer Commanding Middle East Land Forces was appointed Security Commander and an efficient command organisation was established. The various intelligence agencies were also brought under the control of a senior British officer (Brigadier Cowper); but throughout the emergency the lack of reliable information hampered the military.

The deteriorating situation among the tribes 'up-country' added a further complication. The 24th Infantry Brigade supported the Federal forces but incidents continued to increase. The British brought in more troops to Aden itself but the will-o'-the-wisp character of the terrorist tactics made it difficult for them to act before rather than after the event.

It was frustrating for British soldiers to see their comrades killed or maimed with so little prospect of catching terrorists. Aden had long been the British Army's most unpopular overseas garrison and few British soldiers thought the place worth fighting for, let alone dying for. They could trust virtually no one. One British officer's farewell party out at Khormak-

Below: Accompanied by a Ferret armoured car (mounting a 0.3in machine gun) and armed with 7.62mm SLRs, a patrol of Argyll and Sutherland Highlanders moves cautiously through the streets of Crater keeping a careful eye on the rooftops in case of sniper attacks.

sar was abruptly terminated by a grenade thrown, it was thought, by the Arab escort of one of the guests; he was never caught. Pure chance led to the discovery in an Officers Mess of a dining table wired to explode at the time the meal began; only a member of the mess staff could have done it. Another similar attempt failed solely because the terrorists blew themselves up while fixing the charges.

Nonetheless, throughout 1965 the army carried out its counter-insurgency tasks with firmness and formidable restraint – troops were forbidden to open fire first or use heavy weapons – and gradually its policy of covert observation, road blocks, aggressive patrolling and cordon and search operations began to make inroads into the NLF and FLOSY. It is quite possible that in due course the situation could have been brought under control. However, in February 1966 the Labour Government, anxious to slash defence spending, issued a White Paper announcing that the British would not be retaining their base in Aden after all. At best, the average Adeni was completely indifferent to the British presence, but following this announcement even the most dedicated Anglophile dared not assist the security forces for fear of reprisals after independence. Worse, the state rulers were advised that their treaties with the United Kingdom had been abrogated, and from this point the demise of the Federation was a foregone conclusion. The date of the British departure was brought forward to 1968.

Rapid withdrawal

The immediate effect of all this was a sharp increase in British casualties as the NLF and FLOSY vied with each other to demonstrate that they were the true liberators of South Arabia. In 1964 two British soldiers had been killed and 25 wounded; in 1965 six were killed and 83 wounded; in 1966 only five were killed but 218 were wounded. In 1967, as evacuation drew near, these figures rose to an unacceptable 44 killed and 325 wounded.

The British government was at its wits' end over Aden by the end of 1966. Some of the Federal ministers had already decamped to their states or to Saudi Arabia; the Chief Minister of Aden State had thrown in his lot with the NLF. Britain was being taken to task in the UN for its 'colonial misrule' and the Labour Government was anxious only to quit. Sir Humphrey (subsequently Lord) Trevelyan was sent out in May 1967 to replace Sir Richard Turnbull as High Commissioner. Although unannounced, his instructions were plain – to get out fast. The date for British withdrawal was advanced to November 1967.

There was virtually armed insurrection between May and August 1967, fierce battles being fought in Sheikh Othman by 1st Battalion, Parachute Regiment before they re-established control. On 20 June the South Arabian Police mutinied in Champion Lines, and their example was quickly followed by the Aden Armed Police who were quartered in Crater. For a short period Crater itself remained entirely in dissident hands but its bloodless recapture by 1st Battalion, Argyll and Sutherland Highlanders not only restored British morale but also cost the terrorists considerable face within the local community.

The last few months of the British presence saw a brutal struggle between the NLF and FLOSY to decide who would rule Aden. Whatever hostile feelings the two movements may have had towards the British were eclipsed by their hatred of one another.

Over 240 are known to have died in the fighting on the streets and 551 were reported wounded, but these figures are acknowledged to be far from complete. In fact, since it was publicly announced at the end of August that no less than 12 of the Federal states had joined the NLF, the outcome was a foregone conclusion and FLOSY faded away. So did the Federation of South Arabia, yet another ill-fated attempt by the British to solve their colonial problems by the dubious policy of federation. The British Government negotiated a transfer of power to the NLF. But the British soldiers were past caring about Aden and South Arabia.

The final military withdrawal was a masterpiece of logistic and operational planning, the RAF surpassing themselves. One night the Argylls were in Crater and 30 hours later they were passing through London for some well-earned leave. On 28 November the High Commissioner came ashore from HMS *Eagle* lying in the harbour to take a final salute and then flew home. A Royal Marine band sped him on his way with 'Fings Ain't Wot They Used To Be'. At 1345 hours the next day the garrison commander Major-General Philip Tower handed over to the South Arabian Army (formed out of the FRA and elements of the FNG) and left by helicopter for HMS *Intrepid* for passage home. The last British soldier was quit of Aden and no one had any regrets. **James Lunt**

Although many civilians were quick to join the protest movement (top, Adenis tear at street railings in order to place them across streets to frustrate the movement of British armoured car patrols) their protests were very often suppressed with the utmost vigilance by foot patrols (above, a street demonstrator is cornered by British troops as he desperately struggles to get away).

Champion Lines

Where mutineers ambushed British troops

It was around 0900 hours on 20 June 1967 and the 19 men of 60 Squadron Royal Corps of Transport (RCT), who had been firing on the rifle range since earlier that morning, clambered onto the three-tonner which was to take them back to their lines for a shower and breakfast. It was stinkingly hot and looked to grow hotter as the jagged outline of Jebel Shamsan, Aden's extinct volcano, vanished behind the heat haze.

They had not heard the firing from across the sandy waste in Sheikh Othman where the Federal Regular Army (FRA) training centre was located in Lake Lines. Even had they done so it is unlikely they would have attached any importance to it. Rifle and machine-gun fire was part of daily life in Aden as British rule drew to an end.

But the firing had been heard in Champion Lines, close by the range. There, the South Arabian Police (until 1 June called the Federal National Guard) had their training centre. They were tribesmen from up-country with only two or three British officers, their other officers being Arabs. Rumour travels fast in Arabia and is usually garbled in transmission. Soon it was being said that the FRA had mutinied in Sheikh Othman and were being fired on by British troops. The immediate reaction of the police was to storm the armoury, seize the weapons and man the camp perimeter; their officers, who were unable to calm them, took refuge in the main guard room. The rumours were in fact untrue: there had been a minor mutiny in Lake Lines but it had been suppressed by the FRA

Below: While colleagues stand to attention in silence by the graves of their comrades fallen in action, a salute is fired over the cemetery by a salute party after the Aden mutiny of 1967.

itself without the need for British assistance.

Soon the RCT three-tonner came in sight, lumbering down the road on its way to Radfan camp less than a mile away. The police opened fire with everything they had, killing eight soldiers and wounding eight more. A few minutes later two cars came down the road and were similarly greeted, two Aden policemen and a Public Works Department (PWD) employee being killed and another PWD employee wounded.

When the news reached the Federal capital, Al Ittahad, 10km (six miles) away, the government at once requested the aid of British troops to suppress the mutiny. This was soon followed by a mutiny of South Arabian policemen in Al Ittahad itself which was only suppressed by the quick-wittedness and courage of Sultan Saleh al Audhali, one of the Federal ministers.

Meanwhile orders had gone out to Radfan Lines where the stand-by force, C Company, 1st Battalion, King's Own Royal Border Regiment was located. The situation in Champion Lines was to be restored immediately. Major David Miller, Officer Commanding C Company, was told to use minimum force without opening fire if at all possible. The authorities were anxious to avoid any subsequent charge that British soldiers had fired on their Arab comrades and in any case Champion Lines bordered the main runway of Khormaksar airport where planes were landing and taking off.

Since the lines were a Federal barracks they were virtually unknown to the British Army. A collection of huts and tents that normally housed several hundred Arabs under training, the lines were protected by a wide barbed-wire fence with sandbagged emplacements at strategic points on the perimeter. The main road from Aden to Sheikh Othman passed within a short distance of the camp which was joined to it by a tarmacked track. Having issued his orders Major Miller set off with an escort to discover as much as he could about the situation.

Soon after he left, a message arrived insisting on immediate action. The troops then embussed and set off in convoy with a troop of the Queen's Dragoon Guards to support them. They came under fire almost as soon as they started. The machine-gunner in the leading vehicle was killed and eight more men were wounded before the company arrived at the main entrance to the camp and debussed. In the absence of the company commander there was considerable confusion, particularly because the soldiers' tempers were rising as they saw their comrades being wounded. It took highly-disciplined troops with first-class NCOs to 'keep their cool' under such provocation.

Into the camp

Fortunately Major Miller then turned up and ordered 10 Platoon to seize the main guard room where the British and Arab officers had holed up. This was done without bloodshed or firing a shot. The other platoons then started to advance into the camp.

The policemen were still firing indiscriminately in true South Arabian fashion and one wounded soldier required immediate evacuation. He was placed in the only available three-tonner whose driver, Lance-Corporal Vickers, RCT, had volunteered for the mission. So had Private Dickenson of the King's Own Border Regiment who was wounded as Vickers braved a gauntlet of fire, but the casualty was safely delivered to Radfan Lines.

Meanwhile C Company continued to advance cautiously but steadily into the heart of Champion Lines. Not a shot was fired although the supporting Guards Troop fired some rounds over their heads to discourage the opposition. By the end of the morning the situation was back to normal with no more casualties and without opening fire.

This was an action in the highest tradition of the British Army. Although they had seen their comrades shot down in cold blood by men they had until then regarded as friends, and despite the fact that they were greatly provoked by the attempts to prevent them rescuing their wounded, the soldiers of C Company never once lost their heads or took the law into their own hands. Their discipline was beyond praise, as

Below: The Champion Lines mutiny and the death of British troops made headlines in the London *Evening News* of 20 June 1967.

Mutiny, then machine-gun opens up on troops

Eight die answering call for help

ADEN BRITONS GUNNED DOWN

was their courage. They richly deserved the MC awarded to Major David Miller and their two Mentions in Despatches.

When news of their conduct under such provocation reached the Arab troops elsewhere in the Federation all were impressed; indeed it went a long way towards fortifying Arab morale which was close to cracking. The King's Own Royal Border Regiment are unlikely to be permitted to add 'Champion Lines' to the many Battle Honours emblazoned on their Colours, but one thing is certain: never in its history has it or its forbears fought better, nor in more difficult circumstances.   **James Lunt**

Below: Major David Miller (nearest camera) who commanded C Company, 1st Battalion the King's Own Royal Border Regiment. It was Major Miller's accurate assessment of the situation and rapid action that successfully suppressed the mutiny of the South Arabian Police at Champion Lines.

Mad Mitch goes in

The Argylls and the retaking of Crater

By June 1967 the Arab armed forces and police in South Arabia who were cooperating with the British faced an insecure future. The imminence of British withdrawal threatened to leave them exposed to the vengeance of their nationalist enemies in the National Liberation Front (NLF) and Front for the Liberation of Occupied South Yemen (FLOSY). But more than just fear eroded their loyalty; in the heightened atmosphere of Arab nationalism that followed the dramatic events of the Arab-Israeli Six-Day War (5-11 June 1967), many felt the pull of allegiance to Arab nationalism outweigh their duty to the British and the sheikhs. The defeat of Egypt – a severe blow to Arab pride – rendered them intensely sensitive to any slight or suspected insult. It was almost universally believed that the British supported the Israelis, and this both encouraged covert hostility to the colonial authority and aroused irrational fears of British intentions towards all Arabs.

A small incident sufficed to set off a chain reaction which ended in violence. On 1 June the Federal Regular Army (FRA) and the Federal Guard had been reorganised as the South Arabian Army and the South Arabian Police (although the FRA is still called by its former name here, for simplicity). The reorganisation aroused fierce tribal tensions and jealousies within the FRA; it was claimed that officers of the Aulaqi tribe had been shown unfair preference. The problem assumed such proportions that in mid-June four colonels were suspended from duty, one of whom issued

such an inflammatory statement that for the moment discipline within the FRA collapsed. Some units were in a virtual state of armed mutiny. Wild rumours abounded that the British intended to suppress the disturbances without mercy.

On the morning of 20 June, there were mutinies in the FRA at Lake Lines and the South Arabian Police at Champion Lines. Although they were soon suppressed, the sustained firing had led to even wilder rumours within Crater that the British had embarked on a campaign of unrestrained slaughter against their former comrades-in-arms, and that the Aden Armed Police – a gendarmerie unit, not to be confused with the Civil Police – would be attacked in their barracks on Queen Arwa Road in the town of Crater. The Armed Police were predisposed to believe these rumours. Many of them had nationalist sympathies and their ranks had been infiltrated by the NLF. Their internal security duties had been taken over by the British forces, a serious affront to their sensibilities. Torn by conflicting loyalties the Armed Police were nervous and panicky.

The town of Crater is probably one of the most unpleasant on Earth. As its name implies, it is built inside the crater of the extinct volcano Jebel Shamsan. Long ago the seaward wall of the crater collapsed but the remaining cliffs simply serve to contain the immense heat hurled down by the sun and the numerous smells rising from its teeming alleys. Save at two points the towering rocks deny access to or exit from

Above: The wreckage of the Land Rover in which Major Moncur and his companions were killed on 20 June by the Aden Armed Police in Queen Arwa Road, Crater.

Left: 'Mad Mitch', Lieutenant-Colonel Colin Mitchell of the Argyll and Sutherland Highlanders, takes the wheel of a Land Rover. To his left sits the Arab Chief of Police, who had just been warned by Mitchell that his command might be wiped out by the 'wild hillmen' of the Argylls unless they surrendered at once. Above: British troops, with bayonets fixed, move at speed to defensive positions.

Right: A Northumberland Fusilier propels a demonstrator at speed along a street in Crater. The Northumberland Fusiliers had kept effective order in Crater for a year before the mutiny of the Aden Armed Police in June 1967.

Crater, and, depending on one's circumstances and viewpoint, this renders the town either a fortress or a trap. To the east, Marine Drive penetrates the narrow gap between the rocks and the sea and thence proceeds along the waterfront. On the western or harbour side a road climbs to a break in the cliffs known as Main Pass, the summit of which is covered by an ancient Turkish fort; once through Main Pass, this route descends into Crater, to become Queen Arwa Road.

For the past year Crater had been controlled by the 1st Battalion, Royal Northumberland Fusiliers, efficiently and without loss. On 20 June the battalion's Y Company was in position just outside the Marine Drive exit, with the armoured cars of A

Squadron, Queen's Dragoon Guards in support. Inside Crater, Second-Lieutenant John Davies was making a routine patrol in a Pig APC when he noticed suspicious activity within the Armed Police barracks. Shots were fired and after reporting the matter to his company commander, Major John Moncur, he decided that rather than return through the town to Marine Drive he would take the longer route via Main Pass and Khormaksar. At this stage communications broke down and Moncur, not knowing the reason for Davies' delayed return, went in to look for him. His party travelled in two Land Rovers and included Major David Malcolm and two men of the 1st Battalion, Argyll and Sutherland Highlanders, who were due to relieve the Fusiliers within a matter of days. Arriving opposite the barracks, the vehicles were riddled with rifle and machine-gun fire and set ablaze. The sole survivor was Fusilier Storey, who, although wounded, took cover in a nearby building and shot dead one of his opponents. Storey was captured while trying to escape but his life was saved by a senior police officer.

Guns for all

It was now Davies' turn to look for Moncur and from the evidence lying across Queen Arwa Road it was only too clear what had happened. Dismounting with three of his men he sent back his APC with a situation report and remained to observe developments; it was a brave but unwise decision, for none of the four was seen alive again. Altogether, three attempts were made by the Queen's Dragoon Guards to recover the bodies, each of which failed in the face of intense fire which smashed vision blocks and rendered the Saladins' co-axial Brownings useless. Requests to use the 76mm main armament were repeatedly denied by higher authority. Elsewhere, smallarms fire shot down a Sioux helicopter which was lifting a picquet onto Temple Cliff, wounding all the occupants. As dusk fell on what, for the British, had been the bloodiest day of the entire campaign, all troops were withdrawn from Crater.

Inside the town the Armed Police, now fearful of the consequences of their actions, issued 400 rifles to all comers. The gaol was opened and its inhabitants joined a rejoicing mob which subjected several British bodies to a grisly mock trial, following which they were mutilated and ritually hung. The NLF and FLOSY began their fratricidal strife almost immediately. Abdul Bani Makrum Audali, the NLF's military commander, was shot dead, ironically by a recently liberated prisoner; in reprisal, the NLF kidnapped his FLOSY equivalent, Fuad Khalifa, who also happened to be the Mayor of Aden and an executive with Aden Airlines. FLOSY, in fact, had much the worst of the exchange and was ultimately hemmed in among the shanties of the upper slopes.

On 21 June the British responded by sealing the Marine Drive exit from Crater. Simultaneously Main Pass was attacked and secured by the Fusiliers and Royal Marine Commandos. For a while the troops were pinned down by heavy fire from the old Turkish fort and a request for direct gunfire support by the armoured cars received a grudging assent – with the proviso that only *one* round was to be used. That failed to explode and the Queen's Dragoon Guards therefore decided it did not count; the second round burst among the defenders and promptly broke the enemy's resistance. Beyond this the British garrison commander, Major-General Philip Tower, was not prepared to proceed at this stage, a decision which deeply angered the troops who felt that they had taken enough and badly wanted their revenge. In fact Tower's decision was quite logical, for the FRA's loyalty remained shaky and he wished to avoid an open confrontation between it and his own troops; further, there were still several hundred British citizens at risk.

Tightening the grip

The British government maintained its low-key approach, despatching a battalion of the Prince of Wales' Own Regiment of Yorkshire as reinforcements and advising Tower that it would like Crater retaken, provided it could be secured with minimum force and without heavy loss of British or Arab life.

In the meantime the army tightened its grip on Crater. During the next 10 days snipers working among the crags killed 10 terrorists, making a special target of those who carried British weapons captured on the 20th. By night, patrols stealthily penetrated the enemy's positions and established that these were no longer manned with the same regularity or enthusiasm as during the first euphoric days of 'freedom'. The Fusiliers buried their dead, which the Armed Police had handed over on the evening of the 21st, and returned to the United Kingdom having been relieved by the Argylls under the command of Lieutenant-Colonel Colin Mitchell.

A born soldier, Mitchell became a Home Guard when he was aged 14 and joined his regiment in 1945, serving in the Po sector during the final months of the Italian campaign. Subsequently he had been wounded by Jewish terrorists in Palestine, fought in Korea, and served in Cyprus, Kenya and Borneo. Gifted with very evident qualities of leadership, Mitchell lived for his battalion and none of his officers and men would hear a word said against him. On the other hand, he had a flair for self-advertisement and publicity which some in other regiments found hard to take.

Mitchell had a plan for retaking Crater by degrees

Below: A British soldier armed with a 7.62mm SLR dominates a street in Crater. The continued presence of troops on the street tended to prevent crowd action, but similarly presented terrorist snipers with easy targets.

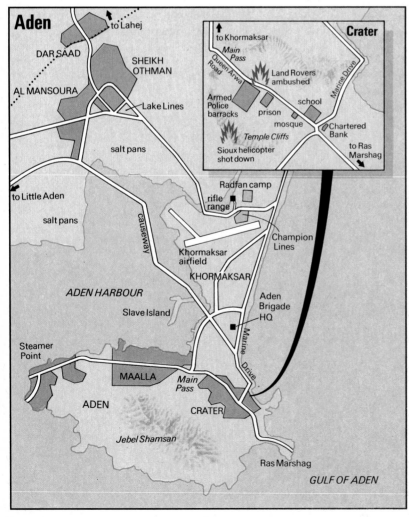

which he code-named Stirling Castle, after the regiment's home headquarters, and this Tower approved. During the afternoon of 3 July one of his companies was lifted by helicopter onto the Ras Marshag peninsula, which had remained in British hands, with orders to link up with the battalion's advance along Marine Drive. At dusk the Argyll outposts indulged in a brief 'hate' against those of the enemy, as they had done on previous evenings, while pipes skirled in the background.

'Wild hillmen'

To the terrorists all seemed routine enough and they would not have noticed the pipers' subtle change to *Monymusk*, the strains of which had preceded every Argyll attack for generations. Mitchell's companies moved off into the darkness, supported by A Squadron, Queen's Dragoon Guards. Near the Sultan's waterfront palace there was an exchange of fire in which two terrorists died but, in the majority of cases, the opposition simply vanished. This had not altogether been anticipated and after the first objectives had been taken, Mitchell requested permission to extend the operation to others. In the temporary absence of Tower this request was granted by Brigadier Charles Dunbar, his deputy. By 0300 hours on 4 July all objectives were secure and Mitchell had set up his headquarters in the Chartered Bank, which was promptly renamed Stirling Castle. By 0530 the Argylls had restored British control of Crater without losing a man. Their pipers brought the Adeni from their beds with the *Long Reveille*, and then the sup-

remely scornful notes of *Hey, Johnnie Cope* began echoing round the ancient volcanic cliffs; the battalion, too, had its dead to avenge. The press had accompanied Mitchell and they joined him as he walked round Crater throughout the morning, smiling and shaking hands with the baffled inhabitants.

There were no smiles, however, for Superintendant Mohammed Ibrahim, the senior Arab officer of the Aden Armed Police; Mitchell told him that the Argylls were wild hillmen who would wipe out his command 'to the last man' at the first sign of trouble. The Armed Police returned to duty, collected all but one of the rifles they had distributed and began re-arresting the criminals they had released. Some days later they held a full dress parade for General Tower, their own pipe band playing *Scotland the Brave* as they marched past. It was a sour, unsmiling affair in which the Argyll officers snubbed their Police opposite numbers.

The Argylls' grip on Crater was never to be shaken. The mosques had already been identified as terrorist havens and were kept under constant covert surveillance; any man seen leaving with a rifle or grenade was instantly shot. After a score of terrorists had been disposed of in this way Crater became the most peaceful area in Aden, in sharp contrast to other areas still nominally under British control where the NLF and FLOSY openly indulged in their private war and drove round brandishing their Egyptian-supplied AK47s. On 25 November, four days before the British evacuation, the Argylls left Crater as neatly as they had entered it.

Bryan Perrett

Below right: Just as the pipes had signalled the entry of the Argyll and Sutherland Highlanders into Crater, so they announced their departure as the regimental flag was piped down on 25 November 1967.

Labour and the Argylls

The Labour Government's choice of a 'softly-softly' approach during the Aden crisis was resented by sections of the British Army, press and public. It was felt that the government's change of policy in the 1966 White Paper exposed soldiers to danger, while 'minimum force' denied them the means to defend themselves.

Advocates of a tough-line with terrorists were outraged by the decision to abandon Crater to the NLF and FLOSY. The retaking of the area made national heroes of Colonel Mitchell and the Argylls; the British public loved it and the army welcomed it. But the Labour government's reaction was ambivalent, because the striking success of Mitchell's direct, 'no-nonsense' approach seemed to discredit the government's caution and reluctance to provoke armed confrontation with the nationalists. Equally, the Labour Cabinet resented Mitchell's outspoken attacks on British policy and his courting of the limelight – 'Mad Mitch' said that British policy in Aden had been so much 'old English humbug'. It seemed somewhat vindictive that his only reward was to be a Mention in Despatches, which could hardly have been avoided in the circumstances. The subsequent announcement that his battalion was to be disbanded was construed as further evidence of government bile, although the truth was that the Argylls were vulnerable in the seniority table. A spirited public campaign to 'Save the Argylls' probably influenced the government sufficiently to prevent complete disbandment.

Bases and budgets

British defence policy of the 1960s

When the Conservative Minister of Defence, Duncan Sandys, presented his review of April 1957 in the aftermath of the Suez Crisis, he failed to resolve a basic dilemma of British policy. Despite a marked decline in the economic and strategic value of Empire and a cut in the size of the armed services as a result of the decision to end conscription, he insisted upon maintaining global commitments. The 'overstretch' was enormous in both financial and manpower terms. The government was trying to retain a facade of world power without the money or manpower to back it up.

The extent of the overstretch became apparent in the early 1960s. On an operational level, British forces found it increasingly difficult to cope with a wide range of consecutive and overlapping overseas commitments – in Kuwait (1961), Brunei (1962), Radfan (1963), Borneo and East Africa (1964) – and this began to affect relations with Europe as Britain's Nato commitment inevitably suffered. The country quite clearly lacked forces large enough to carry out defence roles in both Europe and the Empire.

In addition, such commitments cost money, increasing the pressures upon an already strained defence budget. By 1964-65 the defence bill was £2000 million and this was expected to rise to £2400 million (at 1964 prices) by 1969-70, representing about seven per cent of the country's gross national product in each case. Overseas garrisons, even in areas where operations were not being conducted, were expensive to maintain (by 1964 Singapore alone was absorbing nearly £70 million a year), while the forces to protect them required constant modernisation. Moreover, after 1962 all three armed services had to rely upon volunteer enlistment as the last of the conscripts returned to civilian life, and this necessitated the devotion of substantial funds to such items as pay, just to attract recruits.

The cost of technology

But the real financial problems arose through the need to provide new equipment, for the early 1960s saw a dramatic rise in the number of new developments required to maintain military effectiveness. At a nuclear level, the decision to deploy Polaris submarine-launched ballistic missiles in five boats, taken at Nassau in the Bahamas in December 1962, was expected to cost £350 million by the end of the decade and a further £32 million a year thereafter to maintain; in the air, the projected provision of 150 of the revolutionary TSR-2 aircraft by the early 1970s was likely to cost a staggering £750 million. Add to these a host of other projects – the P-1154 vertical take-off and landing aircraft, the HS-681 medium-range jet transport, the Chieftain main battle tank and the next generation of naval warships – and the extent of the budget squeeze may be appreciated. As *The Times* pointed out in January 1965: 'the defence budget is strained beyond endurance by costly weapons and . . . something has to give; either the budget or the weapons.'

By that time the Conservatives were no longer in office, having been replaced in October 1964 by a Labour administration dedicated to the provision of improved social services. This was likely to prove expensive, requiring a reallocation of resources away from such intangible national assets as defence. No moves were made at this stage to alter the global deployments laid down by Sandys, but after a government meeting at Chequers on 21-22 November 1964, an announcement that the fifth Polaris submarine would be cancelled immediately gave notice of policies to prevent the expected rises in defence spending.

The intention, according to the new Secretary of State for Defence, Denis Healey, was to keep the defence bill below £2000 million a year for the rest of the decade, and the problem of how best to achieve this was delegated to the newly-integrated Ministry of Defence. Its findings were enshrined in official policy in the early months of 1965 and were concentrated against capabilities rather than commitments. Savings were to be made not through a withdrawal from overseas bases but through cuts to equipment programmes. The RAF suffered the most, with decisions to cancel TSR-2 and substitute the American F-111K in its place, to replace the P-1154 project by the subsonic Kestrel (later to be developed into the Harrier) and to purchase American C-130 Hercules instead of the HS-681. In addition, the Territorial Army, occupying an increasingly anachronistic place in the British military structure since the changes to regular Army organisation in the late 1950s, was abolished. It was replaced in early 1966 by a new and cheaper three-tier Territorial and Army Volunteer Reserve (TAVR), designed to provide reservists for a wide range of contingencies. Finally, the Navy's nuclear-powered submarine programme, although retained in the long-term, was delayed.

These changes were estimated to save about £200 million a year, but it was not enough. After various alternatives had been discussed, a more dramatic alteration was announced in February 1966 when it was decided to phase out the Navy's attack-carrier force by the mid 1970s. Both the First Sea Lord and the Minister of State for the Navy resigned in protest, but to no avail. Despite the obvious implication that an absence of large aircraft carriers meant a lack of capability to defend far-flung imperial outposts, the decision remained. Healey, aware of additional savings that were likely to accrue from the end of the Borneo 'Confrontation' with Indonesia and the intended withdrawal from Aden (scheduled for 1968), declared his 'defence review' to be complete.

It was an optimistic claim, for as the year progressed it became apparent that economic growth was slowing down and a balance of payments crisis beginning to emerge. More savings, especially in overseas expenditure, were ordered and a new defence target of £1850 million by 1969-70 laid down. After lengthy discussions, Prime Minister Harold Wilson presented a 'Supplementary Statement on Defence Policy' to

When the Labour administration came to power in October 1964, British defence spending was subjected to a policy of severe economies and the resultant cuts in capability (as opposed to commitment) drastically affected the Royal Air Force development programme. The revolutionary TSR-2 (centre opposite) was abandoned in favour of the F-111 (top left opposite) and the subsonic Kestrel (top right opposite) was brought in to replace the P-1145 development.

the Commons in July 1967. Two major changes were announced. On the one hand, a brigade was to be withdrawn from Germany and, although retaining its Nato role, was to be stationed in the UK to save foreign exchange costs; on the other, forces were to be gradually withdrawn from the Far East, abandoning bases in Singapore and Malaysia by the mid-1970s. The latter move appeared to presage an end to colonial commitment, but in reality it did no such thing, for as the troops withdrew they were to be replaced by strategic air and naval/amphibious units, available for rapid deployment east of Suez should a crisis arise. Such units would clearly be expensive to maintain, especially as their projected tasks bore little apparent relevance to Nato, and as a result the problems of cost and potential overstretch remained.

But the financial crisis was still not over, forcing the government, on 18 November 1967, to devalue the pound. This, in turn, necessitated yet more attempts to curb defence spending. In the short-term,

Below: After the enforced devaluation of the pound sterling by the government in November 1967 further defence cuts were necessary. The Buccaneer naval strike aircraft programme was one area where cuts were imposed and production halted.

Services cuts of 75,000—Official:
OUT of Singapore, Malaysia

FAREWELL FAR EAST!

uneasy DRASTIC CUTS in defen... TOM POCOCK

further equipment cuts were imposed – an RAF order for American Chinook helicopters was cancelled, the carrier HMS *Victorious* was not recommissioned as planned, the production of Buccaneer naval strike aircraft was halted and various re-equipment programmes were slowed down – but there was a limit to the extent of such policies. If money was to be saved on a more permanent basis, something more drastic and far-reaching had to be done.

Europe or the Empire?

The result was to a certain extent predictable and did go some way towards resolving the persistent dilemma of capabilities versus commitments. On 16 January 1968, in yet another 'Supplementary Statement', Wilson announced a complete withdrawal of all British forces from east of Suez (including, surprisingly, the Gulf) by the end of 1971 and, instead of promising specific forces to be committed to these areas in time of future crisis, he spoke of a 'general' capability only, based upon a series of air staging-posts around the Indian Ocean. In addition, as the need for long-range reconnaissance and strike aircraft declined – without the bases there was nowhere they could be stationed east of Suez – the F-111 order was cancelled and, as a final act, the phasing out of the carriers was brought forward to 1972.

These alterations undoubtedly saved money – it was estimated that the defence bill for 1969-70 would now be as low as £1650 million (at 1964 prices), with savings of about £100 million a year in foreign exchange alone – but they did not represent a complete reassessment of Sandys' earlier policy. The garrison at Hong Kong was not touched, all posses-

sions west of Suez remained and air staging-posts at Bahrein, Masirah, Gan, Cocos and Aldabra had to be constructed or maintained to provide the 'general' interventionary capability promised by Wilson. Moreover, a Strategic Reserve of airportable troops, backed by air transports, commando carriers and assault ships, was maintained in the UK and although in July 1968 it was given specific Nato responsibilities, its existence implied a continuance of global pretensions. The government, even under the enormous pressures of deep financial crisis, had still not recognised the reality of Britain as an essentially regional power, dedicated to the defence of Europe rather than the sad remains of a valueless Empire. It was to take another seven years of economic pressure to force such a drastic yet essential change of policy, leaving the armed forces to face an uncertain future, torn between the regional role of European defence and the global responsibility of residual colonial protection.   **J.L. Pimlott**

Although the defence cuts of the 1960s affected many areas of weapons production and development, few overseas garrisons were withdrawn. Hong Kong remained under a military protectorate (top, a British patrol, arms carried to port, moves through the streets of Kowloon) but Singapore was to lose its garrison by the mid-1970s (above, Singaporean Prime Minister Lee Kuan Yew meets Minister of Defence Denis Healey for defence treaty talks in 1966). Above left: The London *Evening Standard* announces the decision to leave Singapore.

Key Weapons

The LEOPARD 1 MBT

The West German Leopard 1 MBT has never seen action but its many virtues have made it an extraordinarily popular tank. German law regarding the export of military equipment is highly restrictive with the result that markets for the Leopard have been limited to Nato allies and Australia. In this narrow field where it has faced competition from American, British and French MBT types, the Leopard 1 has virtually swept the board, becoming the backbone of Canadian, Australian, Dutch, Belgian, Danish, Italian and Norwegian armoured forces. To achieve this it has been seen by its admirers as the equal of its competitors in survivability, power and agility as well as being free of irritating unreliabilities such as the lack of engine power that marred the performance of Britain's Chieftain for so many years. Development of the Leopard 1 began in 1957 when France, Germany and Italy initiated projects for the design of a standard European MBT. In the end, however, each country was to follow up its own development project. Some 26 prototypes of the Leopard were built, followed by a batch of 50 pre-production models. The first production models appeared from the Kraus Maffei works in Munich in September 1965.

The prototype Leopards delivered in 1961 proved to have a number of faults although these seemed correctable with further development and no real major drawback was discovered. Even so, some fairly extensive improvements were made to the first production models which had a larger engine, better suspension, heavier armour, a new transmission and a revised fire control system. They were also fitted with the British 105mm L7 series gun which has continually proved an outstanding success as a tank's main armament in engagements all over the world. Four basic models of the Leopard 1 have been produced, as well as the Leopard 1A1A1 which incorporated additional turret armour to the A1 model. The A2 featured an electronic image intensifier, the A3 was fitted with a new welded turret, while the A4 included a fully automatic gearbox and a new fire control system.

The layout on the Leopard 1 is fairly standard for European and American designed vehicles. It makes provision for a four-man crew with the driver in the front compartment, the gunner in the right-hand side of the turret, the tank commander behind and above the gunner and the loader on the left-hand side. The 10-cylinder MTU diesel engine is located in the rear compartment.

Where the Leopard 1 scored over its contemporary European rivals was in its agility. While the British Chieftain suffered notorious engine difficulties, it was common knowledge that the Leopard had shown greater cross-country speed than the French AMX-30 in comparative trials. This was an important point since both the Leopard and the AMX-30 achieved roughly the same maximum road speed of 65km/h (40mph), but such a road speed is not relevant to combat usage. Engine power, tread width and overall weight can be combined in a formula which might give a tank an exceptionally high cross-country speed but which would be useless in practice because the

Previous page: A Leopard A2 fires its 105mm main armament during Nato exercises. Above left: A Leopard A2 negotiates a sunken track while another A2 makes easy going over rough ground on the German Army tank driving school (above).

Below: The first of the Leopard variants, the A1. The Leopard series is arguably the most successful tank design since World War II.

crew would be injured by the jolting sustained from the swift movement. A tank's agility over the ground, coupled with the efficiency of its suspension, gives its maximum attainable speed in combat and this can only be assessed during trials. This genuine cross-country speed is an important factor in an MBT's combat capability because it represents its power of manoeuvre. Equally important to battlefield manoeuvrability is combat survivability and in the case of an unproven MBT like the Leopard this can only be assessed by comparison with the armour of combat-proven types. The Centurion Mark 13, for example, has considerably heavier armoured protection than the Leopard 1 with armour ranging from 17-152mm (0.67-6.08in) while the Leopard 1's armour is estimated at a mere 10-70mm (0.4-2.75in). The introduction on the A3 and A4 models of an all-welded spaced-armour turret and the recent fitting of appliqué armour to the turret on Dutch and German Leopards has, however, greatly increased available protection while maintaining the high levels of speed and agility for which the tank was designed. The Leopard 1 also has a comparatively low firing height which is especially effective when operating in the hull-down position, a well-designed glacis and turret for the deflection of anti-tank projectiles, and an NBC system.

Main armament on the Leopard 1 consists of an auto-stabilised British 105mm L7A3 rifled tank gun firing a range of ammunition including APDS, APFSDS, HEAT, HESH and smoke. Secondary armament comprises one 7.62mm machine gun mounted co-axially with the main gun, one 7.62mm anti-aircraft machine gun on the turret roof and four smoke dischargers mounted on either side of the turret. When Leopard 1 first went into production laser rangefinders and image intensifiers were distant concepts. Indeed, the British were still using the comparatively primitive method of rangefinding with a machine gun mounted along the gun, a practice that was soon to be found wanting as tanks were required to fire a mix of ammunition types which had different trajectories. The ranging machine gun was discarded on the Leopard and an optical sighting unit was fitted after the tank's initial trials. With the optical sights it was claimed that the Leopard 1 had an 85 per cent first-round hit probability on a stationary target at

1000m rising to 98 per cent with the second round. At 2000m this declined to a 40 per cent first-round probability and a 75 per cent second-round probability. Leopard 1s in service with the Australian, Canadian and Belgian armed forces were fitted with the Belgian SABCA fire control system incorporating a laser rangefinder, analogue computer, seven sensors and a cross-hairs optical sight. The most recent Leopard variant, the A4, is fitted with the COBELDA integrated fire control system.

The crew of the Leopard 1 is provided with a full range of night-vision aids. The original A1 model was

The well-sloped glacis plate of the Leopard A3 can be seen in this photograph (top) and the new welded turret compared with that of the older A2 model (above).

Below: The Leopard A4 was the last of the Leopard 1 variants, and included a new gearbox and an improved fire-control system.

Leopard 1 Main Battle Tank

Crew 4
Dimensions Length (gun included) 9.54m (31ft 3½in); width (including skirts) 3.4m (11ft 1in); height (commander's periscope included) 2.61m (8ft 6in)
Weight Combat loaded 40,000kg (88,000lb)
Engine MTU MB 838 Ca.M500 10-cylinder multi-fuel engine developing 830hp at 2200rpm

Performance Maximum road speed 65km/h (40mph); range (road) 600km (373 miles); vertical obstacle 1.15m (3ft 9½in); trench 3m (9ft 10in); gradient 60 per cent; fording 2.25m (7ft 4ins), with snorkel 4m (13ft)

Armour 10mm-70mm (0.4-2.75in) (estimate)
Armament One 105mm L7A3 gun; one 7.62mm machine gun co-axial with main armament; one 7.62mm anti-aircraft machine gun; four smoke dischargers on each side of the turret

Left: A Leopard A4 prepares to make a river crossing utilising a schnorkel which allows the tank to ford water obstacles to a depth of 4m (13ft).

Below left: A Bundeswehr Leopard A4 drives at speed through a German town camouflaged with local vegetation in an attempt to reduce the vehicle's hard outline. Below: A Leopard driver-training tank which includes a dummy main gun to provide realistic battlefield conditions for student drivers.

Right: The anti-aircraft variant of the Leopard family, the Gepard (hunting leopard) fires its twin 35mm cannon.

Right: The Gepard is a highly sophisticated weapons system which employs twin radars, a surveillance radar at the turret rear and a tracking radar at the front of the turret. Below: A Leopard on night-firing exercises.

fitted with infra-red equipment but on the A2 this was replaced by an electronic image intensifier system which emits no radiation and conceals the tank from detection by enemy infra-red receiving equipment.

Optional equipment developed for the Leopard 1 includes a snorkel which allows the tank to negotiate water obstacles to a depth of 4m (13ft) and a hydraulic blade which can be mounted on the hull front.

In addition to the basic models the Leopard 1's chassis has provided the basis for a number of special-ised variants and battlefield support vehicles. These include an armoured recovery vehicle, fitted with dozer blade, winches and a crane, an engineer vehicle fitted with excavation and earth-boring gear, the Gepard self-propelled anti-aircraft gun, a 155mm self-propelled gun, the Leopard Biber bridgelayer and a training tank.

Of the four Nato contemporaries – the Leopard 1, the French AMX-30, the American M60 and the British Chieftain – the concept behind the first three

was very much the same. Emphasis was on mobility followed by firepower with weight of armour as the least important consideration. Only the Chieftain placed firepower first, protection second and mobility last, so that comparison between it and the others is difficult. For those who did not subscribe to British priorities in MBT construction, the Leopard 1 was a triumph. Its cross-country speed is superior to that of the AMX-30 and of the M60 and it is comparatively easy to maintain in the field. The engine, transmission and cooling system are provided with quick-release couplings so that the entire pack can be changed in 20 minutes and in the same way the gun barrel can also be changed in the same period. This attention to the vehicle's maintainability probably sums up many of the characteristics that have made it so popular: not only is it an MBT which performs at least as well as its rivals but it is sturdy, reliable and without obvious faults. These advantages have been incorporated into its successor the Leopard 2.

Above left: Leopard ARVs (armoured recovery vehicles) on the production line. Above: An ARV hoists a replacement Leopard power pack. Other functions include the recovery of defective vehicles by winch or tow; replacement of turrets and terrain clearing through the use of the front-mounted dozer blade.

Below: The Biber (beaver) armoured bridge layer has a two-element quick-laying bridge for the crossing of waterways and ravines to a distance of 20m (72ft 2in).

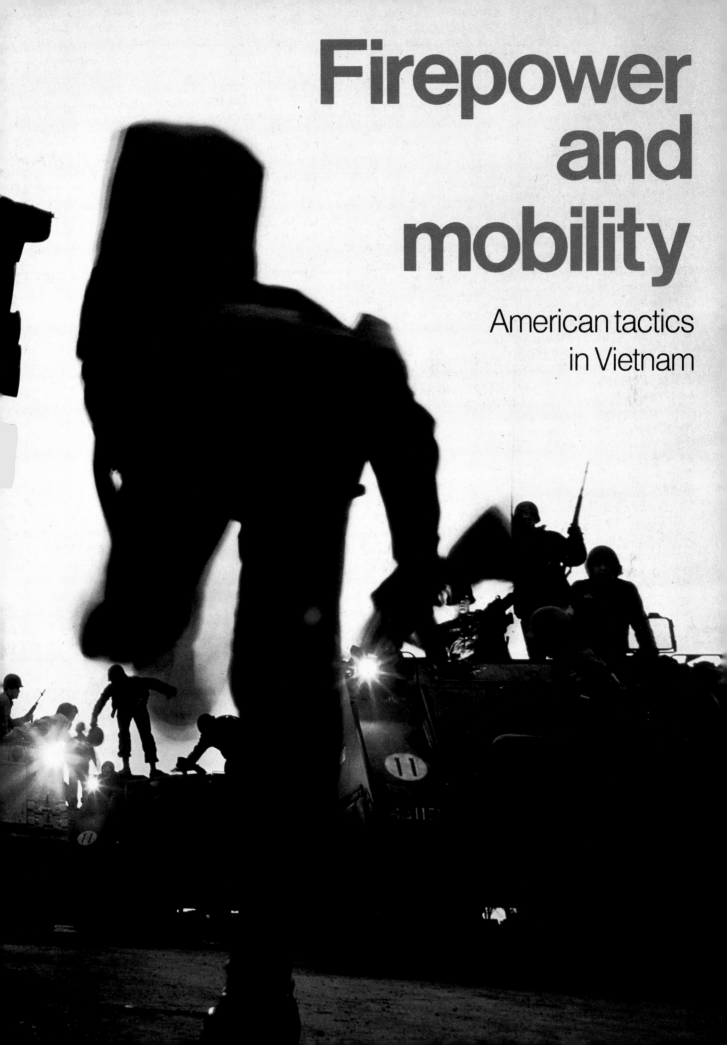

Firepower and mobility

American tactics in Vietnam

Previous page: A US soldier runs to a waiting M113 APC as his unit is 'scrambled' for a night operation. Right: A flight of UH-1D helicopters comes into land at a forward fire base in August 1968.

Left: A gun section of the 1st Cavalry Division (Airmobile) fires against enemy positions in the Bong Son district as part of Operation White Wigg. Although highly manoeuvrable the 105mm guns allocated to the US Army were handicapped by a relatively poor range of little more than 11,000m which meant that isolated fire bases could be vulnerable to long-range NVA fire.

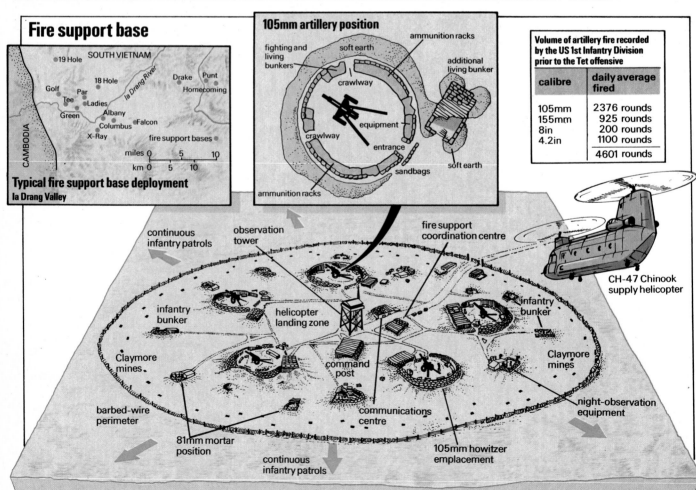

Fire support base

Typical fire support base deployment
Ia Drang Valley

SOUTH VIETNAM

19 Hole · 18 Hole · Golf · Par · Tee · Ladies · Green · Albany · Columbus · Falcon · X-Ray · Drake · Punt · Homecoming

CAMBODIA

fire support bases

miles 0 5 10
km 0 5 10

105mm artillery position

fighting and living bunkers · soft earth · ammunition racks · additional living bunker · crawlway · equipment · crawlway · entrance · sandbags · soft earth · ammunition racks

Volume of artillery fire recorded by the US 1st Infantry Division prior to the Tet offensive

calibre	daily average fired
105mm	2376 rounds
155mm	925 rounds
8in	200 rounds
4.2in	1100 rounds
	4601 rounds

continuous infantry patrols · observation tower · fire support coordination centre · CH-47 Chinook supply helicopter · infantry bunker · helicopter landing zone · infantry bunker · Claymore mines · command post · Claymore mines · barbed-wire perimeter · communications centre · night-observation equipment · 81mm mortar position · continuous infantry patrols · 105mm howitzer emplacement

strategic rethinking of the Kennedy era. As one part of the new doctrine of 'flexible response' the Pentagon had sponsored many studies and training courses in the field, and had pumped British veterans of Malaya and French veterans of Indochina for their experiences. Bernard Fall's classic book *Street Without Joy* was squeezed dry of its insights into why the French were defeated, and fears of a new 'Groupe Mobile 100' or a new Dien Bien Phu came to loom large in the outlook of many American officers.

The planners drew two particular lessons from the French experience in Indochina. One was that ground vehicles, including armour, would be tied to the roads and vulnerable to ambush. The Americans therefore brought a vast helicopter park of some 4000 machines to Vietnam, as compared with the French deployment of just 42. In the event they, too, tended to be tied down – but this time to their landing zones (LZs). It was certainly a mistake not to have brought more armour to Vietnam in the early years, since its great value in cross-country movement, and in close assaults, was soon apparent. This defect in the US force structure was corrected only in and after 1968.

The second lesson learned from the French was just as important to the evolution of the war. It was the need – after Dien Bien Phu – to make sure that any fortified area was always well protected and well supplied by air. The Americans took this lesson to heart with a vengeance.

The standard US fire support base (FSB) in Vietnam was a circular perimeter of foxholes designed to accommodate a company of infantry firing across a cleared field to a range of several hundred metres. This area was sown with mines and obstructed with barbed wire. The ranges and likely lanes of approach were carefully noted. The firepower immediately available consisted of the company's own weapons –

M16 assault rifles, M79 grenade launchers, M60 machine guns, 66mm anti-tank rockets, 81mm mortars and 90mm recoilless rifles. By themselves these lethal machines could often stop an attack in its tracks, but there was more in support. Much more.

An FSB usually included a battery or a battery and a half of artillery (say six 105mm and three 155mm towed howitzers) dug into

The first three years of US mainforce involvement in Vietnam were as decisive as they were experimental. It took all that time for the American war machine to work into top gear and perfect its tactics – but at the end of that period came the Tet offensive and the start of withdrawal. The US military forces failed to adapt quickly enough to the strange environment of jungle warfare in which they suddenly found themselves, and the price they had to pay was heavy.

The war in Vietnam should not have come as such a shock to American commanders, since the South Vietnamese Army (the ARVN or Army of the Republic of South Vietnam) had been created, equipped and trained by Americans, and US advisers accompanied its operations. They saw successes and errors at close hand, and could report back in full. Thus the battle of Ap Bac in 1963 had shown up the need to surround an enemy unit completely, before going in for the kill. On this occasion the ARVN had first suffered heavily in several botched assaults, and had then failed to prevent a Viet Cong exfiltration. In army jargon, there had been no 'Anvil' upon which the 'Hammer' could fall.

The Americans had also gained a wide theoretical grasp of counter-insurgency during the radical

Below: A CH-47A Chinook helicopter airlifts a counter-mortar radar unit into a US Army fire base, still undergoing the rigours of construction.

circular pits and ready to traverse rapidly to cover any point of the compass. These guns would have the task of supporting friendly units operating anywhere within about 15km (10 miles) of the FSB, although in some cases (as at the 'Rockpile' near Khe Sanh) there would be 8in guns, and even 175mm long guns with a range of more than 30km (20 miles). Normally an FSB would be sited within the range of at least one other FSB, thus allowing accurate long-range fire to be added to the perimeter defences. As for the guns within the FSB itself, they could be loaded with direct-fire shrapnel (for the fireplans known as 'Killer Junior' and 'Killer Senior'), with flechette rounds or cluster munitions ('Beehive' and 'Firecracker' respectively). All of these could be devastating at close range.

Many FSBs included a few static tanks or twin self-propelled AA guns, for assistance in the direct-fire role against ground targets. In addition to these, however, there would be an impressive array of 'invisible assets' in the form of airpower. These included Aerial Rocket Artillery (ARA – Huey helicopters armed with 2.75in rockets, organised in the Air Mobile divisions for battery fire in place of conventional tube artillery); fixed-wing flareships

Below: A US soldier parades a manpack personnel detector, or 'people sniffer' as it was called in Vietnam. By analysing chemicals in the air the device was able – at least in theory – to detect the presence of Viet Cong hidden in the undergrowth.

(cargo planes loaded with flare-dispensers and mini-guns, nicknamed 'Spooky', 'Smoky the Bear', 'Puff the Magic Dragon', and so on); 'Slow Movers' (the Cessna A-37 'Dragonfly', or the Douglas A-1 'Sandy'); and 'Fast Movers' (the Douglas A-4 'Scooter', the McDonnell Douglas F-4 'Four' or the Republic Fairchild F-105 'Thud'). Behind these awesome weapons there might be such exotica as the experimental 'Go-Go Bird' (a CH-47 Chinook helicopter gunship, or 'air battleship'); the controversial F-111 TFX 'fighter-cum-strategic bomber'; and above all the trusty B-52, which could approach unheard at high altitude and devastate a kilometre square with its 40,000kg (90,000lb) load of conventional iron bombs (with three planes flying together making one 'Arc Light' strike).

The Americans took firebase security very seriously indeed, and they achieved some spectacular results. It was not uncommon for several hundred attackers to be made casualties in half a night, at the cost of only a couple of dozen defenders. This was the sort of 'body count' ratio that Pentagon planners wanted to see, and it could often be attained when the North Vietnamese Army (NVA) chose to attack an FSB. Few FSBs were ever overrun when they were defended by Americans, and yet they could be built economically and quickly within a single day, even when everything was lifted in by helicopter. In this case, at least, the 'Green Machine' had found something it could do right.

On the other hand, the Americans took some time to realise that in these battles it was the enemy who, in effect, 'selected his own body count'. He attacked FSBs only when he felt he could afford the likely cost, and thereby rendered himself immune from strategic defeat in these operations. It was only by seizing the initiative and damaging the enemy when he could *not* afford heavy losses that the US could make any real progress. They had to be able to penetrate NVA base areas and assembly zones at will – and this proved to be a very tall order.

On the offensive
There turned out to be a certain symmetrical balance in Vietnam between the NVA's inability to seize US firebases, and the US's extreme difficulty in seizing NVA base areas. Quite apart from the political restrictions on cross-border attacks against the sanctuaries in Laos and Cambodia, the Americans found that there were severe tactical problems associated with frontal assaults in areas where the enemy was strong, despite their immensely superior firepower.

The basic unit of manoeuvre for the Americans was the infantry company, which had a nominal strength of around 180 men but which in practice normally went into action with about two-thirds of that number. It was found by experience that isolated platoon units often lacked the resilience necessary to survive a concerted enemy attack, since too great a proportion of the men would be directly involved in the front line. With a company unit only one platoon might be pinned in the immediate firefight, leaving a reserve free to establish a proper base of fire and a line of communication to the outside world. On offensive operations, therefore, the Americans would typically manoeuvre as complete companies.

These companies were difficult to move in the jungle, and in single file on a 'speed trail' they might easily spread out over a kilometre of ground, from head to tail. Such considerations made 'combat flexibility' almost impossible to achieve, and it was rare for more than a single company to be brought into a firefight. Still less attainable was the ideal (after Ap Bac) of complete encirclement of the enemy. 'The jungle mocks manoeuvre,' said S.L.A. Marshall, and that applied even more to reserves inserted after a crisis had flared than it did to the troops who had originally initiated the contact. The NVA was expert in laying secondary ambushes against relief forces, and it could keep an encircling pincer movement at bay for several days at a time.

Fighting in the undergrowth

When a firefight was joined in the course of a mobile US sweep, the American commander would usually lack many of the advantages which he could expect in FSB defence. In particular, he could not pre-register his firepower, but would have to call it up in the thick of a confused and dangerous crisis. The terrain would probably be heavily overgrown, restricting vision, and the enemy would probably be deeply dug in. In these circumstances it was often found that much of the available weaponry was delivered too late to be useful, or that it was too lightweight to make much impression. The rockets of the ARA, for example, would fail to penetrate bunkers or thick treetrunks, while 105mm shells would often tree-burst in thick forest, scattering the ground with shrapnel, but scarcely damaging the enemy soldiers who lurked beneath. Artillery heavier than 105mm was found to be preferable – but it brought its own problems both of availability and of safety. The average engagement range in close country was no more than a couple of dozen metres, so one could not call down heavy ordnance on the enemy without endangering one's own front-line soldiers. Sometimes a deliberate step back was made by the Americans to compensate for this – but such rearward manoeuvres could be misinterpreted, and might give the enemy a decisive opportunity for a counter-attack.

In mobile offensive sweeps the Americans also suffered from the fact that if their own men were on foot, unarmoured and in the open, they were especially vulnerable to the enemy's fire. They could easily be pinned down, and would find it hard to execute the textbook tactic of 'fire and manoeuvre', in which the use of firepower was regarded as no more than a preparation for a final assault to close quarters. It was soon discovered that in the absence of AFVs such final assaults could be extremely costly in friendly lives, and that in a war of attrition these losses would be unacceptable. 'Every time I manoeuvre a man,' said one US NCO, 'I get him shot, and I say to hell with it.' It was much safer to hug the dirt and let the tide of battle roll forward at its own pace.

By 1967 the Americans had developed a new tactical manual based on the principle of 'manoeuvre and fire', whereby the role of unarmoured infantry was reduced from that of an assault force to that of a fighting reconnaissance patrol. It would advance into an NVA base area, become involved in a firefight, and then identify targets for the heavy weapons to destroy. The destructive function was thus allocated to firepower, not to an infantry assault.

This form of action could never destroy enemy units, however many casualties they might suffer. The same was true of the activities of the 'Lurp' or 'Recondo' scouts, specialist light infantry teams sent

to infiltrate secretly behind enemy lines. They would tend to call down artillery as soon as they saw a promising target – and then evacuate the area. Something similar could be said of the roaming Loaches ('Light Observation Helicopters', otherwise known as the OH-6 Cayuse) of the 'air cavalry'. In this case the task was to find the enemy and then administer appropriate fire (from their own miniguns, from supporting helicopter gunships, or from ground forces). The noise of approach militated against any subtlety in use, and so once again there was a high body count unsupported by any serious operational damage to the enemy.

All this proved that firepower could achieve a favourable balance of attrition against the enemy, and especially if friendly infantry did not expose itself in the most dangerous situations. But what firepower could not do was to close with the enemy and destroy his formations in hand-to-hand combat. Such assaults were found to be excessively costly in friendly lives, and hence highly unpopular in a war that the government had billed as 'limited'. What was being implied, in fact, was that the US Army was refusing to pull out all the stops, and would therefore rest content with something less than victory. **R.E.M. Foster**

Above: A US Army patrol wends its way through thick undergrowth. Despite their massive superiority in long-range firepower the Americans had ultimately to go out and engage the Viet Cong in the jungle and here the forces involved were far more equal.

Hearts and minds?

The war in the villages

The United States commanders in Vietnam had a clear theoretical grasp of the need to win the allegiance of the rural population of South Vietnam for the Saigon regime. They also knew what classic counter-insurgency theory dictated should be done: the rural population had to be convinced that the government forces could guarantee their safety against intimidation by guerrillas, and then persuaded to support the government by a 'hearts and minds' campaign of social and economic improvements. But the reality of most US military attitudes was better exemplified by the Marines' slogan: 'Get 'em by the balls and their hearts and minds will follow.' As a British counter-insurgency expert Sir Robert Thompson wrote, 'The American forces fought a separate war which ignored its political and other aspects . . . .'

Vietnamese village society was remarkably stable before the war closed in, with many communities enjoying an unbroken tradition stretching back a thousand years. The mix of Confucian and Buddhist philosophies prevalent in rural Vietnam extolled loyalty to the family and local community, and encouraged a deep fidelity to the ancestral home. This village society, deeply alienated from the Saigon government, was the seedbed of communist insurgency.

In 1962 the Diem government launched a grandiose 'strategic hamlets' programme which US advisers optimistically saw as a great step forward in counter-insurgency. A large part of the rural population was to be relocated in strongholds under military control, protected from Viet Cong intimidation, and offered advanced social services. In fact, the programme was a catastrophe. Villagers deeply resented relocation away from their traditional homes, and the strategic hamlets were often little better than concentration camps. Most of the planned hamlets were never built or swiftly fell apart, and the scheme worsened the rift between the urban-based government and the rural areas. Subsequent renamed variants on the strategic hamlets programme – such as the 'new life hamlets' – met with little more success.

When the US land forces moved into Vietnam in 1965, they confronted a countryside some 80 per cent of which was under more or less permanent Viet Cong control – a situation the peasants accepted either willingly, passively or under duress. At first the US Army devoted its efforts primarily to 'search and

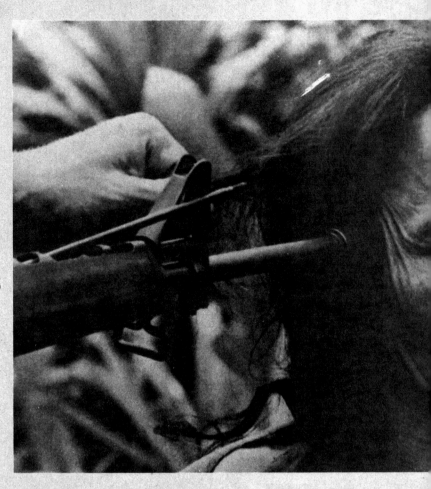

destroy' missions against enemy mainforce units in remote jungle and highland areas, but having realised that 'the Indians were inside the stockade', during 1966 they switched more of their operations to the densely populated areas near the coast. The operational principle was that US forces swept a district clear of Viet Cong units and then South Vietnamese troops moved in to pacify the villages made safe by US action, weeding out Viet Cong cadres and supporters. In fact, the ARVN proved quite incapable of this task. During the day they maintained surveillance, but by night the guerrillas still controlled the supposedly pacified villages.

Destroying villages

As US 'search and destroy' operations grew in intensity, the policy of winning peasant 'hearts and minds' disappeared from view. In principle the rules of US tactics forbade unnecessary destruction of civilian lives and property, but the nature of the fighting made this redundant. The Viet Cong chose the villages as their battleground. Often fortified with firing positions and systems of bunkers, they offered better cover than the open country. US officers were under heavy pressure to minimise American casualties, and the simplest way to do this was to call down a devastating air or artillery strike on any enemy position. The consequence was the destruction of huts, livestock, and peasant property, often with no damage to the Viet Cong who would have swiftly withdrawn. Punitive action, such as the burning down of houses, was frequently taken against villages known to harbour Viet Cong supporters.

The US commander in Vietnam (1964–68), General Westmoreland, was at pains to stress that

The harsh treatment of rural Vietnamese, including interrogation (above) and the burning of villages (below), outraged liberal opinion in the US.

'search and destroy' was not a scorched earth policy, although he admitted that civilian deaths sometimes resulted. But as the ferocity of the war grew and the US forces found the problem of separating out the Viet Cong from the local population more and more frustrating, a policy of clearing whole districts developed. A US official described the process as conducted during Operation Malheur in Quang Ngai province in mid-1967: 'the inhabitants are allowed time to pack their belongings and collect their livestock and then are moved to one of the 65 refugee camps in the province. Shortly thereafter the hamlet is destroyed . . . friendly forces continue to receive fire from such hamlets and encounter mines, but they no longer are inhibited from returning fire and calling in artillery and air strikes.' Often the process was less formal, the population being ordered to leave in messages broadcast from helicopters.

Free Fire Zones

Cleared of civilians, an area could be designated a Free Fire Zone (officially renamed 'specified strike zones' to avoid the suggestion of random blasting away). Any living creature within a Free Fire Zone could be considered a legitimate target. Despite the risks involved – and the dreadful effects of the spraying of these districts with defoliants – many peasants refused to quit their land or returned to it after forced evacuation. It was sometimes unclear to villagers whether their homes lay in a Free Fire Zone – and in practice it often made little difference.

As areas were cleared massive refugee camps opened up – generally 'crowded, dirty and unpleasant' according to an official US report – and the population of the cities swelled. By the end of 1967 there were estimated to be around 1.5 million refugees in South Vietnam. They included those who had been evacuated and those who had fled the ceaseless bombing and shelling. But the growth of the

refugee population was not simply an accidental by-product of war; it was deliberate US policy. In September 1966 the State Department suggested the carrying out of 'military operations specifically designed to generate refugees'. Some US strategists saw this as the only way to separate the peasants from the Viet Cong, and began to use rising refugee figures as a measure of their success.

While these tough policies won the US no friends in rural Vietnam, they also fuelled the small but growing anti-war movement back in America. Press photos and televised images of US troops setting fire to villages or looking on while ARVN interrogators tortured Viet Cong suspects stimulated bitter debates in the US and severely damaged America's standing in world public opinion.

It is now generally accepted that the harsh effect of military operations on the rural population helped Viet Cong recruitment and made an effective hearts and minds programme impossible. But General Westmoreland was probably in fact correct to say that the only way to establish control over certain communist-dominated parts of the country 'was to remove the people and destroy the villages'. The Americans were effectively engaged in the destruction of rural society, rather than in winning its allegiance for Saigon.

R.G. Grant

Right: A Marine uses an axe to break into a Viet Cong rice cache concealed in a hut wall. Many villagers provided food for the communist fighters.

Hammer and anvil

Clearing the Iron Triangle in Operation Cedar Falls

Right: UH-1D helicopters prepare to land at a drop zone; Operation Cedar Falls relied on the mobility conferred by air power. Below: Supported by a rifleman a soldier inspects enemy positions using a Starlight night scope.

For the first two years of direct American involvement in Vietnam, the strategic policy had been essentially defensive in character, coupled with small tactical offensives against known communist sanctuaries. This policy, however, produced only limited and temporary results and tended to leave large areas of the countryside under semi-permanent communist control, while the anti-communist forces held the towns, their operational bases, and as much of the connecting road system as they could keep open by incessant patrolling.

Particularly troublesome was War Zone C, lying between Saigon and the Cambodian border, containing the immense Michelin rubber plantation and, a little way to the south, a notorious communist stronghold known as the Iron Triangle. In September and October 1966 some 22,000 American, Australian and South Vietnamese troops combed War Zone C during Operation Attleboro, the largest tactical deployment in the war to date. Many of the Viet Cong were forced to seek a temporary refuge across the border and it was claimed that 2130 guerrillas had been killed. However, as one somewhat jaundiced US Marine corporal was to comment of his officers, 'The more Regular you were, the higher the body

count was.' General William C. Westmoreland, commander of the US Military Assistance Command Vietnam (MACV), was later to agree that at this period such statistics were indeed 'overdone'.

Apart from penetrations of Boi Loi Forest and Ho Bo Wood on its western perimeter, the Iron Triangle remained largely unaffected by Operation Attleboro. Of the Triangle Westmoreland wrote, 'The Vietnamese, before we arrived, would never dare go in there because it was totally dominated by the enemy. You couldn't go in with companies or battalions; they would have been chewed up, ambushed and decimated. It took a massive troop effort to go in there with safety and get the job done with minimum losses.'

The natural apex of the Iron Triangle was formed by the junction of the Thi Tinh and Saigon Rivers, which also formed two of its sides. The third side followed a line across country from Ben Cat in the east to Ben Suc in the west. The whole was covered by dense jungle in which the communists had located numerous base camps, depots and headquarters. These consisted of tunnel warrens dug on several levels, containing accommodation and storage facilities. There were usually several entrances, some located inside huts, others in close cover or in river banks below water level, and bushes were planted to mask emergency exits. Incorporated in the complex were bunkers which could sweep the whole area with their fire. The obvious approaches to such bases were usually mined and booby-trapped with trip-wires attached to explosive devices, as well as being covered by ambush sites fronted with deadly punji stakes. Holding ground, nonetheless, did not form part of the philosophy of the communists' People's War. If threatened seriously both the Viet Cong and the North Vietnamese Army would quickly break contact and vanish after the initial exchanges, fighting only when cornered; if, on the other hand, they sensed that they held the advantage – as they frequently did within the Iron Triangle – they would attempt to wipe out any unit which penetrated their lines.

The threat to Saigon

Undoubtedly, the most remarkable thing about this apparently inviolable area was the fact that it lay only 25km (18 miles) from the centre of Saigon. Thus, insurgent units, indistinguishable from the rest of the population, found no difficulty in entering the city and a constant flow of accurate intelligence was always available to the guerrillas. For example, the arrival of the comedian Bob Hope and his troupe, in Saigon to entertain the troops, resulted in an immediate bomb attack on the Brink Hotel in which they were staying. The attack itself may not have achieved its ends, but it was an impressive demonstration of the communists' freedom of movement.

By the end of 1966 there were 385,000 American troops in Vietnam and the number was still rising. General Westmoreland was now strong enough to mount the kind of operation that he considered was needed to clean out the Iron Triangle. Aware that the enemy felt no loss of face when disengaging in the presence of greatly superior strength, and that this would in turn be reflected in low casualties among his own troops, he decided that his attack would be made in corps strength.

Detailed for the operation, code-named Cedar Falls, were the 1st and 25th Infantry Divisions and a South Vietnamese infantry division; the 173rd Air-

Left: General William C. Westmoreland, commander of the US Military Assistance Command, believed that superiority in men and equipment would crush the Viet Cong and the NVA in the Iron Triangle.

The destruction of Ben Suc

'The sight of 60 helicopters flying in formation and zooming into Ben Suc at treetop level was one which none who witnessed will ever forget....

'The choppers touched down simultaneously in landing zones to the west, north and east of the town while the "Eagle Flight" guarded the south. In less than one and one-half minutes an entire infantry battalion, some 420 men, was on the ground . . . . The troops occupied blocking positions primarily to prevent movement out of the village....

'Just after the assault ships had departed, helicopters with loudspeakers and South Vietnamese announcers aboard circled the village at low altitude and broadcast the following message: "Attention people of Ben Suc. You are surrounded by Republic of South Vietnam and allied forces. Do not run away or you will be shot as VC. Stay in your homes and wait for further instructions."

'Most of the villagers followed the instructions; those who attempted to evade and leave the village were engaged by the blocking forces....

'By 1030, 8 January, Ben Suc was securely in the hands of the friendly forces and the 2nd Brigade command post had been established in the village. During the two and one-half hours since the initial landing, a total of 40 enemy had been killed in action, with only light friendly casualties....

'After the village was sealed and

the troops had consolidated their positions, a South Vietnamese battalion was airlanded into Ben Suc to search the village and interrogate the villagers.... Following the interrogations and screening, 106 individuals were detained; of these 28 were classified as Viet Cong. Most of them were local Viet Cong who had virtually no information and were of little intelligence value. However, a Viet Cong platoon leader of Group 83 – the major unit in the area – was captured....

'It was to be expected that uprooting the natives of these villages would evoke resentment, and it did. They had lived under and with the Viet Cong and had supported them for the last three years, nor was it easy for the natives to give up their homes and the land they had been working. The villagers were permitted to take with them anything they could carry, pull or herd....

'As the villagers and their belongings moved out, bulldozers, tankdozers, and demolition teams moved in. ... The bulldozers moved through the former Viet Cong stronghold and razed the structures to the ground, crushing ruins, collapsing tunnels, and obliterating bunkers and underground storage rooms....

'One of the major objectives of Operation Cedar Falls had been achieved; the village of Ben Suc no longer existed.'

Extract from Cedar Falls – Junction City: A Turning Point, *by Lieutenant-General Bernard W. Rogers.*

borne Brigade; and the 11th Armored Cavalry Regiment. Together, these made up II Field Force, Vietnam, whose mission fell into three phases. First, the Iron Triangle would be sealed off; then it would be split in half; finally, each portion would be thoroughly searched and all enemy forces and base camps within it destroyed.

Operation Cedar Falls began on 8 January 1967. The western flank of the Iron Triangle was sealed by the 25th Infantry Division deploying the 196th Light Infantry Brigade over a 15km (10 mile) stretch parallel to the Saigon River between the Boi Loi Woods and the northern perimeter of the Filhol plantation, and the 2nd Brigade to the south over the plantation and the village of Phu Hoa Dong. Simultaneously the 1st Infantry Division which included the 2nd and 3rd Brigades, the 173rd Airborne Brigade and the 11th Armored Cavalry Regiment, secured the eastern flank. In the north a battalion of the 26th Infantry, commanded by Lieutenant-Colonel Alexander M. Haig, launched a surprise 60-helicopter assault on the village of Ben Suc, a fortified Viet Cong supply and political centre, while the 11th Armored Cavalry seized Ben Cat. Units of the 3rd Brigade conducted airmobile assaults followed up by 'search and destroy' operations against Viet Cong forces and installations in the Thanh Dien forest area. The following day the 11th Armored Cavalry, less one squadron, drove

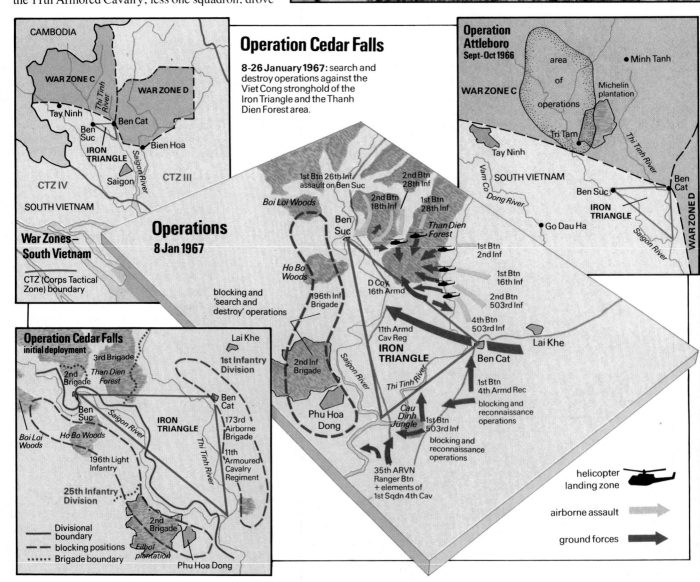

Operation Cedar Falls

8-26 January 1967: search and destroy operations against the Viet Cong stronghold of the Iron Triangle and the Thanh Dien Forest area.

Operation Attleboro
Sept-Oct 1966

WAR ZONE C

area of operations

Minh Tanh

Michelin plantation

Tri Tam

Tay Ninh

SOUTH VIETNAM

Ben Suc

Go Dau Ha

IRON TRIANGLE

Ben Cat

WAR ZONE D

Vam Co Dong River

Thi Tinh River

Saigon River

War Zones – South Vietnam

CAMBODIA

WAR ZONE C

WAR ZONE D

Tay Ninh

Ben Cat

Ben Suc

Bien Hoa

IRON TRIANGLE

Saigon

CTZ IV

CTZ III

SOUTH VIETNAM

Thi Tinh River

Saigon River

CTZ (Corps Tactical Zone) boundary

Operations
8 Jan 1967

1st Btn 26th Inf assault on Ben Suc

2nd Btn 28th Inf

2nd Btn 18th Inf

1st Btn 28th Inf

Boi Loi Woods

Ben Suc

Thanh Dien Forest

1st Btn 2nd Inf

Ho Bo Woods

D Coy 16th Armd

1st Btn 16th Inf

blocking and 'search and destroy' operations

196th Inf Brigade

2nd Btn 503rd Inf

11th Armd Cav Reg

4th Btn 503rd Inf

Lai Khe

IRON TRIANGLE

2nd Inf Brigade

Saigon River

Ben Cat

Thi Tinh River

1st Btn 4th Armd Rec

Phu Hoa Dong

Cau Dinh Jungle

1st Btn 503rd Inf

blocking and reconnaissance operations

blocking and reconnaissance operations

35th ARVN Ranger Btn + elements of 1st Sqdn 4th Cav

Operation Cedar Falls
initial deployment

Lai Khe

3rd Brigade

2nd Brigade

Thanh Dien Forest

1st Infantry Division

Ben Suc

Ben Cat

Boi Loi Woods

Ho Bo Woods

Saigon River

IRON TRIANGLE

173rd Airborne Brigade

196th Light Infantry

Thi Tinh River

11th Armoured Cavalry Regiment

25th Infantry Division

2nd Brigade

Filhol plantation

Phu Hoa Dong

Divisional boundary

blocking positions

Brigade boundary

helicopter landing zone

airborne assault

ground forces

Above: In conjunction with armour and airborne units US troops begin their advance into the Iron Triangle during the Cedar Falls operation. Above right: Air force C-130 Hercules transports unload men and supplies at a forward air strip during the first phase of Cedar Falls.

Below: Men of the 173rd Airborne Brigade prepare to destroy a Viet Cong tunnel in the Thanh Dien Forest of the Iron Triangle.

across the triangle, cutting it in two, and the 'search and destroy' combat teams moved in, their progress assisted by tankdozers where necessary. Many of the Viet Cong managed to slip through the cordon but others were killed while attempting to escape; for example, using tank-mounted searchlights the 2/34th Armor successfully staged a number of night ambushes against communist traffic along the Saigon River. The majority of clashes within the Iron Triangle were with platoon-sized groups but, overall, fighting was light. Since normal ammunition and flamethrowers were ineffective against the enemy's subterranean warrens, these were dealt with by teams known as Tunnel Rats who, having sealed all known entrances with explosives, then pumped the system full of acetylene gas, which was detonated by dynamite charges.

The US mechanised infantry decisively demonstrated their effectiveness. Using M113 APCs, they avoided dismounted action whenever possible. The infantry would only comb an area on foot after repeated armoured sweeps had eliminated every hostile source of fire.

Given the scale of effort directed against an area only 160 square km (60 square miles) in extent, Cedar Falls could hardly have failed. When the operation ended on 25 January an estimated 750 guerrillas had been killed and 280 captured. Material captured included 23 heavy weapons, 590 smallarms, a large quantity of ammunition and uniforms, and enough rice to feed a division for a year. Most significant of all were the 500,000 pages of documents discovered in communist command bunkers, for these revealed the entire Viet Cong and North Vietnamese order of battle as well as detailed operational plans; the acquisition of these papers was described as the greatest intelligence breakthrough of the war. The cost of the operation had been 72 Americans killed and 337 wounded, while the South Vietnamese lost 11 killed and 8 wounded; one tank and three APCs were destroyed, and three tanks, nine APCs and two helicopters were damaged.

Destruction in the Triangle

The plight of the 6000 civilians living inside and within the immediate vicinity of the Iron Triangle aroused great concern in the media. Understandably, the Americans had kept the operation a secret until the last possible moment. As the Americans moved in, the inhabitants were evacuated. The villages were subsequently destroyed by bombing or flattened by bulldozers. The refugees were resettled elsewhere after great hardship – if they had not refused to leave and been killed on the spot. The suffering and damage caused were an inevitable consequence of 'search and destroy' tactics, but to many observers they seemed unacceptable; indeed, to the anti-war lobby in the US the very term 'search and destroy' became anathema.

When, within a week of the operation ending, the Viet Cong began filtering back into the area, they found it transformed. Rome ploughs had carved lanes through the jungle, which had also been sprayed with defoliant. The evacuation of the population not only deprived the communists of local support, but also turned the Iron Triangle into a Free Fire Zone which could be pounded at will. Once described as 'a dagger pointed at Saigon', it was never again the secure base for guerrillas that it had formerly been, although this success had been achieved only by turning the area into a virtual desert.

In addition to its immediate results Cedar Falls marked a turning point in the conduct of the war, with the Americans now firmly committed to a policy of multi-divisional sweeps against the enemy's strongholds. Even as Cedar Falls ended, the units involved were redeploying for Operation Junction City which, between February and May, inflicted such serious damage on the communists in War Zone C that the latter's headquarters was forced to withdraw into Cambodia. **Bryan Perrett**

ARVN
The development of South Vietnam's army

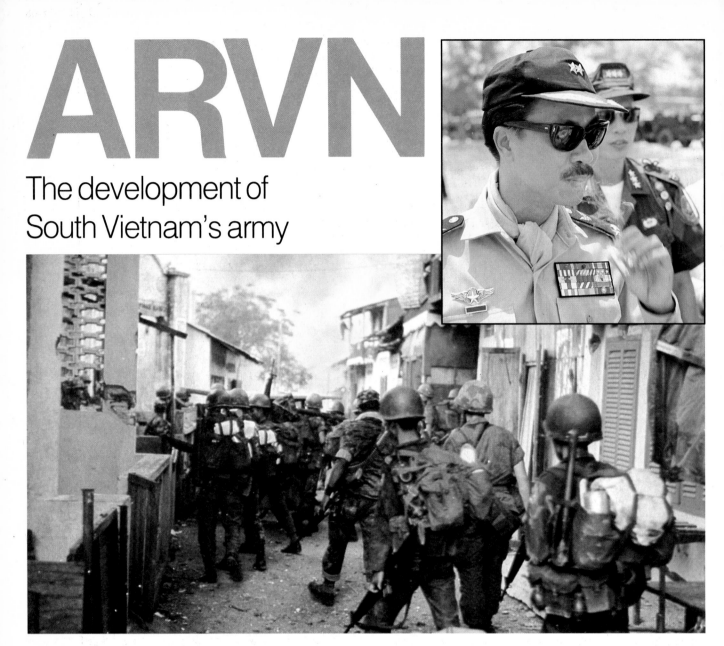

At the time of the ceasefire agreement between France and the Democratic Republic of (North) Vietnam in 1954, the Vietnamese military forces allied to the French consisted of about 200,000 troops organised in 160 light infantry battalions and a few support units. Although there were a small number of ethnic Vietnamese serving as officers and NCOs in the French Army, most of the Vietnamese units were led by French soldiers and there were no native Vietnamese commands or staffs. With the ensuing partition of the country and the replacement of French authority with American advice and support, the armed forces were completely rebuilt. To counter any possible conventional ground attack across the Demilitarized Zone that separated North from South Vietnam, Saigon created three corps headquarters and seven regular divisions, each with three regiments of three infantry battalions each, and a few divisional support units. In addition, there were small parachute (Airborne), Marine Corps, armour and artillery forces and a few air and naval elements. Providing command and control for the ground forces and a small logistical and training base was an operational army staff, a small general staff and a Ministry of Defense.

Independent of the regular armed forces, which at that period never numbered more than about 150,000 men, was a territorial army made up of a 50,000-man Civil Guard and an identical-size Self-Defense Corps. The Civil Guard (later 'Regional Forces') worked primarily for local province chiefs in company-size units, while the Self-Defense Corps (later 'Popular Forces') was a kind of hamlet-level militia. Both were directly responsible to Ngo Dinh Diem, the autocratic president of South Vietnam, and together they acted as a counter to the politically minded army leaders. All these newly created forces were outfitted with World War II-vintage American equipment, as well as a sprinkling of left-over French and captured Japanese gear.

From 1960 to 1964 the armed forces were reorganised and greatly strengthened to combat a growing internal insurgency supported by North Vietnam. With increased American financial, material and advisory support, South Vietnamese forces almost doubled to 250,000 men in 10 infantry divisions and there were smaller but corresponding increases in training and support forces. For anti-guerrilla operations, 20 Ranger battalions and a Special Forces command were established and the territorials in-

Above: ARVN troops of the Airborne Division leave a flaming village after conducting a sweep through Tan Son Nhut on the outskirts of Saigon in the fighting that followed the first round of the Tet offensive. Inset above: The flamboyant Marshal Ky, who was to be one of the major power brokers in South Vietnam's corrupt and ineffectual government.

creased to 264,000 men. More significantly, the country was divided into four regions or corps tactical zones, each controlled by a corps headquarters, and almost the entire army, regulars and territorials alike, was assigned area security missions.

During the same period, American military strength rose to just under 24,000 men, enabling the United States to field a theatre-level military headquarters, an advisory network that stretched down from corps and divisions to battalions, provinces and their subordinate districts, and a rising number of combat support forces from helicopter companies and air transport units to intelligence and communications detachments. In addition, US Army Special Forces began a far-reaching programme organising thousands of Montagnard tribesmen in the interior of the country into a variety of military units that later became collectively known as the Civilian Irregular Defense Groups (CIDG).

All these efforts, however, came to naught when a coup in November 1963 replaced President Diem with a series of military juntas which quickly politicised the entire armed forces. During the months and then years that followed, promotions came to depend more on favouritism than on ability, and appointments on loyalty to one particular general or military clique. Corps, divisions and provinces became almost individual fiefdoms and military efficiency fell dramatically.

Desertions and casualties

As a fighting force, the army appeared to be slowly collapsing from within. Small but serious battlefield setbacks multiplied, losses from desertions and casualties mounted, and the arrival of North Vietnamese Army troops to back up the Viet Cong insurgents in early 1965 seemed to presage the end of the Southern regime. Only the arrival of US ground combat troops that year enabled the South Vietnamese to stave off defeat.

Between 1965 and 1968 South Vietnamese leaders and their American advisers tried to regroup and reform both the armed forces and the government. Initially the two were indistinguishable. In June 1965 a loose coalition of 10 leading South Vietnamese generals formed a Directory to rule South Vietnam. Its chairman was Nguyen Van Thieu and it also included army staff chief Cao Van Vien, air force marshal Nguyen Cao Ky, and the four corps commanders. The Directory generals appointed Ky as 'premier' to run the Saigon administration while Vien ran the armed forces. However, each corps commander remained regional governor for his zone and supervised the civilian administration as well as the military forces within his area. By this time just about all of the provinces and districts were staffed by military personnel and the army dominated the political life of the country. Bolstered by the growing number of American combat forces, the country survived and a kind of stability was achieved, but the army remained entrenched in national and local politics and military professionalism almost vanished.

In the field, South Vietnamese military forces took on what appeared to be a secondary role in the war effort. While American forces, with their superior mobility and firepower, engaged the enemy's larger combat units, South Vietnamese regulars and territorials were given the job of local security. Throughout the length of the country, South Vietnamese soldiers

garrisoned earth and wire forts and barricades which were set up to guard hamlets, towns and cities, roads, airfields and waterways, and other critical installations including their own bases. Recruiting was local and decentralised and units rarely operated far from their home areas. Exceptions were the Airborne and Marine Corps forces and a few of the better infantry units which took part in some of the larger American operations from time to time. But for the large bulk of the army, the long-term static security assignments were debilitating, clashes with the more mobile and elusive enemy were frustrating, and the assumption of political responsibilities proved divisive and ultimately corrupting. As American wealth poured into the country, opportunities for corruption skyrocketed, from the sale of draft deferments and security clearances to large-scale embezzlement, protection rackets and black-marketeering, all encouraged by military pay increases that yet could not keep pace with rapid inflation. Nevertheless, somehow the army was able to survive all this, rebuild its units, and slowly began pushing enemy combat units and political cadres out of the towns, villages and hamlets.

The danger of political involvement was underlined in early 1966 when Buddhist dissatisfaction with the military regime led to a major revolt in the northern corps tactical zone, precipitated by the attempt of the Directory to fire the local corps commander. The rebellion spread quickly, resulting in several clashes between local military units and Marine and Airborne forces loyal to Saigon. Combat operations came to a virtual standstill, but, after several months of stalemate, open civil war was averted and the authority of the Saigon regime restored. In the process the Directory agreed on a transi-

Below: Rough justice – an ARVN Ranger punishes a South Vietnamese farmer for allegedly supplying government troops with incorrect information on Viet Cong whereabouts. Such behaviour did little to endear the central government to the people of South Vietnam whose support was vital if ARVN and US counter-insurgency operations were to succeed.

Above: Kitted-out in jungle uniform a patrol of South Vietnamese soldiers marches past fellow ARVN troops mounted on M113 APCs. Above right: Montagnard soldiers fire a 4.2in mortar during an attack on Viet Cong positions.

ARVN regular force levels

	1954	1964	1967	1968
Army	170,000	220,000	303,000	380,000
Air Force	3500	11,000	16,000	19,000
Navy	2200	12,000	16,000	19,000
Marine Corps	1500	7000	8000	9000
Total	177,200	250,000	343,000	427,000

tion to a civilian government, a step heartily approved by their American advisers. By the following year a constitutional assembly had produced an acceptable plan for a presidential, bicameral government and elections were set for the autumn of 1967. To preserve military power and unity, Ky agreed to back Thieu's bid for the presidency and his successful campaign was followed by a slow but steady effort to separate the military from politics – or at least to eliminate those military cliques hostile to the new president, which was much the same thing.

The physical growth of the armed forces continued apace, regular force strength rising to 343,000 and the territorial forces to 300,000. Most increases were in light infantry units which American advisers felt were easier and cheaper to raise, train and equip. The number of infantry battalions in each division rose from nine to 12 (four per regiment) and the Airborne and Marine Corps forces doubled. Increases in support units were minimal, however, and equipment changes were also small. The armoured units exchanged their old M24 tanks for later models, the artillery turned in their mortars for howitzers and some of the propeller-driven A-1 fighter-bombers were replaced by modern jets.

The most modern weapons, such as the lightweight Colt M16 automatic rifle, were reserved primarily for American units, however, and there were few helicopters left over for the South Vietnamese after the needs of US units had been fulfilled. As before, the air and sea forces of Saigon, as well as their army's technical services, remained small and were only minor adjuncts to the much larger land army. By the beginning of 1968 much of the equipment of all these forces was old and worn, and the small South Vietnamese depots overloaded with work. However, when compared to the material resources of their enemy, the South Vietnamese still enjoyed a marked superiority.

Administratively, the army appeared in much better shape. Desertions had fallen; conscription increased and territorial needs were satisfied almost entirely by voluntary enlistments. After American prompting, awards and leave policies had been relaxed, the military commissary system greatly expanded and a start made towards addressing the needs of military dependents and veterans.

Leadership, or the lack of it, still remained the most pressing problem. But with the passing of the old Directory form of government, American advisers had high hopes that the less able officers could be weeded out without political repercussions and that, with the huge training and military school system that the advisory network had created, the calibre of the South Vietnamese officer and NCO corps could be gradually raised.

Whatever its effect in the United States, the enemy's Tet offensive in early 1968 gave President Thieu the crisis he needed to begin even greater reforms. Many Vietnamese commanders who performed poorly during the heavy fighting were replaced and a series of mobilisation measures pushed through the new legislature, placing the country on a wartime footing. In the field, South Vietnamese troops fought well, especially when defending home bases and local towns, while the enemy was never able to make good the severe losses suffered by the native Viet Cong units.

The attack and its repercussions in the United States also led to a major American effort to modernise the entire South Vietnamese armed forces with everything from M16 rifles to new helicopters and jet fighters. More important, American and South Vietnamese military leaders now began the laborious task of pulling the Vietnamese regulars out of their territorial support roles and putting them back in the forefront of the combat effort. No more US troops would be sent and henceforth Saigon would be expected to take on an increasing share of the major fighting. Whether the ARVN would measure up to these new American expectations remained to be seen.

Jeffrey J. Clarke

The

LEOPARD 2 MBT

The development of the German Leopard 2 MBT resulted from the abortive collaboration by America and West Germany during the 1960s on a project to build a standard new main battle tank designated the MBT-70. Due to escalating costs the project was abandoned in 1970 but the Germans proceeded to develop a vehicle incorporating a number of features of the MBT-70 programme, including the power-plant. In 1977 the Bundeswehr ordered 1800 Leopard 2s from contractors Krauss-Maffei of Munich and MaK of Kiel and the first production models were delivered in 1979. The Leopard 2 is also in service with the Dutch armed forces who placed an order for 445 tanks in 1979, and in 1983 it was accepted by the Swiss Army as a replacement for its Centurions and Pz61s.

In the context of operations on the Nato Central Front, for which the Leopard 2 is designed, advances in Soviet tank design dictated the need for major improvements to the capabilities of the Leopard 1. Developments in automotive technology during the 1970s allowed tank designers more weight without sacrificing mobility and the compromise between firepower, mobility and protection achieved in the Leopard 1 became obsolescent. One of the prime considerations in the design of the Leopard 1 was its battlefield mobility and in order to maintain this capability the Leopard 2 was provided with a turbo-charged multi-fuel engine which developed 1500hp as opposed to the Leopard 1's 830hp powerpack. Track width was also increased from 550mm (21.65in) to 635mm (25in) which, combined with

advanced torsion-bar suspension, provided the Leopard 2 with as high a road speed as its predecessor and excellent cross-country agility despite the 15 tonne increase in combat weight.

In order to meet the new requirements for protection demanded by advances in anti-tank ammunition the Leopard 2 was to be fitted with spaced armour. Rounds such as HEAT and HESH use chemical energy to penetrate armour by detonating an explosive charge directly against the target plate but are only effective against a single thickness of armour. A sandwich of armour, with a space between the inner and outer plates, prevents the hot gases and fragments which are blasted through the outer plate from penetrating the main inner armour plate and reaching the interior of the vehicle. Prototypes of the Leopard 2 were provided with spaced armour but at this stage of development the new British concept of Chobham armour came onto the market. Further collaboration between America and West Germany in the mid 1970s led to the production of a Leopard 2AV (austere version) which was calculated to meet American cost and performance requirements in 1976. This opportunity to alter the original concept allowed German tank designers to incorporate Chobham armour into the design and the Leopard 2's armour is believed to be a combination of spaced and Chobham, providing a high level of immunity against both chemical projectiles and straightforward armour-piercing ammunition.

As tank armour has become more sophisticated and has considerably reduced the efficacy of chemical

Previous page: A Bundeswehr Leopard 2 on manoeuvres in northern Germany. The Leopard 2, alongside the American Abrams and the British Challenger, provides a formidable combination of firepower, mobility and survivability for the Nato front-line arsenal. Above: While its predecessor the Leopard 1 sacrificed weight in favour of mobility, the 55 tonne Leopard 2 is fitted with a rugged 1500hp turbocharged powerpack, allowing its designers to concentrate on increasing the tank's armour while retaining high performance and cross-country agility.

rounds, so tank guns have been uprated to provide a much higher velocity for kinetic energy armour-piercing shot. Although the Leopard 2AV retained the rifled 105mm main armament at the Americans' request, the Bundeswehr opted for the greater firepower of the 120mm Rheinmetall smoothbore gun which was fitted to the Leopard 2. Two main types of ammunition are deployed – HEAT-MP-T (high-explosive anti-tank multi-purpose tracer) and APFSDS-T (armour-piercing fin-stabilised discarding-sabot tracer). An unusual feature of the Rheinmetall ammunition is the combustible cartridge case; this eliminates the problems of spent shell-case ejection since only the base stub remains after a round has been fired and this is easily collected in a bag located under the breech. The 120mm gun is fully stabilised and both the gunner and the commander are provided with stabilised sights, allowing them to lay and fire the main armament on the move with a high first-round hit probability. The gunner is also provided with a laser range finder and thermal image unit linked to the fire-control system. Passive night-vision equipment and NBC systems are standard.

Secondary armament is similar to the Leopard 1 and consists of two 7.62mm machine guns, one mounted co-axially with the main armament and the other on the turret roof on either the commander's or loader's hatch for use against air attack. Eight smoke dischargers are fitted on each side of the turret.

The new generation of Nato MBTs, the American M1, the British Challenger and the Leopard 2 have

Top, left and right, and above: The Leopard 2's ability to survive armour-piercing and chemical anti-tank weapons depends on a combination of spaced and Chobham armour coupled with a good ballistic shape. Left: The squat turret provides a low target silhouette, while the armour arrangement gives good protection against HEAT and HESH projectiles.

Left: A camouflaged Leopard 2 moves through wooded country on manoeuvres with the Bundeswehr.

Right: The Leopard 2's main armament is put to the test on the firing ranges. Despite the proven combat record of the British 105mm L7 series tank gun, the Leopard 2 was fitted with the heavier 120mm Rheinmetall smoothbore gun firing two types of fin-stabilised ammunition.

Below: With its main gun and turret well camouflaged, a Leopard 2 takes up a firing position behind scrub in open country. A 7.62mm machine gun is mounted on the loader's hatch while 16 smoke dischargers are fitted to the turret bustle.

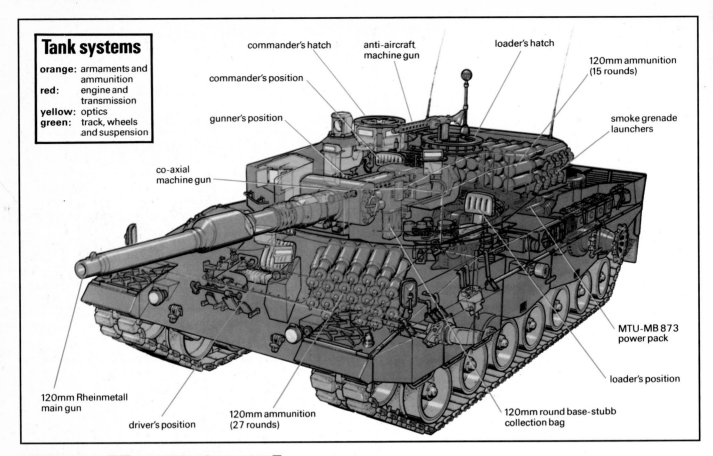

Tank systems

orange: armaments and ammunition
red: engine and transmission
yellow: optics
green: track, wheels and suspension

commander's hatch

anti-aircraft machine gun

loader's hatch

120mm ammunition (15 rounds)

commander's position

smoke grenade launchers

gunner's position

co-axial machine gun

MTU-MB 873 power pack

loader's position

120mm Rheinmetall main gun

driver's position

120mm ammunition (27 rounds)

120mm round base-stubb collection bag

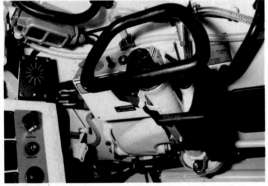

Left: The driver's position on the Leopard 2. In contrast to the Abrams the Leopard 2 is fitted with a steering wheel rather than a T-bar control. Below: A Leopard 2 turret being installed on the tank assembly line at the MaK works in Kiel. 810 vehicles were ordered by the German Army from MaK in 1977 with final deliveries of the Leopard 2 scheduled for 1986.

been criticised for not showing any really radical advance on the capabilities of their predecessors. It is true enough that the Challenger is an obvious descendant of the Chieftain, just as the Leopard 2 is heir to the Leopard 1, but both are considerably improved and more balanced machines with a more equal distribution of the cardinal tank virtues of mobility, firepower and protection than was possible to envisage in the 1950s when the original Chieftain and Leopard concepts were born. The 120mm Rheinmetall rounds can penetrate a standard Nato heavy tank target at some 2200m (2400yds) and the Leopard 2 is considered more than a match for any contemporary MBT.

Leopard 2 Main Battle Tank

Crew 4
Dimensions Length (gun included) 9.61m (31ft 6in); width 3.7m (12ft 1½in); height 2.79m (9ft 2in)
Weight Combat loaded 55,000kg (121,220lb)
Engine MTU MB 873 12-cylinder multi-fuel turbocharged engine developing 1500hp at 2600rpm

Performance Maximum road speed 72km/h (45mph); range (road) 550km (340 miles); vertical obstacle 1.1m (3ft 7in); trench 3m (9ft 10in); gradient 60 per cent; fording without preparation 0.8m (2ft 7½in), with preparation 2.35m (7ft 8in), with snorkel 4m (13ft 1in)

Armour Classified but believed to be a combination of spaced and Chobham
Armament One 120mm Rheinmetall smoothbore gun; one 7.62mm machine gun co-axial with main armament; one 7.62mm machine gun mounted on the commander's or loader's hatch; eight smoke dischargers on each side of the turret

Index

Y

Z